THE
GREAT
MARCH
OF
DEMOCRACY

The Great March of Democracy

Seven Decades of India's Elections

EDITED BY

S.Y. QURAISHI

VINTAGE
An imprint of Penguin Random House

VINTAGE

USA | Canada | UK | Ireland | Australia
New Zealand | India | South Africa | China

Vintage is part of the Penguin Random House group of companies
whose addresses can be found at global.penguinrandomhouse.com

Published by Penguin Random House India Pvt. Ltd
7th Floor, Infinity Tower C, DLF Cyber City,
Gurgaon 122 002, Haryana, India

First published in Vintage by Penguin Random House India 2019

10 9 8 7 6 5 4 3 2 1

ISBN 9780670092284

Typeset in Adobe Caslon Pro by Manipal Digital Systems, Manipal
Printed at Replika Press Pvt. Ltd, India

www.penguin.co.in

To the founding fathers of the Constitution, who laid the foundation of the most trusted institution of the Republic of India.

To Sukumar Sen, ICS, the first chief election commissioner of India, who set up the processes and structures for conducting the largest electoral exercise on the planet.

To T.N. Seshan, who took the Commission to new heights of authority, credibility and visibility.

PREAMBLE TO THE CONSTITUTION OF INDIA, 1949

WE, THE PEOPLE OF INDIA, having solemnly resolved to constitute India into a SOVEREIGN SOCIALIST SECULAR DEMOCRATIC REPUBLIC and to secure to all its citizens

JUSTICE, social, economic and political;

LIBERTY of thought, expression, belief, faith and worship;

EQUALITY of status and of opportunity; and to promote among them all

FRATERNITY assuring the dignity of the individual and the unity and integrity of the Nation;

IN OUR CONSTITUENT ASSEMBLY this 26th day of November, 1949, do HEREBY ADOPT, ENACT AND GIVE TO OURSELVES THIS CONSTITUTION.

Contents

PART FOUR: THE PATH AHEAD

Foreword

प्रजासुखे सुखं राज्ञः प्रजानां च हिते हितम् ।
नात्मप्रियं हितं राज्ञः प्रजानां तु प्रियं हितम् ।।[1]

O n 26 January 1950, the Constitution of India came into operation in a remarkable display of idealism and courage. We, the people of India, gave to ourselves a sovereign democratic republic to secure for all its citizens justice, liberty and equality. We undertook the task to promote to all citizens, fraternity, the dignity of the individual and the unity of the nation. These ideals became the lodestar of the modern Indian states; democracy became our most precious guide towards peace and regeneration from the swamp of poverty that had been created by 190 years of colonial rule. The Election Commission of India (ECI) was constituted a day before the Republic Day, thereby signalling the centrality of this institution—one of the pillars of our democracy. It is a significant metaphor indicating that we received the Indian Republic with the mandate of the people. It is a truly unique body that has supervised our elections freely and fairly for the past seven decades. The National Voters Day was instituted on 25 January 2011 to celebrate the Commission's foundation day. The day is symbolic for many reasons. It is a symbol of hope, empowerment of a people to be able to determine their own destiny by electing their own representatives through universal adult suffrage. So its importance hardly needs any emphasis.

For us democracy is not a gift, but a sacred trust; the Indian Constitution consisting of 395 articles and twelve schedules is not an instrument for administration, a legal document, but a Magna Carta for the socio-economic transformation of the country. It represents the hopes and aspirations of more than a billion people of the Republic of India. From our Constitution flows our nationalism; the construct of Indian nationalism is constitutional patriotism, which consists of an appreciation of our inherited and shared diversity, a readiness to enact one's citizenship at different levels and the ability to self-correct and learn from others. Seven decades later, we've had our ups and downs, but we can proudly state that India is the world's biggest functioning democracy. We were successful in our efforts to build a free country. We have laboured to build a strong democratic foundation. A large number of nations that gained freedom around the same time also adopted democratic systems of governance, but India is one of the very few nations that have been able to strengthen its democratic ethos. Unfortunately, many of them fell prey to autocratic rule. Thus, our history is indeed unparalleled. Our representative institutions embody the hopes and aspirations of our diverse population, and also serve as a platform to echo the grievances. While their responsiveness to public needs is assessed by the people on a continual basis, they are called to account through the medium of elections. Only the conduct of free and fair elections can ensure that we remain arguably the most vibrant democracy in the world. I have lauded the work of the Election Commission of India time and again during my years in public service for this achievement.

To ensure that the Election Commission retains its independence and status fundamental to its functioning, the Constitution of the Republic of India itself vide Article 324 gives it the powers of 'superintendence, direction and control of the preparation of electoral rolls for, and the conduct of, all elections to Parliament and to the Legislature of every State and of elections to the offices of the President and Vice President'. Needless to say, this gives the ECI a lot of responsibility to shoulder and its efficient functioning has a singular bearing on the quality of democracy in the country.

When a newly independent India made universal adult suffrage the basis of elections, not all were convinced of our capability to implement it. However, the successful manner in which the very first elections were conducted put these speculations to rest. Since then, over the years, the Election Commission has been conducting elections successfully and improving on deficiencies to increasing participation in elections. Voters' participation in the electoral process is integral to the successful running of any democracy. The level of participation reflects people's confidence and trust in democracy. The voter is, after all, the focus and the central actor in democratic elections. For encouraging voter participation, I have always appreciated the efforts of the EC to make the process of enrolment easier and convenient, and the voting experience people-friendly. I am happy you see that not only those higher up in the election machinery but also those who worked on the ground level have contributed to the cause of electoral participation. The electorate is increasingly enthusiastic to participate along with various civil society organizations, the corporate sector, educational institutions, the media and many others who have joined the Election Commission in this shared goal. The Election Commission has to not only sustain this consciousness but also strengthen it further. Though the rise of social media and the Internet has raised awareness in our youth population, we still have to pay special attention to those outside the ambit of these digital opportunities.

The Systematic Voters' Education and Electoral Participation or SVEEP, which was borne out of the initiatives taken up by ECI after the Lok Sabha elections in 2009. I am happy to note that today, this programme is spread out across polling stations with an attempt to reach each and every citizen of the country, keeping in mind that those who are not yet eligible to be electors, are prospective electors. In 2013, I was informed that around 2.82 crore new voters were registered across the country, of which 93 lakh were new voters. The efforts of the Commission have indeed borne good results. It is evident in the increase in the number of voters from about 76 crore in 2012 to 79 crore in 2013.

The abuse of money and muscle power to influence voters remains a cause of concern. The spirit of democracy will be subverted if these malpractices are not checked. It is commendable that the Election Commission has taken up initiatives to promote ethical and informed voting. To expand its reach and facilitate eligible voters, the Election Commission launched the National Voter Service Portal or NSVP, which provides a host of services such as online registration, searching names on voter lists, locating polling stations and other related assistance. Hence, the invaluable contributions made by the officials in the ECI over the years in efficiently managing elections, improving voter registration, enhancing voters' participation, educating and motivating voters, fighting black money, influence of money power and paid news during elections, and ensuring a conducive environment for people to cast their vote are praiseworthy.

I recommend these essays to all enthusiastic believers of pluralistic secular democracy and the fierce spirit of constitutionalism. Through increased participation, the electoral process and democracy in India will continue to grow in strength and vibrancy. The success of our electoral systems rests on the strength of our institutions and the entire citizenry will have to constantly engage, philosophically and physically, with political processes in order to uphold the central importance of accountability, fairness and the true freedom of our great nation. The soul of India resides in pluralism and tolerance. The plurality of society has come through assimilation of ideas over centuries, and this volume represents so much of the same diversity.

Pranab Mukherjee

Introduction

'The vote is the most powerful instrument ever devised by man for breaking down injustice and destroying the terrible walls which imprison men because they are different from other men.'[1]

—Lyndon B. Johnson

Real freedom is experienced when citizens can speak freely without fear. Democratic elections provide the platform for citizens to assert their civil and political rights by holding their elected representatives accountable. Elections may or may not ensure that a society will become socio-economically equitable, but they do provide a starting point for justice, equality and good governance. Hence free, fair and representative elections are essential for consensus-driven development.

The value of the vote for every adult has long been recognized by our people. The demand for every man and woman to have a voice in nation-building lay at the heart of our freedom struggle. The history of the demand for universal franchise in India goes back to the nineteenth century. The Constitution of India Bill (1895) was the first non-official attempt at drafting a constitution, wherein it was declared that every citizen living within the territory had the right to take part in the affairs of the country and to be admitted to public office.[2] The Nehru Report of 1928[3] reaffirmed this idea of progressive citizenship, as did numerous such reports and resolutions during the freedom struggle. The electoral process itself was far from a novelty to us, as we already had significant experience of running provincial governments due to the acts of 1919 and 1935.[4] What was lacking was sovereignty—a government of, for and by the people. Hence, despite doubts and fears from many quarters, founders of post-independence India adopted the system of universal adult suffrage without virtually any debate in the Constituent Assembly, thus reposing faith in the wisdom of the common Indian to elect his or her representative to the seat of power.[5]

Needless to say, the socio-economic indicators were appalling when independence came directly in the hands of ordinary people. It was a period when approximately 84 per cent of Indians were illiterate,[6] and an equal number languishing in poverty. The makers of our Constitution were fully aware of the long list of challenges facing this unfathomably diverse country, which was traumatized by the unspeakable horrors of the Partition and plagued by a highly fragmented social structure of caste-based hierarchy. It may be recalled that the UK granted voting rights to women in 1932, about 100 years after its first elections.[7] The US held its first presidential elections in 1789, but women voters had to wait for the nineteenth amendment to their Constitution in 1920 to be able to vote.[8] France and Italy did so only in 1944 and 1945 respectively.[9] But our Constitution ensured that the oppressed masses of India had already voted in many elections before Switzerland allowed its women to vote in 1971 and Australia its aborigines in 1967.[10]

The Indian Constitution was promulgated on 26 January 1950. But Article 324 of the Constitution, which created the Election Commission of India as a constitutional body, was among the very few provisions[11] that was given effect a full two months earlier, on 26 November 1949.[12] Interestingly, the ECI was set up on 25 January 1950, a day before India became a republic.[13] Over the past seven decades, the Election Commission has delivered sixteen elections to the Lok Sabha and over 400 elections[14] to state legislative assemblies, thus facilitating peaceful and orderly transfer of power.

In the past seventy-one years, India has seen a deepening of democracy and respect for constitutional morality. Lowering of the voting age from twenty-one to eighteen years in 1989 was an electoral reform of great significance. Heterogeneity of parties and the rise of coalition politics reflect a bouquet of diverse aspirations and the innumerable positives of power-sharing and consensus-building. The seventy-third and seventy-fourth amendments[15] have enabled the realization of grassroots-level decision-making in our villages and urban local bodies, which embodies the true spirit of 'self-rule' as envisaged by our freedom fighters. The rise of political leaders belonging to the marginalized sections of the society, farmers, women, and minorities to head the national and state governments as well as the upward trend of participation of women, tribals, urban and rural poor in the decision-making process can be traced to the untiring efforts of the Election Commission in conjunction with an increasingly proactive civil society.[16]

A stunning example of the inclusive nature of Indian democracy, which is a source of great pride and satisfaction, is that a country where 80 per cent of the population is Hindu has had four Muslim, one Sikh and two Dalit presidents, including the current one. Several Muslim vice presidents and a Sikh prime minister have adorned the top positions in our country. The largest democracy in the world is now ruled by a prime minister whose mother was a domestic help and who himself worked as a tea vendor to earn a living. There was also a time when four of the largest states (Uttar Pradesh, West Bengal, Tamil Nadu and Rajasthan) and Delhi, the national capital, were governed by women chief ministers. They all came to power through elections conducted by the Election Commission of India.

As India's democracy marches on, our immense economic, demographic and social potential continues to stun the world and even our own selves. The potential of democracy is unparalleled as it accommodates diverse interests and aspirations. This is why Nobel laureate Amartya Sen has remarked that a country does not become fit for democracy, but becomes fit through democracy. [17]

While there is so much to celebrate, it is also imperative to be mindful of some shortcomings in our system that leave a lot of scope for improvement in democratic mechanisms. Many electoral reforms are long pending due to lack of political will or plain lethargy. Reforming campaign finance laws, decriminalization of politics and bringing in a proper law for transparent constitutional appointments to posts, such as that of the CEC, are just some of the many issues regarding which the ECI has repeatedly written to the government. Several important reforms have come through the intervention of the judiciary, which has always acted as a guardian angel of democracy. As the country moves forward, many old and new challenges are surfacing, calling for a swift and decisive action.

As we approach the seventeenth Lok Sabha Elections, it is useful to look back and appreciate our momentous achievements while being mindful of our shortcomings over these adventurous seven decades. This volume aims to do just that—celebrate seven decades of India's unique democratic experiment by compiling opinions on various aspects of the electoral process from eminent voices all around the world who have proven their mettle in academia, social work, public service, industry, journalism and cinema. It is an attempt to look at electoral democracy through different frames of reference: political, historical, social, economic, journalistic and administrative.

The diversity of this volume in many ways represents the diversity of our country. A variety of topics are covered, ranging from women's rights, grassroots democracy, business, electoral reforms, media coverage of elections and the evolution of civil society in these seven decades. The volume includes how the ECI's vast experience with conducting free and fair elections has helped not only India's democracy but many other countries as well. It also touches on what we have contributed to or can learn from neighbouring countries that are transitioning into democracies, such as Bhutan and Nepal.

Needless to say, no such publication can be the work of a single individual. The energy and dedication of a number of people has gone into the production of this anthology of global interest. Words are not enough to acknowledge them all adequately.

My grateful thanks to Bhikhu Parekh, Christophe Jaffrelot, Dasho Kunzang Wangdi, David Gilmartin, Ela R. Bhatt, Gilles Verniers, Ila Sharma, Jagdeep Chhokar, Kabir Bedi, Karamjit Singh CBE, Pramod Kumar, (Late) Somnath Chatterjee, Mark Tully, Meghnad Desai, Milan Vaishnav, Mukulika Banerjee, Naina Lal Kidwai, Niranjan Sahoo, Ornit Shani, Paul Wallace, Rahul Verma, Ratan Tata, Shashi Tharoor, Taylor C. Sherman, T.N. Seshan and Yogendra Yadav for contributing to the volume. They have been extremely patient in responding to the inputs and the various procedures that precede the coming out of the publication. The earlier contributors from among them brooked the inordinate delay with calm fortitude.

My gratitude to Penguin Random House India for taking out the publication at such short notice yet with procedural rigour. My special thanks to senior commissioning editor, Swati Chopra, who worked on war footing to ensure the publication of the book against almost impossible targets.

My thanks to Niranjan Sahoo for helping me organize the book into appropriate sections to make it reader-friendly.

I acknowledge with gratitude the contribution of Mukulika Banerjee, who with help from Meghnad Desai, spent considerable time in 2011–12 gathering the original collection of essays that form almost half of this book. I recognize that she gave all this time at the expense of her own publications to support my efforts.

Shivanshi Asthana, my research associate, was a pillar of strength during the process of putting this volume together. A young scholar with enormous energy and a helpful disposition, she was always there ungrudgingly at all times of the day in pursuit of the project. I foresee a very bright future for her in academics or the civil services, whichever she chooses.

And finally, the Election Commission of India, which shoulders perhaps the toughest and most significant task of conducting free, fair and transparent periodic elections in our country of continental proportions for the preservation of our democratic institutions. I thank it profusely for providing the inspiration and exposure the likes of which I couldn't have got anywhere else in the world. Its reference documents enrich the discourse throughout the book.

S.Y. Quraishi
New Delhi, 2018

PART ONE
Foundational Ideas

I

The Dialectic of Elections

Bhikhu Parekh

Democracy has three essential components—elections, public deliberation and protest. The first ensures that political power is exercised by those authorized to do so by the people; the second ensures that it is exercised for purposes formed by means of public discussion between different points of view and enjoys widespread consensus; and public protests are a bulwark against the misuse of political power and the neglect of national or important sectional interests.

Sole Vehicle of Democracy

In the past few decades in India, the last two components have suffered a decline. Parliament is not the deliberative body it once was. It meets for a shorter period than its Western counterparts do; its business is regularly disrupted; important policies are sometimes made behind its back and legislative measures are rushed through it; and there is little careful deliberation on the great challenges confronting the country. The tradition of well-organized public protests that was developed during the independence struggle has been allowed to decay, and has been replaced by episodic, uncoordinated, ill-planned and poorly led explosions of anger. It seems that the protests are often bought off, co-opted, ignored or brutally suppressed, and those involved are either demoralized, turn

3

to violence, or resort to pseudo-Gandhian fasts and other dubious tactics.

As a result, elections have become more or less the sole vehicle of democracy. They occupy almost the whole of the democratic space, and carry the entire burden of people's aspirations and desire to shape their destiny. They form the centre of Indian political life and excite popular imagination in a way that no other area does. It is hardly surprising that the political history of recent decades is often constructed and told in terms of the chronology and outcome of elections, each forming a neat serial chapter in the national story.

Since elections have come to occupy such a central place, they provide the site where the deeper dynamics of Indian society are played out, revealing and accentuating both its disturbing and healthy trends. Elections, at both national and state levels, structure the political calendar and foreshorten the political horizon in a way that they did not during the Nehru period. For Nehru, they were pedagogical exercises, modes of articulating public opinion, and for electing representatives. Today, they are just vehicles of coming to power. All politics is geared towards winning elections, and policies are made and announced to facilitate this. Not surprisingly, then, they are simplified and reduced to slogans and populist catchphrases. Political parties, with the exception of the Left, are bereft of ideologies and well-considered programmes, and rely for their success on caste, religious and other affiliations and their leaders' personal charisma or dynastic aura. Since they rarely nurture and consolidate their supporters between the elections or deliver on their promises, money plays a crucial role and leads to all too familiar forms of corruption. The electoral support derived in this way is volatile and can easily evaporate with the result that the ensuing legislative majority is unable to count on its stability and lacks the confidence to take bold decisions.

Pros and Cons

The reduction of democracy to elections and the exclusive preoccupation with them also have deeper consequences. All legitimate authority is deemed to be derived from elections, and only the elected representatives are allowed the right to speak for the people. Civil society and NGO activists are told that they cannot claim to represent the people because no one elected them. By this logic, even Mahatma Gandhi would have to be declared an impostor! Once elections are detached from the complex structure of democratic politics and institutions, they can easily go hand in hand with support for authoritarianism. This is why Indira Gandhi was punished, not for imposing the Emergency, which many Indians actually welcomed, but for its 'excesses'. And it also partly explains why, as a recent survey showed,[1] a large body of Indian public opinion supports illiberal measures and a 'firm' and 'strong rule' so long as the government is elected.

While the foregrounding of elections has these and other drawbacks, it has also been a great creative force in Indian politics. Elections have brought new groups into the political system, especially the poor and the marginalized. Too demoralized or apathetic to protest and too inarticulate to influence public deliberation, they find the ballot box an easier route to political influence and power. It does not require argumentative skills or courage. All one has to do is to go to the polling booth and press the right button. Elections have enabled large masses to appropriate and humanize the otherwise alien and impersonal state and put their stamp on it.

Elections are not just what Walt Whitman called the 'Great Choosing Day', but also the Day of Judgement with all its severity and finality. It is the day the wicked are punished, the miscreants chastened, the hypocrites sentenced to obscurity. The sovereignty of 'we the people' is affirmed, and the supplicants of yesterday in their exercise of judicial power pass a final verdict on their erstwhile masters. This adds the elements of contingency and surprise to political life, which no gods or astrologers can predict or prevent, and reinforces popular commitment to it. In their own way, elections are a national spectacle, a collective drama, a deeply bonding experience, and contribute to the political and emotional integration of the country.

Empowering the Electorate

Elections become a source of power only when people are organized. An individual's vote is one among several thousands, and is almost invariably impotent. He or she needs to join hands with like-minded people, and they must cast their votes in a coordinated manner. Not surprisingly, the centrality of elections has thrown up different kinds of interests or identity-based groups that have changed India's political landscape. While these organized groups clash, provoke violence and reduce deliberation to opportunistic negotiations of claims, they also empower individuals and sustain their faith in the system.

Not much research has been done on why people bother to vote in an election in India or anywhere else. After all, it takes up time and energy, and one vote makes no difference to the ultimate outcome. Voters are guided by a variety of motives. They might see themselves as active citizens in charge of the well-being of their community, and think it their moral duty to vote. They might have a fierce sense of freedom and a wish to have a share in determining who governs their lives and how. I am not sure that either of these considerations weighs much with most Indian voters.

Why then do they brave long queues and give up two or more hours of their time? Material reward, given immediately or later, plays a part, but that is declining. My guess is that three factors are far more important. Elections give voters a sense of dignity. They are courted, sought after and valued—an important consideration in a deeply unequal society. The vote also gives them a sense of power. They can, by forming part of a group, make a difference to the outcome of the election and improve their lives. And finally, the vote enables them to humble, even humiliate, and settle scores with those who generally despise or take them for granted. In casting her vote against a higher caste candidate or a government minister in the privacy of a polling booth, the voter silently mocks his pretensions and does what she dare not say or do openly.

Subtly but surely, elections are bringing about large psychological and social changes in India. They could achieve much more and their pathology could be avoided if democracy, currently largely limited to them, were to be extended to other equally important areas of political life as well.

II

The Hidden Wiring of Democracy

Karamjit Singh

It is an honour to contribute to this volume for a number of reasons. The first is a personal one. Both my parents migrated from India to the United Kingdom during the 1930s and the 1940s. I was eleven years old when I first visited India, and my experiences since then have made a deep and lasting impression on me.

The second reason is related to this personal story, which also has a professional dimension. I was appointed in 2001 by Her Majesty the Queen as one of the six founding commissioners for the UK Electoral Commission and was the last of that cohort to demit office in 2010. During this decade in office, I visited India on an annual basis and had the opportunity to interact with each chief election commissioner and his colleagues on these occasions.

The third reason is that as the world's largest parliamentary democracy and with the rich mosaic of religions, cultures and ethnicities that make up the Indian nation state, how can electoral processes make citizens believe that they have a real ability to influence the outcomes of elections? This is a key question not just for India but also for other countries.

An Election in Varanasi

This article contains my personal reflections after visiting one Indian constituency, Varanasi, during the 2009 general elections as a personal invitee of the Election Commission of India.

The voting in this Lok Sabha constituency took place in the first phase of the general elections during April 2009. The parliamentary constituency consists of eight assembly segments and as with all Indian elections, this was conducted under the 'first past the post' system. Postal and proxy voting is only allowed in certain narrowly defined circumstances, such as for allowing voters in the armed forces to exercise their franchise.

During the week that I was in Varanasi, my activities included:

a) Meeting with the collector in order to discuss the overall arrangements and preparations within the constituency.
b) Meeting with the DIG police in order to understand the security issues involved.
c) Meeting one of the three observers nominated to this constituency by the Election Commission in order to understand the issues arising from their visits and the concerns that had been raised with them.
d) Meeting with officials who were responsible for vulnerability mapping, randomization of staff, collection of materials and utilization of transport.
e) Observing how randomization, or allocation of officials for polling duties, was undertaken using computers.
f) Observing the training of electoral staff.
g) Observing the collection of materials by electoral staff.
h) studying the different documentation that related to the electoral process.
i) Monitoring local media coverage of the election, with particular reference to the information that was related to the process.

j)   Visiting fifty-five polling stations at seventeen sites at urban and rural locations across the constituency during polling day and interacting with polling staff, police officers, party workers and voters.
k)   Visiting the collection centre after polling had been completed and observing the receipt of electronic voting machines (EVMs) for depositing in strong-rooms (normally used for storing food grains) and delivery of supporting materials by presiding officers and their teams.

As a precursor to my visit, I had looked carefully at the extensive guidance that is published on the Election Commission's website for those involved at all levels of the electoral administration process. Although political parties, the media and NGOs are major actors in the democratic context, my primary focus was on the electoral process itself. I utilized my unfettered access to all levels of the electoral administrative machinery in Varanasi in order to drill down to the coalface.

Inevitably this meant that I was not able to observe the two other components of the electoral process—compiling the voter register (which would have taken place over some months previously) and the counting and declaration of results (which took place some weeks later throughout India on the same day). However, I noted the emphasis on creating an accurate register that was evident from the information collected about individual voters and (increasingly at that time) a photograph as well. Subsequently, watching the counting and declaration of results on satellite television in the UK, I was struck by the timeliness of this process and the political acceptance of the results.

An important dimension of public administration is public accountability. The background statistics quoted below were made available to me by officials in Varanasi but they were also provided to the local media and published.

The estimated total cost of administration and security for preparation up to and activity on polling day was Rs 3.5 crore for an electorate of just over 24 lakhs (2.4 million voters) or Rs 15 per voter. This was broken down into travel and daily allowances for the police deployed so that Rs 1.7 crore was spent on them and the remainder (Rs 1.8 crore) on civilian staff and associated costs. Rs 12 lakh was spent on refreshments on polling day, 567 buses were hired or used for the movement of election staff, payment for fuel was over Rs 30 lakh, Rs 4.80 lakh was spent on stationery, Rs 11.50 lakh on tents and fencing and Rs 2.50 lakh on polling booths even though most were sited in public buildings such as schools.

The total voters in the constituency are 24,46,608 (over 2.4 million) with 572 polling centres (where one or more polling booth may be sited) and 1573 polling booths with 11,690 polling staff utilized. At 617 booths, the number of registered voters eligible to vote was above 1200 and the remainder was below this figure. The size of polling teams consisting of presiding officers and polling clerks totalled four in each booth, with some also having an additional (female) member of staff to deal with ascertaining the identification of female voters, if necessary.

An estimated 15,000 police and paramilitary personnel were deployed in the constituency. This meant that a total of some 28,000 public servants (civilians and police) were utilized for electoral duties in Varanasi constituency in the period leading up to and including the polling day.

A Transparent Election

A striking feature of Indian elections, from my perspective, was how information technology, communication technologies and the media were being utilized, as well as the collective impact in enhancing transparency and confidence in the electoral process.

The local media was informed that videographers had been deployed at twenty-five polling centres where the number of polling booths sited was eight and above because they were deemed to be sensitive. These polling centres identified as sensitive were also monitored by micro-observers (staff additional to polling staff) and their existence was made known through the local media. Another thirty videographers accompanied teams and supervising officials in the constituency.

At 160 polling booths that had been identified as having the lowest rates of voters with electoral photo identity cards (EPICs), arrangements were made for these voters to be photographed after they had voted using alternative permissible identification and with resulting additions to the register of these photographs as well as issuing cards. I noted the preciseness of this information, which was provided to the local media as well as publishing contact telephone numbers of senior local officials and the three observers acting under the auspices of the Commission. The electorate was made aware of its right to complain about any aspect of the electoral process, and the media highlighted this aspect although some of the coverage was sensational.

During the 2009 general elections, the presiding officer in each polling booth had access to a mobile phone and these numbers were available at each successive tier of the electoral administration system, culminating at the Election Commission level in New Delhi. This information was relayed through national and local media to the electorate, and in Varanasi the local media covered this issue in some depth.

Following public-interest litigation in the Supreme Court some years previously, each candidate had to provide two affidavits listing any criminal convictions and a disclosure of their assets. These affidavits were available for public inspection on the Election Commission's website and attracted a considerable amount of media attention and comment both in Varanasi and elsewhere.

The electorate is not able to observe the computerized process of randomization that allocates staff to polling duties, so any potential risk of collusion is minimized. I observed the three different phases that resulted in staff being allocated to designated segments, areas and polling booths. The teams at individual polling booths did not meet each other until they had assembled at the centres in order to collect the EVMs and supporting materials. Although candidates or their representatives of political parties were invited to attend the sessions when randomization took place, none of them availed themselves of this opportunity.

The EVMs have become a cornerstone of Indian elections by replacing the previous paper-based process and standalone ballot boxes. The technology is relatively simple and easy to understand in terms of its operation. I attended one of the distribution centres the day before polling and witnessed hundreds of presiding officers and their teams testing their EVMs in line with their instructions. Similarly, on polling day, at polling stations I did not witness any voter being unable to understand how to use an EVM. This highlighted increasing voter familiarity but also the effectiveness of media commentary and public information campaigns, and the possibility of education undertaken by political party activists.

Some Conversations

Elections are not just about processes or organizations. They are also about perceptions and people. The three vignettes below (chosen from my many conversations) illustrate different components of the electoral process.

At the distribution centre where EVMs and other electoral materials were being handed out to the staff, I spoke to one of the presiding officers. Our dialogue was as follows:

Q: What is your normal occupation?

A: I am a schoolteacher.

Q: How often have you been a presiding officer or election official in some other capacity?

A: I have worked in every election since 1973 and I have not voted since before then.

Q: How have you found the introduction of EVMs?

A: This has not been a problem. We have received training and as a presiding officer I have now had the experience of four elections where they have been used.

Q: Why do you do this work?

A: As someone who teaches young people, I think it is my personal responsibility to do something to keep the democratic process functioning properly.

Outside an urban polling station I spoke to a male party worker and our dialogue was as follows:

Q: What is your role and how long have you been undertaking it?
A: I am a party worker who lives locally and I have been assigned to this booth as a polling agent for over twenty years. My role is to make sure that local people come here and vote.
Q: What is your view about the EVMs in the electoral process?
A: It is a good thing for the voters but not so good for us party workers.
Q: Why?
A: With the EVMs no one knows how the voter has really voted and we cannot stuff the ballot boxes as we could try to in the past!

Outside another polling station in a rural area, I spoke to an elderly female voter who was coming out of the polling booth and our dialogue was as follows:

Q: Have you just voted?
A: Yes
Q: Without telling me who you have voted for, could you tell me, did you understand the process of how you were allowed to vote?
A: Yes. I went into the polling station with my photo ID card, which I showed to the officers inside. They checked my photo in the register and then they made me put my thumb mark on the paper next to my photo before they put ink on my finger (sic). I was then given a slip of paper that I had to give to another officer before I went behind the curtain.
Q: What happened then?

A: I pressed a button on the machine and there was a beeping sound.
Q: Do you know what that means?
A: Yes. It means that my vote has been registered and no one else can vote instead of me.

These three vignettes highlight a number of themes that are relevant to the electoral process in any context, and certainly well beyond the confines of Varanasi constituency. These are:

a) The commitment of the staff towards discharging their responsibilities in the electoral process. The schoolteacher shone in terms of his personal appreciation of his own role in the democratic process and the notion of providing a public service to his fellow citizens.

b) The perceptions of party activists about the relative strength of electoral processes.

c) Ensuring that the mechanics of the electoral process are understood by all voters, even those who are relatively unsophisticated, so that it is not a system that is only understood by those who are competing politically or those who are responsible for its administration.

d) An implicit sense from all this is that it is important to cast your vote and have confidence in the electoral process and its integrity.

e) The EVM is not just about introducing an electronic voting machine into Indian elections but it has to be linked to inducing a sense of confidence on the part of everyone—the voters at the heart of the electoral process; the political competitors and also those responsible for administration. My observation of the electoral process in Varanasi (and presumably throughout India) is that the EVM is not just information technology hardware added to the electoral process. What has happened is a well-thought-through systems change in terms of processes in which the EVM has taken the place of the original ballot box in which ballot papers were placed. I noted there were high levels of confidence in the robustness not just of these machines but also the procedures surrounding their use.

Unlike some other countries, Indian elections are not conducted by officials who have a dedicated full-time remit for elections. Every level of the administrative process, from the staff in polling booths upwards to the returning officer in each constituency, comprises people from the public sector who are required to undertake election duties for a specified period of time. The only exceptions to this, of course, are the staff at the Election Commission of India and the offices of the state-level election commissioners.

Ensuring Electoral Integrity

My week in Varanasi gave me an opportunity to reflect on how the Indian electoral process has a number of measures embedded within it in order to ensure integrity. These include:

a) Voter registration rolls that (increasingly) have a photograph of the individual voter and other specific details, including name, address, gender and age.
b) Voter identification cards (with a photograph) that a majority of the electorate now has or certain prescribed alternative forms of identification.
c) The randomization process of allocating staff to polling duties in various locations and with colleagues from other parts of the public sector.
d) The collection and use of EVMs (with unique numbers and other electoral materials to record information) with an associated responsibility on the part of the presiding officers and their teams.
e) The checks that were applied at polling booths. In some locations the team inside the booth was augmented by a (female) member of staff checking the identity of veiled women voters. In each of the fifty-five polling booths that I visited, I saw the same process carried out for individual voters.
f) The presence of polling agents, representing different candidates, at each polling booth.

g) The movement of (and in some cases the static presence of) micro-observers and Election Commission-nominated observers and other senior officials responsible to the collector (and who were also accompanied by staff with video cameras) at certain polling booths deemed to be sensitive.

h) The location of the EVM behind a cardboard screen in the polling booth so that the voters could exercise their franchise confidentially. A distinctive beeping noise (which everyone in the polling booth can hear) and red/green lights to indicate whether a vote has already been recorded or remains to do so.

i) Other anti-fraud measures within the EVM include an inability to press or record support for more than one candidate.

j) The high level of awareness of anti-fraud measures in the electorate that has been engendered by public information campaigns and media coverage.

k) The electronic process of recording zero votes at the beginning of the day and the number of votes cast at the end of the day, in the presence of the polling agents representing candidates.

l) The process of depositing EVMs, and supporting documentation, at storage centres after voting has been completed, and the non-release of staff until they have completed this process after making appropriate checks.

m) The retention of EVMs and supporting materials in storerooms that are guarded until counting day and with a facility (if they wish to take it up) for party activists to remain near these storage areas throughout this period. In the case of Varanasi, this timescale was over four weeks (so activists could make their own bedding arrangements and sleep if they wished to).

Achievements and Learnings

A key aspect of good governance is the ability to ensure that citizens perceive governments and elected representatives to be responsive to their concerns, and also that elections allow them the opportunity to express whether or not that mandate should continue.

I believe one of the key achievements in Indian electoral administration has been the introduction of systems and clarity of purpose among staff operating a public service affecting a wide spectrum of urban and rural voters and replacing what has traditionally been a paper-based process with an electronic ballot box (the EVM), which has been sensitively and thoughtfully implemented. In my view, the reason this innovation has been successful is because it was planned from first principles rather than incrementally, and the quality of leadership.

Another achievement is how combating fraud and imbuing a sense of confidence on the part of the voter is seen as an integral feature of the electoral administration process. A continuous system of learning the lessons derived from the application of administrative processes and management of resources plays an essential part here.

The maturity and conduct of the Election Commission itself since its inception several decades ago are other factors. It is no mean achievement to ensure the application of consistent standards in electoral administration and performance throughout elections at national and state levels within India (with some 850 million potential voters).

I consider that another dimension was the quality of human resources utilized, the quality of training they received in order to discharge their responsibilities, and their motivation in what was inevitably an intense and transparent process. A key component in this is the presiding officer, who took decisions at booth level, and effectively embodied the Election Commission to the individual voter. They had to have the appropriate strength of character and insights to interpret and apply Commission guidelines should any unforeseen situation arose.

Of relevance in the administrative context is the extensive documentation published on the Election Commission's website that is made available to all tiers of administrative responsibility as part of their training and the clarity with which different roles and processes are set out therein.

A key feature of Indian electoral administration, from my experience in Varanasi, is the application of general project management techniques to plan the distribution of resources and the implementation of systems. The application of 'kaizen', or Japanese continuous improvement techniques, was evident in the discussions that took place the day after voting in terms of identifying the lessons to be learnt, and recording this as part of an efficient learning system for administration in future elections.

Article 324 of the Constitution confers on the Election Commission the responsibility of superintendence, control and direction in relation to the electoral process. One of the hallmarks of Indian democracy is the widespread acceptance of how the Commission interprets and chooses to discharge its duties, and the actions taken on its behalf.

Using an analogy of electrical circuits, elections are part of the hidden wiring of democracy. As with a power cut or malfunctions in the circuits, it is when electoral processes are not perceived to be effectively delivering (and specifically for the voter) that difficulties arise.

III

Elections and Democracy: The Human Dimension

Paul Wallace

'Elections are a necessity, but not sufficient basis for democracy' is a common statement by electoral specialists. Despite the sophisticated methodology and elegant quantitative analysis that tend to define election studies, the human element tends to be relegated to secondary analysis in the immediate rush for who won and lost in party and celebrity calculations. Long-term human consequences may be equally, if not more, important. Nonetheless, it should be emphasized that elections can be a temporary corrective for democracies that appear to be derailing from their democratic bases.

From Peasant to Farmer

Mani Ram Godara, Bishnoi by caste, and often by identity, reigned as a Member of Parliament (MP) from Hisar district in Haryana as we toured his constituency in 1972 when I held a senior Fulbright Research Fellowship. He proudly pointed out to me the changes in this rural area. Handpumps for water so that women didn't have to walk all the way to a distant well to fill large vessels (they also helped in the irrigation of high-yielding wheat and cotton crops). Healthy, fat Haryana buffaloes gaining national fame. Brick houses on paved roads increasingly replacing mud huts, which further marked the green revolution taking place under Godara's watch. Better and healthier food and milk, especially for children, and rising levels of education and health.

A thin, short farmer demanding more electricity for irrigation suddenly confronted Godara as we approached his dusty farm. Their dialogue turned into a shouting match as the tall, well-built Godara confronted his diminutive dhoti-clad constituent. They finally turned away from each other having exhausted a wide range of colourful swear words without any resolution of their differences.

'That ungrateful peasant doesn't appreciate what I have done for him,' Godara almost shouted at me in frustration. Then he listed the green revolution *vikas* items he had secured for this rural area.

'It's not the development works that are the most important,' I replied after he calmed down. Godara looked at me with surprise. For him, that was the stuff of politics—'delivering the goods' and successfully climbing the ladder of electoral politics, ever since I first met him in Chandigarh after he had lost an election to the Punjab Legislative Assembly. Success since then had taken him to the Lok Sabha in New Delhi from Haryana, a state carved out of Punjab in 1966.

I explained to him that he deservedly should be proud of the economic and social progress, but even more of his role in developing a democratic political culture, however crudely that might be expressed. The farmer confronted him standing upright, I stated. He didn't kneel to the ground and kiss the hem of his pajama trousers. To the contrary, he stood toe-to-toe—or more appropriately considering their relative heights—toe-to-chest with Godara. Demanding more electricity daily to water his fields was a specific demand done in a manner that demonstrated equality rather than beggarly subservience. 'Tomorrow when you can assure him of twelve hours of electricity a day, he will demand even more,' I asserted. 'Then, of course, additional needs in various areas such as education and social areas will follow.' Mobilization, fair elections, party-building and politics are a critical part of this process to which he—Godara—provided key leadership, I emphasized.

Later, as we further explored this topic, I reminded him of our conversation the previous day in a small city of that constituency. Godara had explained to me that the various groups comprising his political base wanted him to resolve their differences. He told them that he now couldn't always be available to deal with factional (he used the term 'petty') differences because as an MP he had to spend considerable time in New Delhi. They had to compromise with their differences, he told them, by themselves. Another remarkable example, I emphasized to him, of a developing democratic political culture that involved a bottom-up rather than the traditional top-down line of authority.

We continued to meet in a regular manner when we were both in New Delhi. I would appear at his government bungalow around 10 p.m. after his chamchas had left. We would eat and drink together and I would ask him endless questions, or what academics call interviews. I learned more from him than he did from me. Before returning to the United States, Godara presented me with a gold Hanuman on a chain. His wife had given it to him the first time he had crossed the dark waters. 'It brought me back safely,' he explained, 'and now it will do so for you.' I have worn it ever since.

Indira Gandhi's Emergency

Subsequently, I reflected upon this experience in an attempt to explain the unsuccessful attempt by Prime Minister Indira Gandhi to alter India's democracy towards authoritarianism by declaring an Emergency on 26 June 1975. Heightened levels of mobilization and the increasing role of the government changed the former autonomous hinterlands, such as Godara's constituency, so that the village and rural society were transformed in contrast to their former limited roles. In the colourful words of W.H. Morris-Jones, 'The little finger has become the whole hand. Government is everywhere and inescapable.'[1]

Instead of upward democratic articulation from the grassroots, such as I had emphasized to Godara, Indira Gandhi had led her regime to increasing centralization and what I termed 'depoliticization', in an article on authoritarian trends in South Asia. Briefly, I argued that depoliticization reversed the democratic progress I had seen, including an open party system, a free press, a vital independent judiciary, and an increasingly participant society. Power became more and more concentrated. Democratic institutions and civil society increasingly came under attack.[2] It is contrary to the actual sharing in decision-making and the structure of authority by a broad range of individuals and groups.[3]

Fortunately for India, a democratic political culture had developed sufficiently so that Indira Gandhi's attempt to legitimize her authoritarian actions was dramatically rebuffed in the elections she felt constrained to hold in March 1977. Elections enabled the dismantling of the depoliticization apparatus. Reversing the 42nd Amendment was particularly critical. It virtually rewrote India's democratic Constitution in November 1976 through fifty-nine clauses that included subordinating the judiciary to Parliament, enabling the prime minister to amend the Constitution by executive order for a period of two years, and replacing Fundamental Rights by a new section on Fundamental Duties. Panchayati Raj institutions again became emphasized for local, rural self-government with additional democratic features recommended for the states in the succeeding Janata Party regime.[4]

The Janata Party's election victories didn't produce governmental success. Non-performance as perceived by the electorate coupled with Indira Gandhi's promise of a government that worked returned her to power in the 1980 elections. Her former emphasis on ideology gave way to emphasizing effective management or, in lay terms, 'delivering the goods'. I introduced a new term, 'Plebiscitary Politics', for the emphasis on the leader rather than the party.[5] The election foreshadowed the 2014 election in which Narendra Modi propelled a plebiscitary presidential campaign for a Bharatiya Janata Party (BJP) national majority.[6]

Haryana's Experience

Several decades after the Emergency, Mani Ram along with India's former Union defence minister Bansi Lal formed the Vikas Party in Haryana. It became Bansi Lal's turn in Haryana in 1996 following Devi Lal who allied with the Charan Singh wing of the Janata Party and Congressite Bhajan Lal, dramatized by the term 'the three Lals'. A former Congress chief minister, then Indira Gandhi's defence minister during the Emergency, Bansi Lal returned to power in the twilight of his controversial political career. He continued to maintain a reputation for shaping the bureaucracy and strongly emphasized his prior achievements in economic development. But, his appearance softened with the years. It was not so much the strong man of the past, but the negative reaction to the two Lal, who had preceded him as chief minister, alliance politics, and positive appeals, especially prohibition, that appealed to Haryana's voters.

Their party formed the state government in 1996 in alliance with the BJP.[7] Party, however, is not the most significant marker for Haryanvis. Devi Lal and his son, Om Prakash Chautala, anchored one part of Haryana's social structure symbolized by the Hindu Jat peasant, about 20 per cent of the state's population. Devi Lal alternatively became a major leader of the state Congress Party, Charan Singh's Lok Dal, V.P. Singh's Janata Dal, which elevated him to the post of deputy prime minister in 1989, and then to minor 'national' parties. In all these cases, whatever the party name, Haryana voters recognized his group as Devi Lal's party.[8] Chautala took the political reins when Devi Lal went to adjoining New Delhi but couldn't match the *tau*. Chautala's rough style of governing turned the innocuous sounding Green Brigade from a youthful support group to a feared gang of enforcers.

The public's reaction to this criminalization of politics resulted in an electoral reaction catapulting the third Lal, Bhajan Lal, into power in 1991 as the state leader of the Congress (I).[9] Bhajan Lal had a longer tenure as a Congress leader. But party loyalty is no more a characteristic that marks him than of the other Lals. The popular Hindi phrase 'Aya Ram, Gaya Ram', denoting the switch from one party to another, originated in Haryana. Bhajan Lal was a master of this tactic, whether it was the wholesale change of his group from one party to another as in 1980, or in persuading opposition MLAs to join his group. A blatant use of money power was the consistent charge of his opponents, whether directed towards buying opponents or in charging for every appointment and service. His core support was in urban areas and among non-Jat groups. Supporters don't necessarily deny the charges of corruption against Bhajan Lal.[10] They insist, however, that he lived up to his promises or returned the money. Chautala, on the contrary, took but didn't deliver, according to Bhajan Lal's supporters.[11]

By March 1996, it had become clear that Bansi Lal would return to power, this time under a regional label, the Haryana Vikas Party (HVP), which he had earlier floated in the 1991 elections. Grassroots reaction to the Green Brigade provided one salient issue. While spending some time in Rohtak University, faculty and students provided me with harrowing accounts of these youthful groups, or goondas as they were called, taking over facilities and behaving in antisocial ways. Tales were told of commandeering *mutts* and forcing religious authorities to 'sell' temple lands to them at almost no cost.

In Ladwa, then a town of over 20,000 people, in Kurukshetra district, women overcame these antisocial elements and forced them to parade in shame on the street. Similarly, the statewide movement for the prohibition of alcohol began in the same district in Jyotisar on the Kurukshetra–Pehowa road. This is the site where local traditions state that Lord Krishna delivered the sermon, enshrined in the Bhagavad Gita, emphasizing dharma and karma to Arjuna and prepared him for the coming battles detailed in the Mahabharata.

Prohibition became a core issue of Bansi Lal's and Godara's Vikas Party. It resonated with Haryana's voters to a surprising degree. A local journalist captured its import with the phrase 'Bansi Lal is the same as in 1991', which meant he continued his autocratic style, 'but he added prohibition and it has clicked'.[12] He described the 'movement' as starting in 1994 in Pabnawa, a village near Kurukshetra. Women made men wear skirts when they misbehaved under the influence of alcohol. It spread with strong support from the Arya Samaj. That is the Kurukshetra perspective. Its roots go even deeper.

In March 1994, while engaged in research in the southern part of the state, in Rohtak district, I accompanied a literacy team to a village. Embedded in the simple sentences of the exercise materials were clear messages about the deleterious effects on society of the consumption of alcohol, especially against women and children. These were repeated in slogans boldly sketched on the walls of houses and compounds. My colleagues told me stories of men returning home from work or the fields being sold shots of alcohol in small plastic containers leading them to beat their wives in drunken stupors. Women and children from all castes were engaged in the literacy programme, enthusiastically welcoming the team, manifesting pride in their developing literacy and becoming increasingly empowered regarding the alcoholism problem. The men didn't manifest any opposition to the literacy group. On the contrary, late in the afternoon, I accepted their invitation to join in their hookah group.

A comparable phenomenon had swept Andhra Pradesh earlier where grassroots mobilization had forced a reluctant state government to establish prohibition. Subsequently, the revenue and enforcement problems became serious. Andhra Pradesh is one of India's largest states while Haryana is comparatively a smaller one. Following the elections that brought Godara's party to power and made him Haryana's home minister, I asked him the obvious questions. How could prohibition be enforced with Haryana bordering Delhi, Punjab, Rajasthan, Himachal Pradesh,

Chandigarh and Pakistan? What about the lost revenues and problems of implementation? Godara acknowledged the problems yet expressed confidence in the continuance of the popular support registered during the elections. All religious and social societies, such as the Arya Samaj and the Sanatan Dharma, supported prohibition, and people cooperated with the enforcement, he maintained. He enumerated prohibition as the number one priority, indicating the serious attention given to the issue. Others priorities were irrigation and water, electricity, security (law and order), and good administration. Corruption, Godara asserted, was also a key problem. He estimated that there was an electricity loss of about 40 per cent due to its theft by corrupt government officials. 'If we can produce cheaply, there is no need for subsidy.' This was especially relevant, he added, as there was a revenue loss of Rs 600 crore over prohibition. Thus, 'other sectors cannot be subsidized'.[13] Godara died in 2009 at the age of eighty-six,[14] following notable yet incomplete political accomplishments.

Prohibition didn't work in Haryana. But the new Vikas Party did respond effectively to the need for protection; too effectively at times. Literacy campaigns directed at vulnerable parts of the population along with increasing mobilization for a variety of purposes, including economic development and political aspirations, continued to build the democratic infrastructure and the values that Godara and I had discussed decades earlier in a farmer's field. One journalist expressed the views of many interviewees in 1996 stating that 'whether you can deliver the goods or not is the major consideration . . . This country will have managers, not ideology'.[15]

Democratic Concerns

Godara represents the human dimension of elections. He wasn't well-versed in the academic rhetoric of democracy. Nonetheless, seeking constituent support for the next elections conditioned his actions. In the process he became increasingly attuned to democratic concerns. These can be summed up in terms of two negatives and two positives: protection and corruption, and development and the larger economy.

a) Negatively, he related to their need for protection. The so-called Green Brigade's excesses provide a clear example, as well as other forms of intimidation and violence.
b) Corruption not only became a significant factor in Haryana elections, but a major reason for the Congress Party's decimation in the 2014 national elections.[16]

Two positives for electoral outcomes that contribute to democratic politics include vikas or development, as in the name of Godara's political party and the larger economy.

a) Development includes electricity, clean water, clean air and toilets as clear examples that are increasingly becoming the staples of Indian politics.
b) The larger economy is always politically important in elections. Jobs, inflation (price of onions as a prime indicator), gross national product and the value of the rupee.

Narendra Modi rode to power in 2014 with these promises. India's 2019 national elections will judge him and the BJP on the delivery of these promises.

Finally, elections are critical in restoring democracy following autocratic periods such as the Emergency. Sri Lanka reversed autocratic trends in 2015, as did Ethiopia, Malaysia and the Maldives in 2018. Central to democratic resurgence is the civil culture embodied by political activists such as Godara.

IV

Law and Politics: A Brief History

David Gilmartin

The complex relationship between politics and law is central to India's electoral history. This is so not because politics and law draw on common principles, but rather, quite the opposite, because the logic of politics and the logic of law have, in the course of India's democratic history, often been in deep tension. Politics is about competing interests, identities, and the competition for power, while law is about rules that theoretically bind the community as a whole. Tensions between the operation of politics and the operation of law have thus been pervasive in India. But the structures of election administration and law in India have, in certain key respects, institutionalized these tensions and contained them within a distinctive electoral structure. The history of India's electoral law and institutions thus provides a key to analysing the distinctive character of India's democracy, and its place within the larger comparative framework of modern democratic development.

Colonial Past

In some ways the distinctive relationship between law and politics that has developed in India is embedded in its colonial past. Though local elections occurred in various contexts in nineteenth century India and earlier, the beginnings of a comprehensive structure of law for Indian elections can be traced to the British colonial reforms of 1919 and their aftermath. This was the moment at which elections, in spite of a very limited franchise, began to play a central role in the structure of colonial administration and politics in India.

Colonial elections were from the beginning built on contradictions. On the one hand, the British sought to use elections to mobilize a structure of intermediaries whose power was tied into India's religious, caste and ethnic divisions, as a counterweight to challenges from nationalists. These motivations were reflected clearly in a British reliance both on an extremely restricted, property-bound franchise and on special electorates for different groups, most famously, but hardly limited to, separate electorates for Muslims. This reflected an old British view of the colonial state as standing above a fragmented Indian society and giving it order through the manipulation of hierarchies of influence.

Yet even as they sought to use elections to maintain state control, the British also introduced a legal structure for voting that reflected a legal vision of the voter as a free individual, a vision that was to have a profound impact on the evolution of electoral law in India. There were thus those among British officials at the time who felt that such a vision was impossible in India, with the power of patronage, caste and religion so deeply entrenched in Indian culture as to render a vision of voter independence meaningless.[1] But the liberal principle of free voting, structured by legal protections for the voter, was, in spite of such reservations, enunciated in accord with international norms as the foundation of election law. Whatever the contradictions, British and Indian officials thus drew up election rules for the first reformed provincial elections of 1920 that were formally structured to protect the independence and secrecy of the individual ballot, to protect the management of elections from excessive government interference or fraud, and to protect the individual voter from bribery, intimidation, and undue influence. Few officials probably believed that these rules could be (or even should be) fully enforced, but they nevertheless came to provide foundations for a structure of law on electoral corruption that embodied an underlying, if idealized, vision of the voter as defined by freedom and choice.[2]

From the beginning, these rules remained in deep tension with the actual operation of electoral politics. Complaints about intimidation at polling stations and about coercive pressures on voting were a marked feature of colonial elections throughout the 1920s, 1930s and 1940s. These complaints focused not only on administrative failure in the conduct of elections, but also on various forms of social coercion exercised by local power-holders, including religious leaders, government ministers, and other locally powerful people (not excluding both local British officials and leaders of the Congress). The result was a developing case law focused (among other things) on the legal protection of voters from what was called 'undue' political influence, that is, influence projected as undermining freedom of choice.[3]

This case law drew initially on the precedents derived from election decisions in the United Kingdom, but it fast developed its own Indian precedents. The tensions between free voter choice on the one hand, and the dangers of coercive pressures of government and society on the free will of the voter on the other, provided the framing conflict defining the meaning of elections as constituted by law. Whatever the electoral outcomes, the tension between law and politics thus came to be central to the meaning of elections as a process.

However limited the colonial electoral franchise, the process of colonial elections thus provided a critical backdrop to the framing of the principles that after 1947 linked elections to the concept of 'people's sovereignty'. In some respects, India's constitutional drafters envisioned the electoral system, much as the British initially had, as a framework for strengthening and legitimizing the state. Yet, they now cast the authority of the state as linked to a unitary conception of the Indian 'people', imagined as a collective of free individuals cast against the local pressures that constituted social division and everyday politics. This was a conception that drew significantly from the structuring of law and politics as linked, yet also opposing, realms that had shaped the dynamics of colonial electoral law. Yet nothing indicated the new vision of elections after 1947 as a 'people's' arena more clearly than the elimination of the old colonial property qualifications for voting and the establishment now of universal adult franchise.

Post-Independence Complexities

Universal adult suffrage signalled an identification of the state with the 'people' of India as a whole. The sovereignty of the 'people' was directly embedded in the Constitution, and the imagination of the 'people' as a unified entity was signalled by the general elimination of the old separate electorates for different groups that had marked the colonial system. Yet the leap to adult franchise only heightened in the eyes of many the projection of law as a necessary counterpoint to politics in defining India's electoral structure. As one of India's later chief election commissioners, S.P. Sen Verma, noted in a subsequent commentary on the coming of universal adult suffrage, 'A democratic form of Government cannot but be turbulent.' For this very reason, it was essential that men devise 'institutions, means and devices to act as restraints until the time shall come—if it comes at all—when by some means individual self-restraint and self-control shall be a sufficient guarantee for the successful functioning of . . . democratic government.'[4] Central to the 'institutions, means and devices' necessary for democracy was law.

The tensions between politics and law that had defined the structure of election law under the colonial regime took on new meaning after 1947. The structure of law—and electoral litigation—that had developed in the colonial era was thus strengthened in the years after 1947, most notably in the Representation of the People Acts of 1950 and 1951.[5] Though separate electorates were generally eliminated (in spite of the maintenance of some reserved seats for Scheduled Castes and Scheduled Tribes), the law sought to expand limitations on the operation of 'undue' electoral influence, adding to the limitations on appeals to official and religious influence that existed in colonial law, bars to appeals for votes on the basis of caste. Subsequently, in the wake of the bitter linguistic rivalries that marked the 1957 general elections in some regions, electoral appeals to language were added to the law's electioneering limitations.[6] All of this reflected a continuing recognition of the tensions embodied in electoral politics, tensions now configured in terms of a vision of the 'people' as a unified, abstract, sovereign entity, a vision in which the law was central, which was juxtaposed against the lived realities of parochial division and social conflict that marked Indian elections.

Meanwhile, electoral litigation accelerated in the years after 1947, as appeals for votes on the grounds of 'religion, race, caste, community or language', though technically labelled as 'corrupt' practices, remained ubiquitous in actual electioneering. From the first general election onward, evidence suggests that issues of caste and community-based voting played a central role in many, probably most, electoral contests. Nevertheless, the law played a critical role in India's constitutional development by upholding the unfettered free choice of the individual voter as an *ideal*, however much the reality of electoral practice might threaten this. This was underscored by the significant volume of election cases in the subsequent decades. Even though most election outcomes were upheld, a sufficient number of election outcomes was overturned to maintain the clear *principle* of the law's operation as a vital counterpoint to politics.[7] Though rooted in colonial precedents, the structure of election law thus took on critical new meanings after 1947 as a critical element in the Constitution of the sovereignty of the people. The idealized vision of the free, individual, voter, protected in law, came to be central to the basic vision of a sovereign people, however much that ideal gave way in practice to the realities of political division, conflict and influence that marked Indian society.

Yet, as a practical structure for regulating electoral practice, the problems in the law's operation were also manifold after 1947. It was not simply that the rules on electoral appeals were, in the context of real elections, largely contradictory and often unenforceable, but that the structure of electoral litigation itself produced highly inconsistent results, as the courts themselves sometimes recognized.[8] The delays that were inherent in the filing of post-election petitions, and in working their way through election tribunals and court appeals, made the results of many of them moot by the time decisions were finally handed down. Efforts to streamline the process, as in the elimination of election tribunals in the late 1950s and the sending of cases directly to the high courts, had some impact, but hardly enough to change this basic situation.

Election Commission's Role

As a practical framework for policing the conduct of elections, the structure of litigation in the courts was thus of limited practical significance, however critical this structure remained to the ideal of the people's sovereignty. Far more important to the actual operation of India's electoral system was the role of the Election Commission of India, which was established by the Constitution to oversee the real-time administration of India's elections. Unlike the structure of election law, the ECI was an institution for which there was no precedent in British colonial law or practice.[9] In some ways, its establishment in the Constitution can be seen as a reaction against the perceived problems of official interference in elections that had marked the late colonial era. Its role as a national body, conducting both national and state elections, also signalled, like the establishment of universal adult suffrage, a vision of the sovereign people of India as a unitary national entity, thus requiring a distinct national entity for running elections that encompassed the legal management of elections at state and central levels within the same unitary structure.[10]

Yet the Election Commission, though drawing on the framings of electoral law developed in the courts, has operated, in some ways, in counterpoint to the courts' adjudication of elections. As an autonomous authority, commanding administrative personnel from the state and Central governments, its mandate was to manage elections in real electoral time. Its relationship to the authority of the courts was thus defined by a structure of cyclically shifting jurisdiction. The ECI had full authority to run elections during the official tenure of election campaigns, with the courts barred during that period from hearing legal electoral challenges or disputes. But once the results of elections were officially announced, the jurisdiction of the Election Commission ceased, and election petitions challenging the announced results on the basis of corruption or legal irregularities were referred to tribunals or (after the late 1950s) directly to the high courts for judicial decision.

In its early years the main energies of the Election Commission went into the massive administrative task of preparing the electoral rolls and making the administrative arrangements for voting on a massive, hitherto unprecedented scale. Ramachandra Guha has captured well in his history of modern Indian democracy the massive effort it entailed. As the first election commissioner, Sukumar Sen, put it, it was 'the biggest *experiment* in democracy in human history'.[11] The logistical problems of providing access to voting for a huge, and partly illiterate population, dominated the ECI's concerns. Oversight of electoral corruption, and dealing with election disputes, while certainly within the ECI's quasi-judicial purview, were given less attention, as the ECI remained acutely aware of its limitations. But the roles of the ECI in hearing and settling disputes and dealing with charges of corrupt electoral activities within the time frame of electoral campaigns evolved over time, often in response to the changing political pressures that the ECI faced. Its powers to register and recognize political parties were enhanced, for example, by the Election Symbols (Reservation and Allotment) Order of 1968, a power that was exercised by the chief election commissioner, S.P. Sen Verma, in his adjudication of claims to the Congress Party symbol after the party's great split in 1969.[12]

But the Election Commission's importance in India has arisen not just from its ability to carry out the administrative tasks necessary to the conduct of elections (however important that might be), but also from its evolution into a symbol of the central role of law in balancing politics in the definition of democracy. Perhaps the most important marker of the evolution of the ECI's role in this framework was the development of the model code of conduct for elections. The code grew initially not out of any explicit constitutional or statutory authority given to the Commission, but rather as a result of its ongoing negotiations with the political parties in structuring electoral arrangements. According to a later ECI report, the first model code developed from discussions among the political parties in Kerala in 1960, and this spurred the developments of such voluntary codes in some other states as well. Subsequently, the ECI began to circulate suggested rules of conduct to the parties, and a formal model code of conduct was issued by the ECI in advance of the general elections in 1972.[13] The fact that the code itself did not have the force of law (even though many of its provisions were contained in statute and could thus also be litigated through post-election petitions) was itself a marker of the ECI's evolving moral authority. The significance of the model code lay not in its determinative impact on political behaviour (though that has perhaps become greater over time), but rather that it came to be a symbol of the moral claims of the ECI to stand above politics and set rules for electoral behaviour. It thus became a symbol of the moral standing of rules (and law) as a critical counterweight to the self-interest and group conflict that marked electoral politics.

Enforcing Model Code of Conduct

It was not until the tenure of T.N. Seshan as chief election commissioner, from 1990 to 1996, however, that the code gained central importance as a symbolic statement of the ECI's claim to a special moral authority, balancing the self-restraint of law against politics. Seshan gave new teeth to the code by using the ECI's power to fix the dates for election campaigns, threatening to suspend the campaigns midstream of those whose violations of the code were blatant. Most important to his power to enforce the code, however, was his ability to *publicize* model code violations, holding up to intense public scrutiny those politicians who openly violated it, in an era in which the reach of the media in India was expanding markedly. This propelled the model code (and with it, the role of the Election Commission) into popular consciousness as never before.[14]

Seshan's success in using the model code did not come without considerable criticism. Nor did it suggest an Election Commission that operated entirely outside politics. In many ways, Seshan's expansion of the power and presence of the ECI was a product of the balance of political forces between the Congress and the BJP in the early 1990s that made room for an activist—and less politically controllable—ECI during this period.[15] At the same time, his policies were facilitated by a number of important legal decisions by the Supreme Court in the ECI's favour, which underscored the ECI's association with a vision of law cast as an antidote to the dangers inherent in uncontrolled, and self-interested, political competition.

One Supreme Court decision, for example, underscored the Commission's constitutional power not only to secure from state and Central governments the staff they needed to conduct elections, but also to discipline this staff according to its own rules, thus shielding them more effectively from political pressure.[16] Another SC decision confirmed the full power of the ECI to set the official dates of an election campaign, thus giving it power to control the time period in which the model code would be in force.[17] All of this strongly reinforced the ECI's autonomy, and sharpened its image in the popular imagination as an institution standing outside the workings of everyday politics, and thus able to act, in the name of the Constitution's legal mandates, to make 'free and fair' elections possible. Like the protections for the voter's freedom of choice embodied in election law, this was a vision of authority that seemed to capture the ideal of the people's sovereignty, an ideal standing outside the pressures of everyday politics.

None of this is to suggest, of course, that the powers of the ECI that were evident during Seshan's tenure actually empowered the ECI to stand fully outside politics or to fully manage the political pressures that at times compromised the fairness of elections. For all their enhanced scope, the powers of the ECI remained limited and dependent in critical respects on its image among the voters as a body that stood apart from the political parties, yet was willing, at least on occasion, to call politicians—and the political parties—to account. Though the ECI has remained, particularly since the 1990s, a potent force in the popular imagination, it has hardly been able to control fully the various, and in some cases increasing, threats to the functioning of Indian democracy, not least the growing influence of money in politics.

Still, in a world in which political threats to the functioning of democracy have been growing, the model of electoral administration and election law that had developed in India has gained increasing salience around the world. Particularly (but hardly exclusively) in the United States, where the problems of fragmented, localized and politicized electoral administration have gained increasing attention since the fiasco of the 2000 presidential election, the vision of a powerful and apolitical Election Commission has attracted increasing attention (even as the salience of such a structure within the American constitutional structure remains questionable).[18]

Indeed, the power of India's system lies in the fact that its unique balancing of politics and law has come to define a distinctively Indian approach to the concept of 'people's sovereignty', which is gaining increasing attention in worldwide discussions of the meaning of democracy more broadly.

V

What Is Distinctive about Indian Elections?[1]

Yogendra Yadav

In my contribution, I offer a key to answering two simple, related and rather obvious questions about the state of democracy in India. What is wrong with representative democracy in today's India? And what can be done about it? Questions of this kind are considered too simple, too general or perhaps too large for students of politics to answer. I suspect that in its search for *clever* questions and *novel* answers, academia often loses sight of *significant* questions and good answers. I suggest that good answers to these questions are not global answers. An attempt to answers these questions would lead us to understanding the distinctiveness of electoral politics in India.

Let me first clarify the questions. The first one contains two questions within it. Does the system of competitive elections succeed in representing the people in terms of what they demand, what they desire or what they need? If it does not—at this stage let me not get distracted by the fascinating distinction between these three terms and how these set up three different ways of measuring the gap between the actual and the ideal—then the natural question is, why not?

There are many obvious candidates for an answer here: the quality of political leadership, the nature of political parties and party competition, the institutional rules of electoral competition and popular beliefs, attitudes and values. How much weight do we assign to these possible explanations? An understanding of what and why should give us some clues about how we can go about correcting the democratic deficit. Where should the thrust of the attempts at political reforms be directed? Does it call for constitutional and legal redesigning? Or should we look at institutional modifications? Or does the answer lie in the domain of political action?

I cannot hope to answer all these questions here even if I were to pretend to know the answers. But I do wish to suggest a general way of thinking about and answering these questions in the Indian context. In this sense my argument is specific to India.

Established academic wisdom plays little role in shaping political common sense on this issue in contemporary India. Scholars would, of course, put it down to the illiteracy of politicians and public intellectuals. But it could also be read, equally plausibly, as a sign of disconnect between political science and political sense. India has rich, almost obsessive, public debates on what is wrong with representative democracy and what can be done about it. Political common sense on this question is forged by political debates in legislatures and committees, jurisprudence and the legal discourse, 'civil society' recipes for political reforms and media debates around specific instances of lack of accountability and responsiveness in politics. Yet this debate has virtually no point of contact with the professional knowledge of politics listed earlier.

Three Objections Met

Let me begin by responding to three possible objections to the line of inquiry that I undertake. It could be argued that the questions I ask are not worth pursuing because: a) India is not quite a democracy, or b) there is nothing really wrong with the outcomes of democracy in India, or c) one should not expect democracy to address issues like mass poverty.

In defining democracy, I follow the 'minimalist' tradition of defining democracy as a form of government in which those who rule are elected by the people in competitive elections and run the risk of losing power in regular elections. According to this definition, the election of rulers by the people is subject to some qualifications:

a) The election should be competitive in that there should be more than one serious contender.
b) The opposition should have a fair chance of winning, should they have popular support.
c) The electoral mandate cannot be revoked by the loser and the winner should get to exercise the highest political power.
d) The elections should be held at regular intervals irrespective of the wishes of the incumbent.

It seems fair to categorize India since independence as a 'democracy'. To be sure, there has been more than one instance where these minimum rules have been violated. The illegitimate, though strictly speaking not unconstitutional, extension of the term of the Lok Sabha during the state of national Emergency imposed by Indira Gandhi (June 1975 to March 1977) was one such instance at the national level. There are several instances of gross violation of the minimum requirements of democratic rule at the state level, where the overall verdict of the elections could not be described as a fair reflection of popular choice. In that category, I would put all elections that took place in the state of Jammu and Kashmir before 2002 except the one held in 1977, all elections in Nagaland before 2003 and in Mizoram before 1987, the state assembly election in West Bengal in 1972, Assam in 1983 and Punjab in 1992. This is an embarrassing but finite list of exceptions that otherwise serves to prove the rule that India since independence must be characterized as a democracy in the minimalist sense of the term.

The second objection can be met by pointing to one gross failure in India since independence—the continued existence of a vast population well below a floor of minimum goods and services required for dignified living.

Why are we surprised at the coexistence of democracy and mass poverty? Simply put, majority rules in democracies and we should be surprised if those who (can) rule do not use this power to improve their conditions of life. This is not to say that the desire or demand of every kind of majority is routinely fulfilled in any democracy. Clearly, the strong desire of an overwhelming majority of the electorate in all the democracies to have clean, accountable and efficient government is routinely frustrated. The point here is that the non-fulfillment of this expectation calls for an explanation. There is nothing new in this expectation: democracy was always seen as the rule of the poor. Before the recent spread of the democratic form of government all over the globe, democracy was the dread of the propertied classes and the hope of those who believed in radical redistribution of power and resources.

In fact, the paradox of the coexistence of democracy and mass poverty is deeper in India than in many other societies. Some of the common reasons why democracies do not care for their poor do not hold true for India. First of all, the institutional design of Indian democracy (parliamentary system, asymmetrical federalism, flexible Constitution amendment) is not 'demos-constraining' in that it does not put significant obstacles to the democratic popular will. There are not too many veto points that might account for the failure of floor-securing social policies to be legislated and implemented. Second, the party system is intensely competitive with very high electoral volatility. The first-past-the-post system accentuates the effect of voters' volatility into dramatic change in seats and government formation. Though the level of volatility has come down in this decade as compared to the previous one, a ruling party in an Indian state has just about a 50 per cent chance of coming back to power. Parties cannot afford to be complacent and overlook issues that might concern a significant proportion of population. Third, the state capacity in India is higher than most comparable poor countries; it still commands the force to impose its will and is not crippled by absence of resources to meet some of its key projects. All this makes it even more intriguing that the ruling parties/coalitions should not (be able to) muster adequate political will to carry out anti-poverty policies.

Finally, what makes it truly intriguing is that the poor have not opted out of democratic politics in India, at least not from routine participation in electoral politics. The evidence put forward by

National Election Studies[2] in India shows that the participation level and the sense of efficacy and legitimacy of the system are still fairly impressive in the case of the poor. While electoral participation rates are declining in older democracies, turnout at the state assembly level has risen in India. Turnout in Indian elections goes up as one goes down the multiple tiers of democracy; the highest turnout is recorded in local level elections. Unlike Europe and North America, the participation rates do not decline in India as one travels down social hierarchy. Citizens at the lowest rung of the hierarchies of caste, class and education turn out to vote in numbers as great as, if not greater than, those at the top. Villagers vote more than city dwellers and women's participation level is catching up with men's.

To sum up, the coexistence of a functioning democracy and mass poverty does constitute a paradox that we need to think about, especially in the case of India. A meticulous way to respond to this paradox would be to take up each link in the chain of argument summarized above and specify at each level the mechanisms that do not let this expectation be realized. Many of these mechanisms would turn out to be nearly universal and are fairly well understood. Grossly unequal distribution of private wealth and the constraints it imposes on the nature of democratic politics are good examples of such universal factors. I take these into account while proposing the way forward, but let me focus here on some of the mechanisms that are distinctively Indian.

Across countries in terms of the impact of the electoral system, the structure of political choices offered by the party system, the social basis of political preferences, agenda-setting and public opinion formation, the invisible role of issues and ideologies, interests and identities are seen to be the keys to making sense of elections. Yet we simply assume that elections perform the same role everywhere. The end result of this similarity is that the experience of electoral politics in societies like India is interpreted in the light of the narrow historical experience of Western Europe and North America. Hence the need to understand the distinctiveness of the Indian experience of elections.

One of the first things that strikes any observer of Indian elections is their centrality in India's political life. Banners, posters and crowds fill the streets; massive processions and rallies are a norm; the media is full of election news and every street corner is buzzing with political gossip. Though on a steady decline of late, this kind of visibility in Indian elections symbolizes the pivotal role elections have come to play in Indian politics. If tension between pre-existing social form and borrowed legal-political structure provides the basic frame for understanding Indian democracy, the history of Indian politics is an attempt by millions of ordinary people to write their own political agenda in an alien script. An encounter such as this, if it is to lead to meaningful outcomes, requires bridges or hinges that connect the two different worlds. The institution of elections came to perform this crucial role in India. It became the hinge that connected the existing social dynamics to the new political structures of liberal democracy, allowing for reciprocal influence.

An election is often the site for a fusion of popular beliefs and political practices with high institutions of governance. Thus an election is an occasion for the transfer of energy and resources from the 'unorganized' to the 'organized' sector of democracy. This is the moment when the legal-constitutional order of liberal democracy makes contact with the messy social and political reality of India. The 'formal' sector is highly visible, it leads a legal-constitutional existence, it involves 'civil society' groups and NGOs or a certain segment of political parties, it speaks a familiar modern language, mobilizes secular identities and is easy to incorporate into a global register of democracy, even if it draws modest energy and participation.

Every political actor is aware of another 'informal' sector, often seen as a source of embarrassment. Political organizations and movements that inhibit this sector speak a homespun hybrid language and fall back upon identity-based mobilization. Though political practices in this sector lead an invisible, often paralegal, existence below the radar, this sector remains the most happening political site in terms of popular mobilization and energy. The chasm that separates the two worlds and the absence or non-functioning of the other possible bridges has resulted in the unusual salience of the institution of elections. This unique role is what accounts for the continued dynamism of the electoral process in India, while a number of other imported institutions and processes are floundering.

Elections in India perform many more functions. For a post-colonial country like India, successful elections are still a symbol of a national political community, something of a festival of collective identity. For the poor and the marginalized, who are excluded from the normal functioning of the state, elections are an affirmation of their citizenship and are seen as a sacred ritual of political equality. Notwithstanding a robust media that routinely uses public opinion polls, elections are still the principal site for the dissemination of political ideas and information and also the only reliable method to gauge public opinion on the big issues facing the country. Elections force political parties to consider ideas, interests and entities that do not lend themselves to easy aggregation through instrumentalities of the 'organized' sector. Thus, elections often appear as the only bridge between the people and power, as the only reality check in the political system.

Elections are also an occasion for settling, unsettling or resettling local equations of social dominance and the arena of struggles for social identity and dignity. Elections are a site for contestation for social dominance in a locality, leading to assertion by dominant social groups and protests by subaltern groups. Attempts by clever political entrepreneurs to manufacture a social majority often involve building a local coalition of castes and communities. This often leads to an invention of community boundaries and sometimes the jerrymandering of settled boundaries. In a micro as well as macro setting, elections are an occasion for distribution and redistribution of resources. This is the time for patronage distribution as well as the occasion for the ordinary citizens to collect their 'dues' from the political class. All this accounts for the festival-like character of the Indian elections and the fierceness with which they are contested here. At the same time, this compression of multiple decisions into a single act also results in an under-emphasis on the representational functions of elections.

Two other structural features of Indian elections have accentuated this difficulty. One of these has to do with the problem of scale in politics. The design of representative democracy in India simply lifted a system meant for much smaller communities and applied it to a polity of continental scale. This resulted in a manifold increase in the scale of representation and led to a qualitative difference in the nature of the relationship between the representative and the represented. A member of Lok Sabha typically represents a population exceeding two million and a member of the state legislature in one of the major states represents anything between 200,000–500,000 persons. A comparison with the scale in Britain (less than a hundred thousand for each member in the House of Commons), which served as the model, brings out the sharp contrast. The mega-scale of the system of representation has had many consequences for the nature of political representation. The minimum requirements of resources and information needed for this kind of election result in a very high entry barrier for a new entrant to the system. The impossibility of face-to-face interaction between the representative and the represented has necessitated an army of rent-seeking intermediaries and is beginning to lead to the mediatization of constituency-level politics.

Finally, a system with multiple levels of governments and its corollary of multiple non-corresponding electoral cycles in a parliamentary system have introduced a peculiar disjunction between different levels of government and elections. Over the years, state-level politics has become the principal arena of political contestation. But the design of Indian federalism allocates principal power and resources to the Central government. And most of the principal or at least immediate problems faced by citizens require a solution at the level of local self-government. In the absence of well-functioning local bodies with matching resources or accountable local officials, elections to parliament and state assemblies also perform a routine municipal function of attending to local grievances and connecting the people to the administration. Parliamentary elections often reflect the verdict for or against the state government. This conflation in levels has meant that the Central government is simultaneously under-accountable and over-accountable. It is over-accountable, for every round of state assembly elections are politically sensitive for the national government. At the same time, the Central government can be under-accountable, for its fate is largely determined by what some other governments do.

Political Lessons for Our Times

An overwhelming majority of India's population still lives below the acceptable minimum level of access to goods, services and dignity. They use every available opportunity offered by universal adult franchise and open political competition to secure better conditions of life. Very often they don't succeed, for the political menu on offer is very narrow and hard to alter, especially at a time when mainstream political parties are more insular and party organization is very fragile.

What, then, needs to be done? If the argument offered above has any force, it points in two directions. The first and a pressing need is a package of political reform that reduces some of the institutional constrains that prevent the needs of the majority from being translated into political signals leading to political will for social policies. Let me provide here a checklist of the changes required. The basic idea is not to bring India in conformity with the global practices, for 'deviance' has been the strength of the Indian system. Nor do we need to change India's electoral system or de-crowd the electoral arena of contestants, as many enthusiastic reformers have suggested in recent times. What we need is, first of all, decentralization of political power by creating smaller states, greater assured resources to state governments, autonomous district-level governments, greater funds, functions and functionaries to local bodies. Second, we need measures to strengthen other mechanisms of accountability and responsiveness by instituting independent regulatory institutions and reforming the bureaucracy and the police to bring them closer to people. Third, we need measures to reduce the asymmetry of information, such as a genuine public service broadcaster, regulation of cross-media ownership, checks against private treaties and stronger disclosure norms for public functionaries. Fourth, we need measures to reduce the inequality of resources in politics, such as public funding of elections by vote-linked cash reimbursement on a non-discriminatory basis and tax support for political contributions. These reforms are urgent, for their absence would hurt not just the prospects of social democracy but also the existence of democracy itself.

A Representative Democracy

A fairly common way to think about representational deficits in India is that representative democracy in India has not yet evolved to the level of 'advanced' democracies. There are too many parties, too much caste-based identity politics and too little ideology, which allows political entrepreneurs to take advantage of ill-informed citizens. The view invites us to be patient with the maturing of Indian democracy and encourages legal interventions to nudge it in the right direction.

This reading gives us a different perspective on what's wrong with representative democracy in India. The problem is not that the people are uneducated and lack ideological orientation; the problem is that popular preferences do not get translated into politically relevant signals by the media. The problem is not that caste mobilization subdues other cleavages, but that the multiplicity of cleavages fractures the majority. The problem is not that the proliferation of parties leads to fragmentation, but that an increase in parties is compatible with a shrinking of political choices and the capture of parties by special interest groups. Finally, the problem is not with the first-past-the-post (FPTP) system, but with the massive scale and multiple levels of representation.

This reading recognizes the need for some corrective measures: lowering the scales, reducing the asymmetry of information, monitoring the media and levelling the playing field in terms of resources. At the same time, it also reminds us that democracy cannot be made responsive and accountable by tinkering with institutional design alone, that the quality of democracy is in the last instance a function of the intensity and nature of politics.

VI

Why Does India Vote?

Mukulika Banerjee

Data from the Election Commission of India has provided clear evidence of rising voter turnout in each election, which has raised the question: why do people vote? Do people vote mainly to support their candidate or a political party? Or do they vote because they are intimidated by political parties? Or do they vote because their votes are bought? Or is it due to peer pressure? To add to the ECI data, data from Lokniti's National Election Survey (NES) data in 1998 revealed that demographically, it were the poor, rural and socially disadvantaged, who were the most enthusiastic voters. As a result, it was possible to make the assumption that their motivations for voting were based on their lack of education and poverty.

I have tried to provide some explanations for this question— why does India vote—on the basis of qualitative research into voter motivations. In a paper titled 'Sacred Elections', I argued that Indian citizens vote because they feel that they have an inviolate, almost sacrosanct, commitment to participating in elections (Banerjee 2007). My explanations for people's enthusiasm to vote were based on long-term ethnographic research conducted while living in two adjacent villages in West Bengal. These villages were poor, had high levels of adult illiteracy and displayed voter turnout above 85 per cent in all three tiers of elections, so they were typical of the national trend identified by the NES surveys. Research revealed that people voted to support a party that was the most likely to improve their material needs, and for candidates who they thought could achieve this for them.

Right to Vote

Surprisingly, evidence shows that the act of voting itself is an important reason for voter motivation as it expresses citizenship and popular sovereignty, which in a context of ubiquitous social inequality is especially meaningful. There is widespread awareness even among the most socially disenfranchised that as citizens they have a right to vote and they feel a duty to discharge this right. They feel a deep sense of gratitude and obligation towards the Election Commission of India for making elections accessible, free and fair. Thus, elections provide in the lives of citizens a unique moment of procedural fairness, equality, rule of law, efficiency, unity of enterprise, citizenship, meaningfulness and festivity, such that they have taken on the mantle of ritual in the deepest sense that transcends quotidian experience. It is for this reason that elections have come to be regarded as sacrosanct in modern Indian public life.

In 2014, the findings presented in 'Sacred Elections' were tested as hypotheses in a national study. A team of twelve researchers investigated whether elections were sacrosanct everywhere in India by studying the national elections of 2009, in which they documented the reasons voters gave when they were asked why they voted, how they received the message of election campaigns, what their personal experience of casting a vote in a polling station was. The researchers paid particular attention to the adaptability of Indian languages in inventing new terms and catchphrases and poetry to disseminate political messages. The result of this countrywide study was the volume *Why India Votes?* and it confirmed that despite enormous political variations across different regions of the country, the reasons why people voted remained largely the same (Banerjee 2014).

In the past decade or so since then, the study of Indian elections has expanded exponentially and a variety of exciting scholarship has emerged. It has covered a wide range of themes: the making of the Election Commission of India and its current processes, analyses of elections through available quantitative data such as polling booth results, innovative techniques that have created new visualizations of data, research projects on issues of elected representatives and their social background, and factors that determine voter choices. The study of the conduct of elections themselves has also become more thorough and nuanced. The role of money in particular has dominated these writings, and scholars have paid particular attention to legislative loopholes, criminality and the role of business in generating the enormous amount of cash that changes hands during elections.

Ethnographic studies have deepened our understanding of what role vast sums of money actually play during elections, rejecting outright a 'vote-buying' argument and offering more nuanced explanations. The management of elections and electoral strategy of political parties and candidates have also been studied, especially given a growing professionalization of electoral management by teams who work across political parties. Thus, our understanding of the role of money, media and management in Indian elections has deepened. Our knowledge of Indian elections is, therefore, more sophisticated and nuanced than ever before, and includes a variety of scholars from a range of different social sciences.

Understanding the Voter

In this rich tapestry of election studies, what remains relatively less understood is the voter herself. Research questions of election studies are driven by a processual view of elections that aims to analyse or predict electoral results and scrutinize political actors, such as politicians and middlemen, through their social background or political alliances. The voter becomes salient to explain how they vote, which political party they are likely to support and what determines these choices. These studies have made our comprehension of elections detailed, of course, but our understanding of the voter is mainly on the basis of *how* they vote rather than *why* they vote at all. This is a question worth pursuing mainly to explain rising turnout but also because political parties repeatedly fail to deliver on their campaign promises and social inequality continues to grow. Thus, it could be expected that in India, like in other older democracies, voter apathy can set in. But as we know, the opposite is true.

Why India Votes? aimed to address this gap and the main findings from this study pointed out that Indian voters vote for a number of reasons, some of which are obvious and the others, less so. Voters tend to vote for the candidate who they think best represents their interests, and caste and community often determine their choices. As some voters said to our team in 2009, they gave their votes like their daughters' hands in marriages, only to those who belonged to their castes. Poor voters tend to reward parties that work for them, even if they have a reputation for being an outfit of the rich. Incumbents are punished for non-performance and there is a healthy appetite for change to test new politicians. The research during the 2009 Lok Sabha elections also revealed the counter-intuitive finding that some people always voted for the underdog who had no chance of winning just so that he would not lose his deposit or will. The need for keeping political competition in a democracy was keenly felt—a chapati has to be cooked on both sides and needs to be flipped over from time to time, people explained. But voters were in complete agreement about the venality of all politicians, and explained that politics was like quicksand that sucked you in and made you dirty.

From these above explanations, it is clear that along with the support for a particular political party, voters were also committed to some basic principles of democracy, such as the need for political competition and rising above identity politics to reward performance.

Affirmation of Citizenship

The biggest revelation, however, of the 2009 Lok Sabha elections, augmented by a further study conducted between 2012–15 on assembly elections in over six states, was how important elections were in reinforcing a sense of citizenship. Across India, voters pointed out that casting their votes at polling booths was unlike any other social experience they had ever had. Anyone who had their electoral photo identity card was allowed to stand in queue to vote and this created genuine social mixing in a way that no other public space in India allowed. People queued in the order in which they arrived and no preference was made on the basis of wealth, status or any other social marker, and so the polling booth was perhaps the only public space in India with no 'VIP' culture and the otherwise ubiquitous factors of class, gender, work, age, skin colour, or disability that dominated Indian public life. Thus, often middle-class voters found themselves standing behind their domestic staff, and landowners behind agricultural workers.

For this fact alone, the experience of voting in an Indian election is unique and welcomed by voters, especially those who come from socially disadvantaged sections. This small but significant detail is further reinforced by the civility of polling officials towards all voters and their care towards those who need help. The business of voting itself is thus accessible, efficient, takes minimum effort and the public holiday declared on polling day adds a festive note to it. For those who are routinely discriminated against on the basis of caste, colour, class and religion in everyday life—and millions of Indians experience these acutely—this extraordinary glimpse of egalitarianism is deeply valued.

Voting has thus become the most assertive way for citizens to inscribe their presence on the body politic. By showing up to vote, they avail of the chance of being counted and reminding the elite and the powerful that they exist, and in large numbers, and can therefore determine their political fates at elections. 'The vote is our weapon' is a statement often used to describe this sense of empowerment. The voter is conscious of making the correct individual choice, which is always open to the influence of a caste group, kin or community or indeed money and muscle. But the secret ballot offers an opportunity to escape this pressure. As one man put it, 'One cannot express political loyalties inside a village, it is too risky. But we can in the vote.'

It is for this reason that the totalizer machine is urgently required. Currently, votes are counted by EVMs, making polling booth data available through the ECI. This allows political parties to know exactly which communities have voted for them and which have not, leaving voters vulnerable. The totalizer is able to electronically 'mix' ballots before counting, in a way that large drums were used for mixing paper ballots. In order to protect the secrecy of the ballot, it is imperative that the totalizer is implemented.

A Fundamental Right

Election officials revealed that they too were fully aware of the responsibility of elections vested in them and anticipated their duties with a mixture of excitement and dread. As Government of India officials, a mistake committed while on election duty could lead to a black mark in their annual report. It is no wonder that one of them said, '*Yeh pariksha bhi hai aur shaadi bhi!* [It (elections) feels simultaneously like an exam and a wedding!].' In order to serve as officials, they are required to undergo training in three stages to learn their way around the electoral procedures and the enormous paperwork that it entails. Much of the training also anticipates what needs to be done when things go wrong or when the unexpected happens, such as the case of a visually impaired voter who requires help with the EVM. The commitment of election officials towards the proper conduct of elections is recognized by voters. To vote in India has, therefore, become a means of being taken seriously, as one man put it: '*Vote se hamar pehchan banta hai* [The vote gives me recognition].'

Research has shown that voting is seen as a duty to exercise a foundational right (*maulik adhikar*) that each citizen has and one that underpins all other claims—to food, education and security. Some even refer to it as their birthright (*janam siddh adhikar*). Indian voters see their electoral participation as fundamental to their engagement with the state, and their names on the voting list as a rare but valued official acknowledgement of their existence by a system that otherwise neglects their interests. Fulfilling the duty to vote is an important responsibility and as one voter put it, 'It is my right to vote and it is my duty to exercise this right. If I don't discharge this duty, it is meaningless to have this right.' A person in Kolkata referred to Election Day as 'Vote Puja' (worship) to capture this meaning as an inviolate and sacrosanct duty.

The responsibility to vote was further reinforced by tremendous peer pressure to not waste a vote. This was inadvertently created by the simple procedure followed by election officials of marking the left index finger of those who voted with a short vertical line in indelible black ink. While this is done to prevent fraudulence, it also creates peer pressure particularly in close-knit communities, as it is impossible to lie about having voted. To not have the ink mark on one's finger results in suspicion and questions about the reasons for not voting.

Therefore, to not vote is unthinkable for many marginalized citizens and is expressed in emphatic terms by many. 'Vote *toh debe hi karo* [Of course, I will vote].' And because of this potency, to be able to vote is a cherished right that people express in emotive terms as one man did, 'Vote *na diye toh aisa laga jaise maa se baccha bichad jata hai na* [For us not to vote is like a child to be separated from her mother].' Thus, as with other borrowed words, the original meaning of 'vote' is rather expanded in its Indian usage. While 'to vote' continues to indicate a mechanism to express support for a chosen candidate or political party in an election, it has also acquired an affective meaning.

NOTA Option

The most concrete evidence that perhaps people often vote not just to support a particular party or candidate but for other reasons has been the growing numbers of votes cast against the NOTA button, a new option on all electronic voting machines available across the country for the 2014 Lok Sabha elections. NOTA allowed voters to 'spoil the ballot paper', which was not otherwise technically possible on an

EVM.[1] The uptake for this option was immediate and in 2014, 1.1 per cent of all votes cast across India were registered for NOTA and an average of 10,000 votes was cast for it in every constituency. In every subsequent election, NOTA registered more and more votes, and while 1.1 per cent is not a large figure in absolute terms, in at least nineteen constituencies, NOTA votes could have affected the final results as its vote share was higher than the winning margin between the first and second candidates. In the Bihar state elections in 2015, NOTA polled more than the winning margin in a significantly high number of twenty-three seats and in Chhattisgarh's state elections held in 2013, NOTA had polled more than the winning margin in fifteen seats.

In the state of Odisha during the 2014 general elections, NOTA polled more than 4 per cent of the votes.[2] There may be several explanations for this but we can conclude that whatever the motivation, those voting for NOTA view the act of voting *as an end in itself*. By bothering to turn up, with the correct ID and the willingness to queue, only to press a button that doesn't support any individual or political party, significant numbers of voters appear to be sending the message that they believe there is some intrinsic merit in the act of voting without necessarily using it to support anyone in particular. The figures for NOTA votes thus draw attention to the act of voting itself and raise the possibility that the vote is not used only instrumentally to achieve a particular result but perhaps also to achieve a symbolic meaning.

Thus, the act of voting is rich with meanings in India and adds additional texture to our understanding of elections and democracy everywhere. A vote does not merely indicate electoral choice but encodes a faith in values and a hope for a better future. India's functioning electoral democracy contrasts with its rather poor record of according basic democratic rights of security or justice to most of its population. Also, it is ironic that despite India's high economic growth rate figures as compared to other nations and the growing size of its economy, the most common demands by voters across the country, in rural and urban areas, remain *bijli, paani, sadak* (water, power and roads), and sanitation, housing, good government schools and primary healthcare centres. It is for this reason that elections in India have become so burdened with hope and expectations as an opportunity to usher in change. Indian voters continue to invest their energy into elections by showing up to vote, as elections still have meaning, standing as they do for a plethora of values associated with the democratic ethic that is missing in everyday life. India's challenge is to extend her democracy beyond elections so that her citizens continue to vote in large numbers.

References

Banerjee, Mukulika. 2014. *Why India Votes?* Exploring the Political in South Asia. New Delhi, London: Routledge.

Banerjee, Mukulika. April 2007. Sacred Elections. *Economic and Political Weekly of India.*

VII

Elections Enshrine India's Democratic Pluralism

Shashi Tharoor

India has a culture that values modesty in conduct and speech, but one boast we have not been shy of making is that we are proud of being the world's largest democracy. It is India's conviction, from its experience in maintaining this distinction, that democracy is the only form of governance that gives each citizen of a country a strong sense that her destiny and that of her nation is determined only with full respect for her own wishes.

Democracy, Winston Churchill famously wrote, is the worst system of government in the world, except for all the others. One of democracy's defining characteristics is its unpredictability, since it reflects the wishes of large numbers of people, expressed in the quiet intimacy of the polling booth. The wonders of democracy have startled the world as the voters of India have repeatedly confounded all the pundits and pollsters to place the country in the hands of different governments led by different parties or coalitions. India's first prime minister, Jawaharlal Nehru, would have been proud of this. His greatest satisfaction would have come from the knowledge that the democracy he tried so hard to instill in India had taken such deep roots, despite many naysayers claiming that it would never work in a developing country.

As a result, India has managed the process of political change and economic transformation necessary to develop our country and to forestall political and economic disasters. Much as it is tempting to do so, this cannot, in all good conscience, be accredited to some innate beneficence that one acquires along with the right to an Indian passport. Rather, I credit Indian democracy, which is rooted in the constitutional rule of law and free elections.

Every Indian general election is inevitably the world's largest exercise in democratic franchise—with some 850 million registered voters, that is hardly surprising. And look what happens in these elections: governments are routinely voted out of office, and voters hold politicians accountable for their development promises. And they do so within India's extraordinary framework of diversity: for instance, in May 2004, India witnessed a general election victory by a woman leader of Roman Catholic background and Italian heritage (Sonia Gandhi) making way for a Sikh (Manmohan Singh) to be sworn in as prime minister by a Muslim (A.P.J. Abdul Kalam) in a country that is 81 per cent Hindu.

India's democracy has flourished while pursuing some of the most intractable challenges of development the world has known. India has in the last decade and a half become a star amongst the countries and regions described as emerging markets. Of course, politics remains a significant impediment to India's development, since reforms are pursued with the hesitancy of governments looking constantly over their electoral shoulders. But this also ensures the acceptance of reforms when they are eventually made.

India is also proud of being able to demonstrate, in a world riven by ethnic conflict and notions of clashing civilizations, that democracy is not only compatible with diversity, but preserves and protects it. No other country in the world, after all, embraces the extraordinary mixture of ethnic groups, the profusion of mutually incomprehensible languages, the varieties of topography and climate, the diversity of religious and cultural practices, and the range of levels of economic development, that India does. Yet Indian democracy, rooted in the constitutional rule of law and free elections, has managed the processes of political change and economic transformation necessary to develop our country.

India is united not by a common ethnicity, language, or religion, but by the experience of a common history within a shared geographical space, reified in a liberal Constitution and the repeated exercise of democratic self-governance in a pluralist polity. India's founding fathers wrote a Constitution for this dream; we in India have given passports to their ideals. Instead of what is sometimes known as the 'narcissism of minor differences', in India we celebrate the commonality of major differences. To stand the famous phrase on its head, India is a land of belonging rather than of blood.

So, the idea of India (a phrase coined by Rabindranath Tagore and minted by many others since) is of one land embracing many. It is the idea that a nation may endure differences of caste, creed, colour, culture, conviction, cuisine, costume and custom, and still rally around a democratic consensus. That consensus is about the simple principle that in a democracy you do not really need to agree all the time, except on the ground rules of how you will disagree. The reason India has survived all the stresses and strains that have beset it for fifty years, and that led so many to predict its imminent disintegration, is that it maintained consensus on how to manage without consensus. Indians are comfortable with the idea of multiple identities and multiple loyalties, coming together in allegiance to a larger idea of India.

In India, the Election Commission plays a pivotal role in husbanding our democracy. The largest electoral exercise in the history of humanity, the sixteenth general election for our Parliament, was completed on 18 May 2014. It was a mammoth election, with over 554 million voters, out of the 834 million eligible to do so, casting their votes in 927,553 polling booths, over a period of six weeks. An astonishing 8251 candidates from 464 political parties took part in the polls. Though as a victor myself, I can celebrate the election, the government of which I was a part was turned out of office, and my own party lost 80 per cent of the seats it held. Yet I can say with great pride and satisfaction that the exercise itself, and not just the outcome, demonstrated the vital strength of democracy. Democracy is also about how to lose, and that is something Indians have repeatedly learned, as multiple changes of governments have confirmed. Democracy is a process and not just an event; it is the product of the exchange of hopes and promises, commitments and compromises that underpins the sacred compact between governments and the governed.

Of course, as I have written elsewhere (*India: From Midnight to the Millennium*, published by Penguin Books in 1997) the singular thing about India is that you can only speak of it in the plural. There are, in the hackneyed phrase, many Indias. If India were to borrow the American motto, 'E Pluribus Unum'—out of many, one—it would have to read 'E Pluribus Pluribum'! Everything exists in countless variants. There is no single standard, no fixed stereotype, no 'one way'. This pluralism is acknowledged in the way India arranges its own affairs: all groups, faiths, tastes and ideologies survive and contend for their place in the sun. At a time when most developing countries opted for authoritarian models of government to promote nation-building and to direct development, India chose to be a multi-party democracy. And despite many stresses and strains, including twenty-two months of autocratic rule during the 'state of Emergency' declared by Prime Minister Indira Gandhi in 1975, a multi-party democracy—freewheeling, rumbustious, corrupt and inefficient, perhaps, but nonetheless flourishing—India has remained.

The Indian voter has long since resolved the 'bread vs freedom' debate so beloved of intellectuals: the question of whether democracy can literally 'deliver the goods' in a country of poverty and scarcity, or whether its inbuilt inefficiencies only impede rapid growth. Some still ask if the instability of political contention (and of makeshift coalitions) is a luxury a developing country cannot afford, but they do so with diminishing conviction. No one seriously suggests any more—as they were prone to when three governments fell between

1996 and 1998—that, as today's young concentrate on earning their bread, they should consider political freedom a dispensable distraction. Not only is democracy *not* incompatible with economic growth and progress, it is the only guarantee that growth and progress will be stable and self-sustaining.

This is where lies the great hope for the survival and success of India's pluralism. No one identity can ever triumph in India: both the country's chronic pluralism and the logic of the electoral marketplace make this impossible. In leading a coalition government, and then in losing office, the Hindu-inclined Bharatiya Janata Party has learned that any party with aspirations to rule India must reach out to other groups, other interests, other minorities. After all, there are too many diversities in our land for any one version of reality to be imposed on all of us.

Equally, democracy is vital for India's future. While there is no easy way to cope with the country's extraordinary diversity, democracy is the only technique that can work to ensure all sections of our variegated society the possibility a place in the sun. Elections are the instrument for ensuring this. What is encouraging for the future of democracy is that India is unusual in its reach; in India, electoral democracy is not an elite preoccupation, but matters most strongly to ordinary people. Whereas in the United States a majority of the poor do not vote—in Harlem in ten Presidential elections before 2008 (when a black candidate ran), the turnout was below 23 per cent—in India the poor exercise their franchise in great numbers. It is not the privileged or even the middle class who spend four hours queueing in the hot sun to cast their vote, but the poor, because they know their votes make a difference.

The experiment started seven decades ago by India's founding fathers has worked. Though there have been major threats to the nation from separatist movements, caste conflicts and regional rivalries, electoral democracy has helped defuse them. Separatism in places as far afield as Tamil Nadu in the south and Mizoram in the northeast has been defused in one of the greatest unsung achievements of Indian democracy: yesterday's secessionists have, in many cases, become today's chief ministers. (And thanks to the vagaries of democratic politics, tomorrow's Opposition leaders.)

It's still true that in many parts of India, when you cast your vote, you vote your caste. But that too has brought about profound alterations in the country, as the lower castes have taken advantage of the ballot to seize electoral power. The explosive potential of caste division has been channelled through the ballot box. Most strikingly, the power of electoral numbers has given high office to the lowest of India's low. Who could have imagined, for 3000 years, that an 'untouchable' (Dalit) woman would rule as the chief minister of India's most populous state? Yet Mayawati has done that three times in Uttar Pradesh, based on her electoral appeal.

On the fiftieth summer of India's independence, K.R. Narayanan, a Dalit—a man who was born in a thatched hut with no toilet and no running water, whose university refused to award him his degree at the same ceremony as his upper-caste classmates—was elected the president of India. He led an India whose injustices and inequalities he had keenly felt as a member of an underprivileged community; yet an India that offered—through its brave if flawed experiment in constitutional democracy, secularism, affirmative governmental action and change through the ballot box—the prospect of overcoming these injustices. Five years later, he was succeeded by a Tamil Muslim, a fisherman's son who sold newspapers on the streets as a boy, and who happened to be the father of India's missile programme. Today, in 2019, the highest office in the land is again occupied by a member of the Dalit community. If the presidency symbolizes the Indian state, it is still a symbol of India's diversity, and its egalitarian democracy.

The question of whether democracy and development can go together has also been answered convincingly by India. Some experts have argued that democracy does not lend itself to rapid development, that the compromises that are essential elements of democratic governance, and the need for decision-makers in a democratic society to take the wants of their constituents into account, were distractions that less-developed states could ill afford if they were to make the hard decisions necessary to improve their futures.

Of course, this argument rests on a set of assumptions that India has never accepted. The most significant of these assumptions is that development is solely about generating wealth. The Bible (in three different places) offers the undoubted wisdom that 'man does not live by bread alone', and neither, I might add, does woman. After all, why does man need bread? To survive. But why bother to survive, if it is only to eat more bread? We recognize that life is about more than survival. But we are also, perhaps uniquely among the large democracies, very well aware that neither man nor woman, nor country nor state, will live well or long unless some attention is given to the baking of bread, the boiling of rice, the rolling of a chapatti.

And just as we are aware, and proud, of modern India's strong democratic traditions, we are also aware of our responsibility to develop, to seek to bring our people into the twenty-first century with comfortably full bellies and comfortably fulfilling occupations. Democracy and human rights are fundamental to who we are; but human rights begin with breakfast.

So modern India has struggled to come to terms with what has sometimes been seen as the competing demands of freedom and development, just as it has struggled with the need to fully respect diversity and at the same time strengthen and pay homage to our sense of identity. Democracy, as precept and practice, will never wear the mantle of perfection. I have written in my books of the many problems that India faces, the poor quality of much of its political leadership, the rampant corruption, the criminalization of politics. And yet, corruption is being tackled by an activist judiciary and by energetic investigative agencies that have not hesitated to indict the most powerful Indian politicians. (If only the rate of convictions matched the rate of indictments, it would be even better . . .) The rule of law remains a vital Indian strength. Non-governmental organizations actively defend human rights, promote environmentalism and fight injustice. The press is free, lively, irreverent, and disdainful of sacred cows.

I believe that the India of tomorrow is one that is open to the contention of ideas and interests within it, unafraid of the prowess or the products of the outside world, wedded to the democratic pluralism that is India's greatest strength, and determined to liberate and fulfil the creative energies of its people. That is the transformed India of the early twenty-first century, and its place in today's world is well worth looking forward to.

The American editor Norman Cousins once asked Jawaharlal Nehru what he hoped his legacy to India would be. 'Four hundred million people capable of governing themselves,' Nehru replied.[1] The numbers have grown, but in 2019, 550 million voters will demonstrate yet again to the world how completely they have absorbed his legacy. More than five decades after Nehru's death, that offers our nation one more cause for celebration.

VIII

How We Can Strengthen Parliamentary Democracy

Somnath Chatterjee

The completion of seven decades by the Election Commission of India is, indeed, an occasion to celebrate its role in the overall consolidation of our parliamentary democracy. I feel, it deserves not only recognition but also appreciation for the relentless efforts it has made, and continues to make, in providing a secure foundation to our democratic structure as contemplated by our founding fathers, in which the people of our country should have full faith and confidence.

The holding of periodic elections, for the due composition of our houses of Parliament as well as the legislative assemblies and councils in the states of our country, with more than 800 million voters, is a task of such gigantic proportions that it requires not only a tremendous organizational set-up and a well-functioning machinery but also a deep commitment to upholding the basic objectives and the true spirit of our Constitution, by conducting them in a fair and transparent manner. I feel that it has been a commendable achievement on the part of our Election Commission to have discharged its constitutional and legal obligations in substantial measure. However, all concerned, including the Commission, should take lessons from those occasions when some controversies had been raised, for good or bad reasons, so as to avoid them in the future.

Electoral Challenges

I believe that a vast majority of the people of our country are fully wedded to the principles of our parliamentary democracy, as provided by our Constitution. I also believe that there is no suitable alternative to the same. Thus, to my mind, it is imperative that every citizen of India and every political party uphold in the fullest measure the true principles of parliamentary and participatory democracy. Of these principles, the holding of free and fair elections is the most important one since it gives full opportunity to the electorate to give due expression of its choice through the electoral process. When we talk of our representative democracy, it can only be true to its name if we are able to maintain the primacy and purity of our electoral system, free from the vitiating influence of money and muscle power, and from attempts at exploiting divisive issues and taking recourse to violence and other undesirable activities.

Our country, for its size as well as varied geography and climate, its large population, multiplicity of political parties, languages, religious practices and ethnicities, poses a huge task for adequately organizing a free and fair exercise of franchise in every nook and corner of the country. We cannot but admire those deeply committed and sincere officials who have performed usually in the most unobtrusive but dedicated manner over the years, particularly those employees who have covered 45 kilometres in knee-deep snow to collect thirty-seven votes or who have waited at a booth in a forest teeming with Asiatic lions for one whole day for a single voter.

To my mind, it is essential that all political parties, large and small, taking part in our electoral process should be fully committed to seeking a free and fair verdict from the electorate. For this, what is needed is scrupulous adherence to the principles of parliamentary democracy and all electoral laws, rules and regulations for giving primacy to the unhindered expression of choice by every member of the electorate and total elimination of all questionable methods to influence the voters. When elements endeavour to pollute the system by taking recourse to methods that include violence for their own partisan interests, it becomes much more difficult for the Commission to hold elections in a free and fair manner.

Those who actively participate in the electoral process should conduct themselves in a manner that will give the fullest opportunity to the electorate to express their views without any fear or favour. And if all the participants truly believe in the primacy of the electorate's choice, then it is the duty of each one of them, and particularly of the political parties, to see that the Election Commission of India is able to discharge its onerous duties and functions without any interference or pressure from any quarters. To my mind, the Election Commission not only has to provide the logistics for holding elections, but also needs to see that the purity of the elections is maintained by weeding out methods, processes and activities of different parties and participants who seek, for ulterior purposes, to misuse, if not destroy, the system.

The Constitution of India, a product of the sagacity, vision and the collective wisdom of a whole generation of our nation's leadership, is an embodiment of the values that we as a nation deeply cherish. Those who hold public office take an oath to uphold the Constitution, which is based on a value system. It is a codification of our fundamental objectives and methodology as perceived by men and women endowed with a broad and inclusive national vision. A commitment by all participants to fundamental democratic values is central to it and must manifestly prevail in all electoral matters.

Polarized Politics

Regrettably, over the years, it appears that growing sections, representing practically all walks of life, particularly the political class and most worrisomely even some in the judiciary and the media, have begun to think that values and principles are dispensable and that an assumption of power or authority or making quick money is what counts. Politics is no longer seen as a noble vocation in the service of the people, but it is all about the 'art of the possible', which signifies that neither the means nor the end matters. No society can insulate itself from the consequences of such politics for too long. All the major maladies our society is afflicted with today have their roots, in my view, in politics devoid of values, of which the political community seems unmindful as having any importance to them. It is the end that matters and not the means, although politicians might preach otherwise for public consumption.

Unfortunately, we have a fractured polity in the country, which is almost totally governed by the politics of confrontation, if not hatred of each other. The country is overtaken by intolerance, divisiveness, corruption, senseless violence, untruth, false propaganda, conflict and disrespect for democratic dissent, which are seriously vitiating our political life as well as social cohesion. This kind of confrontational politics seeks to mould public opinion around caste, creed, language, region and religion-divisive issues. Sections of our political spectrum depend on these to get political advantage by emphasizing what divides the people rather than what unites them. Leadership based on such dangerously divisive factors and actuated by a hunger for power seems to be oblivious of our most cherished national values such as secularism, socialism, respect for pluralism, inclusiveness, decency, probity, tolerance and co-existence, thus vitiating our electoral process.

What is even more worrisome is the fact that political polarization is sought in the name of sub-national, narrow and divisive identities, whose preferred language is often that of violence, rather than the democratic and civilized methods of discussion and dialogue. Several recent incidents in our country have exhibited politicians and even so-called cultural organizations taking recourse to violent and unethical means dependent on crime and rabid antisocial elements.

Criminals are being used to settle political scores and, in the process, they are crossing the border and entering politics. This has led to criminalization of politics, or rather what I call the 'politicization of crime'. The violent behaviour we see in our legislative bodies at every level is the result of not only the entry of people with questionable background into politics, but also sections of political leadership taking recourse to questionable means, which they believe will help them politically whatever its effect on the people. It is, therefore, imperative to stress that parliamentary democracy cannot be strengthened, unless those who indulge in behaviour incompatible with the established traditions of democracy or who, without real faith in healthy democratic methods, deliberately resort to unethical means, are made accountable for their wrongdoing. The only way to do so is by separating them from the democratic institutions they have come to be associated with, sometimes through questionable means.

One most unfortunate trend, which has emerged in recent times, is that Parliament, the lofty temple of our democracy, has come to be the playground for acute confrontational and competitive politics. The floor of the house has great sanctity as a forum, where the government is made to listen to the demands and aspirations of the people, who are the real masters in a democracy. That sanctity is grievously violated when members behave in a manner that invites public opprobrium.

It is essential not only for those connected with the proper functioning of our elected bodies but also for citizens as a whole that our most important representative bodies, constituted by the exercise of franchise by the people who participate in the electoral process with great hopes and aspirations, individually and collectively look into their problems and find out solutions that will usher in a new order through which the country's progress will be ensured. The people expect that the institutions at the highest level will, through dialogue and debate, consider and discuss what ails the nation and, if necessary, make laws that are needed for meeting the needs of the people and for the advancement of the country as a whole. It is obviously the expectation of the people that although different political parties take part in the elections, whichever party is able to form the government will discharge its duties and functions for the benefit of the people.

What we have been witnessing for the past few years is that our political parties think that the functioning of elected bodies, particularly the houses of Parliament, in a proper manner is not

relevant for their partisan purposes. Examples such as both the Lok
Sabha and the Rajya Sabha not functioning for more than two weeks
throughout the winter session are matters of the greatest concern
and the people can reasonably ask the question as to the relevance
of constituting these important bodies after spending huge amounts
of taxpayers' money if even the budget and important public issues
are not discussed on the floor of the houses. To my mind, a belief
seems to have developed in the minds of different political parties
that disturbances of the proceedings of the houses of Parliament will
be politically more productive than allowing the houses to function,
probably because disturbances of the proceedings get larger media
coverage than making good speeches that are hardly noticed far less
reported.

It will indeed be a tragedy if ordinary people come to believe
that the whole electoral process has become irrelevant, a means
somehow to acquire power, and that the proper functioning of
elected bodies is of no importance. To my mind, it will be a great
danger if people lose faith in the functioning of our political parties
and in our electoral process and thereby in our constitutional set-
up. The weakening of our democratic structure will result not
only in anarchy but in the ultimate degeneration of our polity
towards dictatorship or some other form of government, which
our founding fathers had expressly rejected. This will also seriously
affect the importance of our electoral system and thereby of the
Election Commission.

'Right to Recall'

This is the time when the people in general and the political parties
in particular should ponder which way our polity is going. We should
introspect whether each one of us, individually or in groups through
different political entities, is duly discharging obligations as citizens
of an independent country.

It is essential that the right-thinking members of society not
surrender their rights under the Constitution by remaining inactive

or becoming despondent about the state of affairs. It is the right of every citizen to demand that his or her elected representative discharge their obligations in a manner that will sustain democracy rather than weaken it.

What is the option available to the electorate if their representative is not functioning to their satisfaction? If any elected representative is found to be corrupt, irresponsible, inefficient or indifferent towards people's causes, the citizens are left with no choice but to wait till the next elections. This brings us to the question of how to express our disapproval of the erosion of values in politics. I strongly believe that it is time we thought of incorporating the concept of 'Right to Recall' in our Constitution.

In the Fourteenth Lok Sabha, some members were disqualified for raising questions on the floor of the august House for pecuniary considerations. The voters who elected those members were powerless to take any effective action. It was the House that took the bold step. If only the electors had the right to question and hold their representatives accountable for their acts of omission and commission without having to wait till the next elections, our public life would, perhaps, become better. The public must be empowered to initiate action when the situation so demands. This is a question the nation must debate seriously.

For the last several decades, no single party nationally has been able to get a majority of its own. The result has been that both at the Centre and in the states, governments have been formed on occasions by political parties with disparate programmes and ideologies, who combine only with the object of acquiring power, forming unprincipled coalitions and even by encouraging defections from one party to another. There have been many more instances of post-poll understandings or adjustments than before between different political parties, only for the purpose of forming a government. The instability of such governments and the adoption of questionable methods to remain in power, often compromising basic political and constitutional morality, have seriously eroded people's faith in the system.

Non-Partisan Election Commission

In my view, unless we have a political system where honesty, probity and commitment to values prevail, it will be idle to expect that our electoral system will be free from maladies or deficiencies or that the Election Commission will alone be able to maintain the sanctity of the electoral process or earn the confidence of the people. All should cooperate with the Commission in discharging its responsibilities in a proper manner.

It is, however, essential for the Commission to convince the people that it is wholly neutral and non-partisan in all its actions and decisions and it should not give any impression of taking sides in any matter whatsoever. Its duty is primarily to see that the electors are able to cast their votes fearlessly and of their free will. In the face of terrorist threats to disrupt elections or the risk of violence, it will be the particular responsibility of the Commission to ensure safety and security to all participants not only on the date of the polls but throughout the election campaign. It should not condone any violation of the rules, regulations and the Code of Conduct. This has become extremely important because of some parties resorting to violent methods to serve their purposes.

What is also needed is a system of appointing 'observers' in constituencies that is not merely a ritual but is effective in curbing illegal and criminal activities. Observers should discharge their functions without any partisan motivation and without fear and favour. Unfortunately, my experience from having taken part in the Eleventh Lok Saba elections is a mixed one. The Commission must cautiously and scrupulously select observers who can, indeed, play a significant role in keeping a watch over happenings but also over the use of huge amounts of money, which some candidates spend during elections when they even make attempts to purchase voters.

Though the Commission has been carrying out its duties in a manner that has generally earned the approbation of the people, it has not yet been able to eliminate corrupt practices and violent methods by parties or candidates both during the campaign and most importantly on the date of the poll. To achieve this, more plenary powers may have to be conceded to the Commission, which I hope will never compromise with forces of destabilization and those who take recourse to anti-democratic methods.

It is for the Commission to establish its credentials that it will strictly adhere to its constitutional mandate and will not succumb to threats or illegal persuasion and ensure that the farce of an election as was experienced during the election to the West Bengal assembly in 1972 is never replicated anywhere else.

PART TWO

A Tumultuous Journey

I

Origins of Trust in India's Electoral Process

Ornit Shani

The Election Commission is one of the most trusted public institutions in India. This is supported by survey data and studies from a range of disciplines over the last two decades.[1] The vibrant Indian electorate has, on the whole, accepted electoral outcomes, which has made the peaceful transition of power from one elected government to another possible for almost seven decades. But at Independence, during the preparations for India's first elections that took place in 1951–52, it was not obvious at all that India would establish successfully the means for conducting democratic elections under universal adult franchise, and to embed trust in the electoral process among its vast electorate.

This democratic endeavour had to be achieved in the midst of the partition of India and Pakistan that was tearing territory and people apart, even as 552 sovereign princely states had yet to be integrated into India. Partition led to mass displacement of an estimated 18 million people, and the killing of approximately one million people. Moreover, about 85 per cent of the prospective electorate of over 173 million people had never voted for their political representatives in a legislative assembly and a vast majority of them were poor and illiterate. How then, under such adverse circumstances, were trust and a belief in the electoral process bred among the prospective electorate?

Beginning the Process

This chapter explores the origins of the building of a credible political culture of electoral administration in India. In particular, it traces its roots to the preparation of the first electoral roll on the basis of universal adult franchise for the first elections. An electoral roll prepared and maintained as accurately and as up-to-date as possible, was the plinth upon which the institutions of electoral democracy would rest. The design and management of this stupendous task on the basis of universal franchise was underway already from September 1947, ahead of the enactment of the Constitution, by the Constituent Assembly Secretariat (CAS), a small and newly formed interim bureaucratic body of the state-in-the-making. Only in March 1950 was the task handed over to the first chief election commissioner of India.

I argue that the way the Secretariat, as the election management body at the time, dealt with the registration of voters, and particularly with the many challenges that arose in that process, cultivated the engagement and trust of the future electorate. From the earliest stages of the preparation of the draft electoral roll, the Secretariat instituted practices and norms of openness and responsiveness towards citizens' contestations over a place on the roll, which resulted in a widespread sentiment of ownership of electoral democracy. These factors, combined with the competence exhibited by the Secretariat, demonstrated the trustworthiness of this ambitious project to a wide public, eventually resulting in an electoral process that is largely trusted. To demonstrate the dynamics of these contested interactions the chapter focuses on the challenge of registering Partition refugees on the electoral roll.[2]

The instructions for the preparation of the rolls set out that a voter had to be a citizen of or above twenty-one years of age, with a place of residence in the electoral unit where he or she was to be registered for a period of no less than 180 days in the year ending on 31 March 1948, i.e. no later than 30 September 1947. The qualifications for citizenship were based on the anticipatory citizenship provisions in the draft constitution of February 1948. Soon after the Secretariat sent detailed instructions for the preparation of the rolls, and provincial governments began issuing their instructions to local administrators, letters began arriving at the Secretariat, asking whether and how refugees should be enrolled. Indeed, refugees' citizenship and residential status—two key qualifying criteria for registration as voters—were unclear and soon became a contested matter. A large number of refugees migrated after 30 September 1947, which was the deadline for the prescribed residency qualification. Letters of complaint also arrived at the Secretariat from a wide range of citizens' organizations and ordinary people, raising questions and concerns over the registration of refugees.

Registering Refugees

The President of the East Bengal Minority Welfare Central Committee, Calcutta, for example, cautioned in a letter to the Secretariat that unless new 'definite' directions were given with respect to the residential qualification of 180 days 'the immigrants from Pakistan are likely to be omitted from the draft electoral rolls now to be prepared.'[3] The committee proposed that the question of residence 'should be very leniently applied at least in the preparation of the first electoral rolls. Mere declaration as to intention of residence should be accepted as residential qualification.'[4] The committee also reported that in some parts of Assam attempts were being made to leave out the immigrants from the electoral rolls.

Indeed, several letters referred to a circular that the Reforms Commissioner of Assam issued on 28 May 1948 to all district officers, containing detailed instructions for them and their staff regarding the preparation of the electoral roll.

'The Government desires to draw your personal attention with regard to the floating and 'non-resident' population of the District. These people are not qualified to be registered as voters. They may be staying with friends, relatives or as refugees or labourers. Great caution will be necessary on the part of your staff to see that not a single individual of this class manages to creep into the electoral roll by any chance.'[5]

The CAS acknowledged that the residential qualification of 180 days up to 31 March 1948 would cause hardship to refugees for reasons beyond their control. Seeking a solution to the question of refugees' registration, the Secretariat decided to tackle it on an all-India basis. Members of the CAS initially explored international precedents. The CAS's research officer prepared a report that summarized how European countries dealt with the refugee problem since the beginning of the First World War and in the wake of the partitioning of the Ottoman Empire. The report concluded that there was no book, documents or adequate precedents, which dealt with this minute question.

Members of the CAS reviewed the summary report, as well as the suggestions and requests made in this regard by citizens' organizations. The undersecretary noted that 'the refugees are always on the move, and, therefore, no residential qualification can be prescribed for them, if they are to be given the right of vote in the next elections'.[6] The Secretariat ultimately decided to register all refugees on the electoral rolls at that stage on the mere declaration by them of their intention to reside permanently in the town or village concerned, irrespective of the actual period of residence. It is noteworthy that one of the citizens' organizations that wrote to the Secretariat suggested a similar solution.[7] The Secretariat sent the new directives on the enrolment of refugees to all the provinces and the states. It then replied to all the queries of citizens' organizations, telling them about the solution they found. The Secretariat also issued a detailed explanatory press note in the matter.

Nonetheless, problems arose when provincial governments issued instructions to their staff for the registration of refugees, based on their own interpretation of the Secretariat's directives. The Government of Assam, for example, set a court-fee stamp of the value of eight annas to be affixed on the declarations to be filled by refugees for inclusion in the preliminary electoral rolls, even though no fee was stipulated to the order to relax refugees' registration on the roll. It also set that such declarations should be made in writing before the circle sub-deputy collector before 30 September 1948. In the face of that, numerous citizens' organizations and ordinary people submitted complaints to the Secretariat.

Various citizens' organizations wrote to the Secretariat that the Government of Assam's instructions 'will have the inevitable affect (sic) of disenfranchising the majority of the refugees'. The Assam Bengalee Association, for example, warned that if the Assam procedure for the registration of refugees was not modified it would 'nullify the intent and purpose of the declared object of the Govt. of India for granting citizenship right to the refugees in an easier method'.[8] Specifically, citizens' organizations demanded, first, the cancellation of the court-fee charge, claiming that it was an economic blow for the refugees. Second, they asked that the male heads of the households be allowed to file a declaration on behalf of his wife and other women in the family, explaining that a large number of women were *purdanashin* (observing rigid rules of seclusion), and that it was impossible for a pregnant woman to appear in person. Third, citizens' organizations asked to extend the time limit for the submission of declarations.

Some organizations reported in detail about the misconduct of specific local officials. Thus, the Tinsukia Bengali Association complained that although the deputy commissioner's directives specified that declarations from refugees were to be accepted on 4 September 1948 until 3 p.m., the sub-divisional commissioner who was authorized to receive declarations stopped working at 1.15 p.m. They wrote that a few hundred refugees, 'including about a hundred ladies' were waiting to file declarations 'in the scorching sun for hours'.[9] In Hojai, wrote the Assam Citizens Association Nowgong, the sub-deputy collector Kampur, who was set to receive declarations on 24 September 1948, did not show up. As a result, '[a]bout 500 Refugees including females, who had come from distant villages . . . had to go back disappointed.'[10]

In these struggles over the refugees' place on the electoral roll, citizens' organizations entered into ongoing discussions with the

CAS on their future democratic franchise and citizenship rights with great passion.

Guaranteeing Inclusion

Confronted with disparate exclusionary practices in the registration of the refugees on the ground, the Secretariat became the principal guarantor of inclusion on the electoral roll. Its members acted with accountability. The staff of the Secretariat acknowledged the receipt of all letters and responded, often in great detail, to explain the procedures and the actions that were taken or that already took place. The Secretariat replied within at most two weeks from the day they received a letter, but usually even earlier. Before replying, they considered each and every letter. They acted rapidly to redress problems that arose with local governments. For example, they summoned the Reforms Commissioner of Assam to Delhi following several complaints from citizens' organizations in Assam. He was asked to withdraw the court-fee charge he imposed on refugee declarations. He agreed to extend the deadline for the declarations of refugees by a month and to give due publicity to this extension. He also agreed that in the case of women refugees it would be enough if their husbands or parents signed the declarations on their behalf. The Secretariat asked for a report on the actions agreed at their meeting.

The Secretariat also made inquiries into complaints about specific incidents of abuse in the registration of the refugees at the local level. It thus asked the Reforms Commissioner of Assam to account for breaches in the registration, such as the one reported by the Tinsukia Bengali Association against the sub-divisional commissioner. The Reforms Commissioner investigated the complaints with his district officers, deputy commissioners and sub-deputy collectors, and sent a detailed report to the CAS.

The Secretariat also made the public aware of their activities. They published a comprehensive press note, which told in detail all the problems that arose with faulty procedures and how these were redressed.

Henceforth, the Secretariat regularly asked provincial authorities to respond to written inquiries they received from citizen organizations. It forwarded these letters to local authorities with a proposed draft reply and asked to be kept informed with a copy. In doing so, the Secretariat delegated authority to provincial officials and strengthened their competence; it also created a mechanism for overseeing their activities while endeavouring to achieve as much uniformity in the implementation of the procedures for the preparation of the rolls as possible. Provincial governments often used the Secretariat's proposed draft reply in their responses.

Notwithstanding the CAS's inclusionary efforts, clarifying press notes, substantial correspondence with citizens' organizations, and remedial measures, infringements in the registration of the refugees did occur. The Secretariat's responsiveness to peoples' letters fostered a sense of personal proximity and of being taken into account. This, in turn, empowered people to express growing and passionate interest in their right to vote. In their modus operandi while dealing with one of the first challenges for the preparation of the roll, that is, the registration of Partition refugees as voters, the Secretariat can be said to have tutored bureaucrats and the public in the institutional and procedural principles of an electoral democracy. The Secretariat proved itself to the prospective voters and administrators time and again to be trustworthy with the way it handled occasional attempts to disenfranchise whole groups of people from the roll. This was the basic precondition for the ability, for example, later on ahead of the first elections, to educate the largely illiterate voters into the technicalities of the actual voting. Moreover, embedding trust in the electoral process was about much more than the mere technicalities of registration and voting. It was also about the values and purpose of democracy. This point was clearly demonstrated by the solution the Secretariat found for the exceptional circumstances of the refugees so that they would not be disenfranchised. If a way of relaxing the residential qualification of 180 days for the refugees was not found, millions of people would have been disenfranchised. In this case the value of the franchise, the spirit of the law, took precedence over the application of the 180-day residency rule.[11] In making their judgement call, the Secretariat imbued the values and purpose that underlay the right to vote among administrators at all levels and the voters. The true demonstration of the spirit of democracy it exhibited was indispensable for the democratic imagination to resonate in the minds of Indians.

Altogether, the Secretariat's way of tackling the question of the refugees' registration contributed to developing the 'forms of democracy', particularly customs of accountability in India's institution of electoral democracy at its inception. It was, however, in dealing with the public that the Secretariat fostered what S. Radhakrishnan, a philosopher and the second president of India, referred to as electoral democracy's 'habit of mind . . . its spirit, that sensitive adjustment . . . to the infinitely varied demands of other persons.'[12] This was not simply a result of the Secretariat's impressive responsiveness to citizens' organizations' letters. It was rather related to the terms and style of engagement, which the Secretariat, as the election management body at the time, developed. For a start, they took seriously people's grievances, queries and suggestions. Some of their decisions in redressing problems reflected proposals that some organizations put forward. Moreover, the Secretariat was authentic and transparent in their correspondences, repeating, sometimes word for word, their internal notes or the content of letters they sent to provincial authorities. The internal office notes, the official letters to provincial and state authorities, and replies to letters from the public were entirely consistent and based on identical wording. These principles and practices that the Secretariat developed and instilled in administering the first steps of making the universal franchise, particularly the way it tackled the question of the refugees' registration, were passed on to the first Election Commission, forming the foundation of a credible culture of electoral administration in India.

II

The First and Last General Election in Hyderabad State

Taylor C. Sherman

Looking at the first general elections in 1951–52, it is clear that India was still in a period of transition during this contest. In these elections, some princely states and centrally administered territories held elections separately before being amalgamated into the rest of India by the reorganization of states in 1956. Looking at the history of these elections in the princely state of Hyderabad, we can begin to grasp what an enormous administrative task it was to hold elections on the basis of universal adult franchise so quickly after Independence, Partition and the integration of the princely states into the Indian Union. Moreover, the main features of what later came to be seen as the Nehruvian consensus of the first decades after Independence had yet to been firmly established—after the success of the national movement, the boundaries of legitimate opposition politics were still being laid; the substance of Indian socialism was uncertain as, for example, land reforms were still being debated; and the place of regional, religious and linguistic identities within a larger Indian national identity was anything but settled. In addition, we can see some incipient concerns about how those in government positions can use their position to the advantage of their party during elections, and about the ways in which campaigning can rouse passions that could undermine India's democracy.

A Society in Turmoil

In the years before the general election, Hyderabad State had experienced upheavals that were, arguably, unprecedented in its history. As a princely state, Hyderabad had not been covered by the terms of the deal to partition British India, and the Nizam of Hyderabad, Bahadur Osman Ali Khan, like other princes, had been given the choice of whether to join India or Pakistan. The nizam, however, refused to decide, and his ministers spent the first year after August 1947 in increasingly frustrating negotiations with the Government of India, which insisted on nothing less than Hyderabad's full accession to the Indian Union.

During this period, Hyderabad's internal situation collapsed. The state was already coping with a communist insurgency in its Telangana region, but when the nizam failed to accede to India, Hyderabad's different political parties, including the Hyderabad State Congress, the communist Andhra Mahasabha and the Majlis-e-Ittehadul Muslimeen and its Razakar volunteer force, fell upon each other as they tried to persuade the nizam and one another to either join or remain out of the Indian Union. Hyderabad's internal political fissures did not precisely match the religious divisions that had dominated British India during Partition, but the structure of rule in the state, where a government with a predominantly Muslim character appeared to be in conflict with a population the majority of which was Hindu, made it seem as if Hyderabad was deteriorating into communal war. Concerned both about the communist movement and the potential spread of communal violence, the Government of India decided to send troops into the state in September 1948, arguing that the move was necessary to restore order.[1] The 'Police Action', as the invasion was known, ultimately secured the accession of the state to the Indian Union.

From September 1948 until the first general election, Hyderabad was governed by unelected officials. In the first year after the Police Action, the state was ruled by a military governor, Major General J.N. Chaudhuri. When Chaudhuri departed in late 1949, M.K. Vellodi replaced him as the head of the new civilian government in Hyderabad and became the state's unelected chief minister. Vellodi brought a small number of 'popular representatives' into his cabinet in June 1950, but these men, from the Hyderabad State Congress party, were not elected. Initial plans for a Constituent Assembly that would decide the fate of the state were delayed and eventually shelved in favour of simply participating in the general election. Thus, although there were elections to some municipalities in the early months of 1951, the first general election really did mark a transition to democratic rule in Hyderabad State.

Preparations for an election in Hyderabad State began as early as 1949, because an election had initially been planned for representatives to be sent to the Constituent Assembly. With the state's seventeen million residents spread across 82,000 square miles, much of which was not served by transport links, the task of enumerating voters was 'colossal'. The Government of Hyderabad not only called upon its 60,000 village officers to assist, but also employed 450 election inspectors, 500 lascars, 142 assistant tehsildars and 174 clerks to help in compiling the electoral rolls. [2] Village officers were paid according to the number of names they enrolled, with, for example, patwaris paid Rs 4 for the first 200 names, and another rupee for every additional 100 names they enrolled.[3]

Enrolling Voters

The task of enrolling voters was not easy in a state where taluq and district boundaries were not known with precision. Indeed, official records had been kept in such a haphazard manner that, 'there were "ghost" villages on some records and there were actual villages unmentioned in records'.[4] In Hyderabad city, an outbreak of plague meant that 10,000 houses had to be enumerated separately. Because

five languages were spoken in the state, electoral rolls were prepared
in Telugu, Marathi, Urdu, English and Kannada, using forty-seven
local presses and eighty-three presses in surrounding states.[5]

In the first attempt, around 50 per cent of the adults were
registered. This was in part because women voters, as in other parts
of India, did not give their own names, preferring 'to be enrolled
under the names of their husband or father'. But the enumerators
defended their work, noting that this figure 'certainly compares
favourably with that of Asiatic countries like Burma, Iran and Turkey
on the one hand and countries in the Western zone like Canada,
Great Britain and Australia on the other', whilst in neighbouring
Madras, the percentage of adults included on the rolls was 'more or
less the same'.[6] Political parties were requested to assist in bringing
the rolls up to date, and the main parties urged their supporters to
get themselves enrolled if their names were not on the list.[7] For
the general election at the end of 1951, the rolls were prepared and
opened on 1 October 1951.[8]

The main parties in the general election reflected Hyderabad's
particular politics more than national trends. The Hyderabad
State Congress, which had been established little more than a
decade before Independence, was a party divided along many lines,
including over several of the main issues in the elections. In addition
to the rather fractious Hyderabad State Congress, the other main
party contesting the elections was the People's Democratic Front.
The PDF was an alliance of Left-leaning parties formed largely of
members of the parties associated with the Telangana Movement.
Many prominent communists remained in jail, and although they
were allowed to vote and run in the elections, the Communist
Party and the Andhra Mahasabha had both been banned. Those
disenchanted with the State Congress, including Jaisoorya, leader of
the Democratic People's Party, and Govindas Shroff, the Marathi
leader of the Socialist Workers Party, also ran under the banner of
the PDF.[9] The Front adopted 'the red flag with the hammer and
sickle' as its emblem.[10] Smaller parties included the Socialist Party,
the Scheduled Castes Federation and the Shetkari Kamgar Paksh.

Political Prisoners

In the three years between the Police Action and the general election, Hyderabad had experienced a great deal of turmoil. Razakar threats against the population, both violent and non-violent action by Congressmen against the nizam's forces, the uprising under the communist Telangana Movement and anti-Muslim violence, which swept many parts of the state after the Police Action, had all left a mark on Hyderabad's politics. This was reflected in the central issues debated during the campaign.

Several communists remained in detention, as did several Muslims who had fallen under suspicion because of their position in the previous regime. It is perhaps unsurprising, therefore, that the release of political prisoners was one of the central issues of the election. The Government of Hyderabad had agreed to allow detenus to vote, and permitted several communist detenus to run for election, though they had to submit their nomination papers from jail.[11] The manifesto of the PDF included a call to release all political prisoners, including the Razakar leader, Kasim Razvi.[12] The demand for the release of political prisoners had some backing from the press,[13] and some declared that elections in Hyderabad could not be free so long as these men remained imprisoned.[14]

Members of the Hyderabad State Congress, however, were alarmed that released communists 'would very seriously affect the success of Congress candidates in the Telangana area during the elections', and were not keen on such a move. In fact, Burgula Ramakrishna Rao, who was a minister in Vellodi's unelected civilian government (and would become Hyderabad's first elected chief minister after the first elections), personally approached Vellodi to attempt to persuade him to have releases 'postponed till after the elections', but Vellodi demurred at this request.[15] Indeed, the Government of Hyderabad released around 2000 low-level communist detenus to participate in the elections, and later, on 5 December 1951, released on parole four prominent communist candidates—Ravi Narayana Reddy, Makhdoom Mohiuddin, Chandra Gupta Chaudhuri and Baddam Yella Reddy.

Radical Agricultural Reform

If the demand for the release of political prisoners arose partly out
of the Telangana Movement, so did the second big issue in the
campaign: the call for radical agricultural reforms. Land grievances
had been a central part of the peasant uprising in Telangana. Under
the 'sheer pressure' of popular sentiment, the Andhra Mahasabha had
done more than adopt the slogan 'land to the tiller'. The party had
also overseen an extensive land-redistribution programme.[16] Guided
by Nehru, who had visited Hyderabad State in December 1948
and declared, 'The tiller of the soil should be made the free man,'[17]
the military government in Hyderabad had initially expressed no
desire to reverse the redistribution undertaken by the communists.
However, the government later succumbed to pressure from large
landholders and began a programme to restore land to its 'rightful
owners' and settle land disputes.[18] Vellodi's civilian government
followed this with agricultural reforms in the form of a Tenancy Act
passed on 15 May 1950. This Act promised greater protection for
tenants, as well as the automatic right to buy the land they had been
tilling from their landlord at a fixed price. Although the legislation
promised nothing less than the 'elimination of all intermediate
interests between the cultivator of the soil and the State',[19] it fell far
short of this aim. The government suffered from a shortage of staff
to record holdings and inform tenants of their rights. An absence
of proper record-keeping in many areas meant that peasants could
not verify their claims to land, and many landlords simply evicted
tenants before the provisions of the Act came into force.[20]

During the election, therefore, the PDF was essentially able
to run on the strength of its record when it came to land reform,
at least in Telangana. A secret communication by the communist
party issued during the campaign boasted that in 3000 villages across
Telangana, 'One million acres of land were seized from the landlords,
rents were abolished, [and] land distributed to agricultural labour and
poor peasants.'[21] Four members of the State Congress, by contrast,
had been associated with Vellodi's government during the period of

implementation of the Tenancy Act, and suffered from association with the rather less successful reforms of 1950. Nonetheless, many State Congress candidates campaigned on the promise of more radical change. One of these was Swami Ramanand Tirtha, whose proposals for agricultural reform included a ceiling on landholdings with compulsory confiscation above the ceiling.[22]

Agricultural reforms tied into the broader question of economic development, which in turn was woven into the question of how to find work for Hyderabad's many unemployed people. Like much of India, the state had a large number of educated unemployed, but problems of unemployment had increased because of the changes introduced by Hyderabad's new governors after September 1948. The military governor had not only disbanded the nizam's army, but had also undertaken a sweeping programme to change Hyderabad's services. When the Government of India began governing the state, there was a widespread perception that Hyderabad's police and bureaucracy employed a disproportionate number of Muslims relative to the size of the Muslim population in the state. Reducing the number of Muslim employees, therefore, was viewed in the new administration as an essential component of the Government of India's plans to stabilize and democratize the state. In government it was believed that, 'non-Muslim opinion both in the State and outside demands a very radical and rapid change in the proportion of Muslims' in the services.[23] This was done through forced retirement, prosecution for minor and major offences, and the introduction of regional languages in government business along with a requirement that government employees pass a test in Telugu, Kannada or Marathi. By the time of the elections, therefore, the problem of unemployment had become a central feature of Hyderabad's political contests.[24]

State Identity

The issue that overshadowed all others during the campaign was the question of whether Hyderabad State ought to even continue as a separate political entity. Many of Hyderabad's political parties favoured the partition of the state along linguistic lines. The communists, who had forged alliances during the Telangana uprising that included not only those from Telangana but also communists from the Andhra region of Madras, demanded the creation of 'Vishaal Andhra'. Most of Hyderabad's other political parties, including the Scheduled Castes Federation, supported the demand for linguistic states.[25] The Socialist Party and the Shetkari Kamgar Paksh also agitated to break up the state.[26]

The Hyderabad State Congress, however, was troubled by the question of whether to support the breakup of the state during the election: a few in the State Congress, including Janardhan Rao Desai, opposed the idea of partitioning Hyderabad.[27] In contrast, Swami Ramanand Tirtha believed that Hyderabad State had been 'the centre of gravity of the British Empire in India', and true swaraj could only be realized if the state was completely dismantled.[28] Moreover, the Congress party in the state had been organized along linguistic lines, and provincial congress committees had long advocated the creation of a Karnataka state, Samyukta Maharashtra, and Vishaal Andhra. However, when Nehru declared during the election campaign that 'having known and suffered the consequences of partition once he was not prepared to accept it again' through the creation of linguistic states,[29] this posed a problem for the State Congress. Digambarrao Bindu, president of the State Congress, was forced to clarify the party's position, saying that 'the party would eventually insist on the disintegration of the State, though they would naturally have to be guided in this behalf by their central organization.'[30]

Voting Day

With these issues in their minds, Hyderabad's nine million voters went to the polls between 21 December 1951 and 17 January 1952. Despatching their votes in 71,000 steel ballot boxes,[31] they chose between 560 candidates for 175 Legislative Assembly seats in the state,[32] and between seventy-two candidates for twenty-five seats in the Lok Sabha.[33] Voting seemed to have progressed reasonably smoothly, although there were a few small glitches. Given the association between the national movement and the Congress government in the country, the presence of national symbols at voting stations could prove contentious. Thus, when the chief minister noticed a tricolour flag flying above a police station serving as a polling booth in Thumkunta, he had it removed, 'lest it should be construed to be partial to a particular party'.[34] When the prominent communist Ravi Narayana Reddy arrived at his polling station in Bhongir Tehsil in Nalgonda district, he found that the office was adorned with pictures of Gandhi and Nehru. When the presiding officer asked if he wanted the pictures removed, the communist leader said he did because the portraits 'might influence voting'.[35]

Unfamiliar with the passions of a general election, some expressed concern at the fervour aroused by the campaign in the state. Thus, the Urdu daily *Siasat* warned against 'dirty election propaganda' and expressed dismay at the tenor of some of the campaign tactics. For example, on one wall where a Congress election symbol had been painted next to the names of a Congress candidate, someone had scrawled, 'vote for black-marketers'. And in a rally for one party, someone had raised the slogan '*murdabad*'. *Siasat* worried that this 'contemptible' behaviour would harm not only 'the dignified traditions of this magnificent city', but also the 'collective interests of the country'.[36] There was also some anxiety that the excitement of the campaign would upset the fragile 'peace and tranquility that had been established with much difficulty' in Hyderabad after the turmoil of the communist movement and the Police Action. *Siasat* warned that 'passion and anger' could be tolerated during the campaign 'to a certain extent', but after voting had ended such 'nonsense cannot be tolerated'. The paper urged 'every person and organization . . . [to] move forward forgetting the past', and work together for the sake of the country.[37]

In the end, these anxieties proved to be unfounded. And, after an election that cost an estimated Rs 50,00,000,[38] the people of Hyderabad obtained their first elected representatives. In the

Legislative Assembly, the State Congress won ninety-three seats and the People's Democratic Front took forty-two, mostly in Telangana. Independents took fourteen, the Socialist Party grabbed eleven, the Shetkari Kamgar Paksh won ten, and the Scheduled Castes Federation filled five seats.[39] The election brought Hyderabad State its first and only fully democratic government, with Burgula Ramakrishna Rao taking up the post of chief minister.

The debates during the campaign were not forgotten. The new government quickly set about devising more radical land reforms, but these had to be moderated because of the constitutional protections provided to property-holders. The big issue of the election, the reorganization of southern India along linguistic lines, rose again in 1952, as many political parties in the state, including some segments of the State Congress, began agitating for the state's breakup. The creation of linguistic states on 1 November 1956 ensured that Hyderabad State's first general election was also its last. Even though Hyderabad State ceased to exist, the issues raised in its only election would be central to Indian politics for many decades to come.

III

A Tumultuous and Glorious Seventy Years

T.N. Seshan

The Election Commission of India should be proud of its achievements for the reason that through it the people of India have been able to sweep parties and politicians in and out of power the way they have felt fit. And part of the credit for the continuous and unbroken strain of democracy in India should go to the Election Commission. It has not been easy, the Commission has had its fair share of fights, and it has had to struggle with the goal that every voter should have his free say and every vote should matter. There is much to do still.

A democracy, by definition, rests on the central idea of voting rulers into place, and because of that the processes related to elections need to be protected, as they were the bedrock of democracy itself. The founding fathers did well in conceiving an independent Election Commission. They knew that for democracy to sustain, elections should be clean. They did their utmost to ensure that the Commission remained autonomous and independent of the executive.

In fact, after giving shape to the Election Commission, the only fear they expressed was that it would be difficult for the nation if the person in power at the Commission were to become a stooge of the executive!

Miracle of Elections

The first general elections in 1952 were a landmark since they brought the first Parliament into being and because they also laid the foundation for the elections that were to follow. The first chief election commissioner, Sukumar Sen, was meticulous. It is marvellous in the sense that about 70 per cent to 80 per cent of the method devised and applied at that time continues to be used even today. But for the EVMs, the percentage would have been even higher. It took six months to complete those elections, which was still a feat considering the fact that they were the first-ever general elections in India. There were no computers, and our country was back then, as it is now, the largest democracy in the world.

Indeed, elections in India are nothing short of a miracle. After the counting starts, the verdict of a total of 834 million Indians, 60 per cent of whom on an average cast their franchise, is declared in a matter of a few hours (it took two days even when EVMs were not in vogue) in a country with a diverse geographical setting, ethnicity, language and demographic variations, inclusive of a great amount of illiteracy.

That is not the end though; the Election Commission's hardships are not restricted to these 'simple' challenges. Somewhere down the line, the Election Commission, which was designed to be autonomous of the executive, increasingly found itself subjugated by the executive. Not that the chief election commissioners did not assert themselves. A former CEC even went so far as to declare the election of a prime ministerial candidate null and void. At the same time, it can also not be forgotten how once a CEC wrote a letter to the law ministry for clearance to purchase a book costing Rs 25. The scant respect given to the constitutional position of the Commission could be seen when the acting CEC was appointed despite there being no constitutional provisions whatsoever for such an arrangement.[1] Evidence shows that women came out in fewer numbers than men for voting and the reason could easily be attributed to the fact that they did not feel secure enough to vote.

Evidence also shows that certain backward tribal communities were systematically denied entry into polling booths. Criminal elements rode roughshod over the voting process by intimidating voters. The aim was to capture as many booths as possible in order to place their own people in the legislature. Needless to say, action had to be taken by the Election Commission, and it should be proud that throughout its history, efforts were made to counter such malpractices.

A Tough Phase

The Election Commission probably had the toughest time in the early 1990s. It had to bat on several fronts. On the one hand, the elections were getting violent and out of hand. On the other, the model code remained a toothless document. The government of the time was not interested in playing ball, and, finally, the permanent executive played every game in the book and out of it to prevent the Election Commission from taking charge during the elections despite its constitutional authority to do so.[2] On questions of protocol, it wished to keep the Election Commission under its thumb.

Without doubt there was a need for the Commission to reset itself. Given the laws passed by earlier governments (not a single law was passed in the early 1990s to facilitate the efforts of the Commission), a battle had to be fought on all fronts to ensure that the Election Commission continued to be the watchdog of democracy.

In order to keep the process of conducting elections updated and abreast of emerging challenges, many measures were taken. These were related to cleaning up of electoral rolls, staggering elections, positioning security forces, annulling elections won through wrong means, fine-tuning the counting processes, calibrating media involvement in the election process and counting votes after mixing of ballots.

There was a model code of conduct that was already in place, an excellent document thanks to the work of political parties and the Election Commission of the early 1970s. But the problem, as we have just seen, was that it had no teeth and it was reduced to a showpiece of pious intentions. But not to be deterred, laws were dug out of other statutes of the land, which could be used to ensure that the model code was implemented.

With the limited control that the Constitution gave to the Election Commission during the run-up to the elections, members of the bureaucracy were taken to task for not maintaining decorum. Orders were passed related to the use of loudspeakers, keeping the campaign within the time limit, putting a stop to splattering city walls with graffiti, keeping expenses under the prescribed ceiling, getting ministers to not misuse their advantageous positions, and so on. The model code gained its required force.

EC versus Political Establishment

The fight with the permanent executive came to a head when it repeatedly denied the Commission the right to punish offending officials who had failed to do their election duties properly. Some officials at that time thought that deputation to the Election Commission for electoral duties was some kind of voluntary work that they were at liberty to do if they pleased. Despite quoting from articles and clauses, when the authorities in the bureaucracy failed to see light, when the government at every level sat on the issue for months on end and when, at last, the Election Commission was not allowed to go by its perception of the requirement of security at a particular election to be enforced, there was no other way for it to assert itself than to pass the order of 3 August 1993, postponing all elections by three months (which could be extended by the Commission for three months, if required).[3]

All hell broke loose; the executive ran helter-skelter and did not know what to do apart from queering the pitch. The media began with a chorus of condemnation only to follow it up with another of praise once the significance of the move sank in. The Supreme Court passed an interim order saying that indeed the Election Commission did have the right.[4] The very next day, the elections were allowed to continue. Looking back, this victory went a long way in asserting what the Constitution wanted for the nation. Executive-driven elections have always been disastrous for all free nations.

The fight with the political establishment was highlighted by the fact that the chief election commissioner was twice lined up for impeachment and on one occasion a special session of Parliament was called by the ruling party to do the honours. The media dubbed the bill 'anti-Seshan', and the session was called the 'Seshan session' of Parliament. But to the credit of a few foresighted legislators, the embarrassing moves of the political fraternity did not go on for very long. After attempting everything under the sun, including offering the CEC all kinds of ambassadorial and governorship roles, the Commission was expanded.

It was an interesting order in the sense that it almost said there would be three chiefs of the Election Commission. Is it not ridiculous to say the prime minister is too powerful, so let's have three prime ministers who will act on a majority decision! The executive said that it wanted to strengthen the Commission, but people who have studied power dynamics know that a three-member group is the weakest formation. It said that the members were added to help with the workload, but work was slack in the Commission. In two months' time, a stay order came from the Supreme Court.[5]

With this verdict from the Supreme Court and the verdict in support of the 3 August order, the Commission had the freedom to go ahead with the cleanup of the process of elections as most of the hurdles in its path had been removed.

Cleaning up of Electoral Process

The idea of issuing identity cards was already afloat by that time. Thankfully, Parliament later found it important enough to be implemented across the board. But at that time, when the Commission asked for it in order to clean up the issue of voter impersonation, there was an unusual chorus from some state governments against it. Every method possible was used by the Commission to move the process forward but at every step it met with remarkable resistance. The law for issuing voter ID cards requested by the Commission was not passed. The Commission had to use an order that could be implemented in a constituency and multiply it by the total number of constituencies so that eventually the card could be asked for all constituencies in India. And even as hard as the Election Commission tried to get everything done, the opposition stalled, and dragged, and whined, and did everything it could to say that the issuing of cards was impossible, that too in just fifteen months! It was, anyway, achieved in half the time by some states.

Going by the Constitution, the view of the Supreme Court over the enacted law held over all the other views, and as such the new arrangement came to be formalized. With the new arrangement in place, the challenge was to ensure that the advantages won by the Commission were not lost, and the 'three-equals' arrangement worked to the strength of the Commission. The three commissioners devised a method in which a file was circulated repeatedly among them until no one wanted to make any more changes. This ensured that the strengths were added through the contributions of all three commissioners to the extent possible. Though this slowed down the process, it ambled along without stumbling.

While initiative has been relatively restricted, consolidation has occurred. Thankfully, the Election Commission has held on to the ground gained in the early 1990s, if not improved upon it. EVMs, which were merely tried out in the early nineties, have now become a mainstay of elections.

The three-member Commission has so far worked reasonably independently, though the scope of the executive to play mischief still exists. But then, that is another story and, probably, a battleground for another fight. Somewhere along the line, if the need arises, the Supreme Court may hopefully still take up the matter in a larger context for, after all, the Constitution is paramount and its tenets cannot be twisted and turned to cater to individuals.

As for the Election Commission, may it cherish its beholden duty to our fledgling democracy. May it continue to gain strength and hold its autonomy with glory so that the fate of the citizens of this nation and the hopes of yearning democracies all over the world is held in the bosom of trust.

IV

T.N. Seshan and the Election Commission

Christophe Jaffrelot

The Election Commission was conceived by the Constituent Assembly as an autonomous body vested with the power to supervise the smooth conduct of elections. Even before Independence, the sub-committee tasked with deliberating on fundamental rights came up with the idea of such a commission in July 1947.[1] Finally, Article 324 of the Constitution provided for the preparation of electoral rolls and the conduct of elections to Parliament and legislatures of the states under the 'superintendence, direction and control' of the Election Commission. The latter was composed of a chief election commissioner and as many members as the president of the Indian Republic deemed useful.

The members forming the Election Commission continue in office till the age of retirement. Appointed by the president, they can only be removed—like judges—through impeachment. Ahead of every election, the president also appoints, after consultation with the Election Commission, chief electoral officers, who supervise the election work in the states.

Criminalization of Politics

The task of this institution became increasingly important and tricky with the degeneration of political practices. If criminals seek the protection of politicians—mostly for being released from jail—the latter, in turn, more readily solicit their help. Many among them thus consider it necessary to have henchmen to execute their dirty work, particularly for organizing vote rigging or electoral fraud. Till EVMs were introduced, the most common method in this regard was booth capturing: candidates suspecting that victory would elude them, hired an armed gang for snatching one or many ballot boxes of the constituency on polling day. During the 1971 general elections, eleven such cases were recorded, eight of which were in Bihar, a state known for the direness of political violence.

In 1980, almost sixty polling booths—twenty-one in Bihar, twelve in Uttar Pradesh and nineteen in Kashmir—witnessed comparable incidents or tensions that led to the polls being cancelled.[2] In 1984, re-polling was ordered in 265 booths, and in 1989—the most violent elections, ever—in 1670 booths.[3] During the 1991 general elections, 460 companies of the Central Reserve Police Force (CRPF) were deployed around polling booths after violence marked the election campaign, already recording seventy-five victims, fifty of whom were in Bihar.[4]

These practices sometimes come in addition to booth-related problems: clashes between party workers as well as violence by gangs aimed at suspending voting when their 'boss' feel they are in a tight spot. In 1989, such violent clashes claimed around a hundred lives. Even though such cases remained rare, settling scores targeting the candidates themselves was on the rise. In 1989, a Congress (I) rival contesting the Uttar Pradesh assembly polls—in the same constituency where Rajiv Gandhi was in the fray for a Lok Sabha seat—was shot in the stomach.[5]

In 1990, Om Prakash Chautala, son of deputy prime minister Devi Lal, was implicated in a series of violent pre-poll incidents to intimidate certain sections of voters to dissuade them from voting in Meham constituency, where he needed a win to retain his post as the chief minister of Haryana. In 1994, the inquiry commission that had been appointed by the government, the Saikia Commission, concluded in its report that the actions of Chautala and his men had resulted in the death of an independent candidate, Amir Singh.[6] The leaders of his own party (Janata Dal) obtained his resignation only after much kerfuffle, and while his career came to a temporary halt, it was not compromised.

A New CEC

As the criminalization of Indian politics was affecting elections as never before in the late 1980s and the early 1990s, the Supreme Court initiated a new form of 'judicial activism'. But the Election Commission contributed in its way to boosting the rule of law. The shift came with the appointment of T.N. Seshan at its helm in December 1990, where he would serve for six years. The Commission had always discharged its duties with care, but its measures became more stringent under its new chief's impetus.

Tirunellai Narayana Iyer Seshan, an IAS officer since 1955, saw his career soar in 1988 when Rajiv Gandhi had him appointed as secretary heading the defence ministry. As defence secretary, he so ably defended the interests of the Congress (I) during the Bofors affair—a scandal that placed the ministry in the line of fire—that he was promoted to cabinet secretary of the government in March 1989. Seven months later, the new prime minister, V.P. Singh, demoted him to a member of the Planning Commission.

It was Singh's successor, Chandra Shekhar, who, in December 1990, appointed Seshan as the head of the Election Commission. Seshan then displayed a certain amount of bias: during the 1991 elections, the Election Commission zealously monitored the bastions of the Janata Dal (V.P. Singh's party), where elections were deferred or cancelled on sometimes flimsy grounds. Generally, Seshan behaved unpredictably, even capriciously. He thus cancelled the Punjab assembly elections a few hours before polling was scheduled, spurring the governor's resignation.

In 1992, the Left parties called for impeachment proceedings to be initiated against him. This move did not succeed apparently due to an understanding between Seshan and Narasimha Rao, who thought he could use the Election Commission.[7] But Seshan turned out to be tough to manipulate. Finally, the prime minister had the president expand the Commission with two additional members in 1993. Seshan challenged the appointment in the Supreme Court, but its verdict in 1995 was unequivocal: not only was the appointment of these two men deemed to be valid, but the judges also conferred parity on them, ruling that the Commission's decisions had to be made with an absolute majority.[8] The Supreme Court justified its decision by underscoring that '[Seshan's] public utterances at times were so abrasive that this court had to caution him to exercise restraint on more occasions than one' and that his numerous interviews to the media 'gave the impression that he was keen to project his own image'.[9]

The 'Seshan Effect'

Nevertheless, even the most virulent critics of his megalomaniac and autocratic tendencies recognized Seshan's unprecedented efficiency in protecting the electoral process. Often, he would stagger voting to deploy additional forces and thus reduce the risks of booth capturing and violence near polling booths, which aimed at dissuading so-called hostile voters (e.g. Dalits who, it was feared, would not vote for their upper-caste candidates) from turning up. In Uttar Pradesh, the booth capturing count fell from 873 in 1991 to 255 in 1993, and the number of polling day killings from thirty-six to three. As for constituencies in which polling had to be suspended or deferred, the tally was a mere three as compared to the previous seventeen.

It is true that the 1991 elections were held in a particularly tense background—Hindu–Muslim clashes on the one hand, and caste conflicts on the other dominated the campaign. Moreover, many state assembly elections had been scheduled at the same time as those of the Lok Sabha, which was not the case in 1993. However, there was still a 'Seshan effect', as the press termed it. Seshan's policy partly explains the higher voter turnout (+10 points in Uttar

Pradesh): the security provided around polling stations encouraged a greater number of voters to cast their ballot, especially the Dalits, whom gangs were no longer in a position to intimidate.

The 'Seshan effect' was again at work during the 1996 general elections. The Election Commission dispatched 1500 observers (an average of three per constituency) for monitoring the elections.[10] Around 600,000 enforcers of law and order were deployed near polling stations run by approximately 1.5 million state employees. Over 300,000 people were placed in preventive detention (125,000 in Uttar Pradesh[11] and 59,000 in Madhya Pradesh, where 87,000 firearms were also seized[12]). These arrangements helped contain incidents near polling booths: voting was cancelled and reorganized in 1056 booths against 2614 in 1991. A little under half of these (471) were in Bihar, 231 in Andhra Pradesh, ninety-six in Assam, thirty-one in Rajasthan, forty-three in Uttar Pradesh, twenty-two in Orissa[13] . . . Poll-related violence, too, was spatially concentrated, as out of fifty-one deaths, forty-one took place in Bihar.[14] The number of violent incidents at the polls declined from 3363 in 1991 to 2450 in 1998 and the number of deaths from 272 in 1991 to 213 in 1996, sixty in 1998 and five in 1999, including twenty-nine people who were killed in landmine blasts engineered by Naxalites in Bihar.[15]

Enforcing Model Code of Conduct

Seshan also waged war against the tendency of politicians to flout the model code of conduct, which they were supposed to abide by. Polling was suspended in a Madhya Pradesh constituency as a serving governor campaigned for his son, ultimately leading to his resignation. In Uttar Pradesh, a minister was forced to quit the dais at a rally as the campaign period had just ended. Above all, Seshan harried politicians by constraining them to limit their election expenditure. This policy was executed vigorously from April 1996, when the Supreme Court accordingly mandated the Election Commission, which then ordered political parties to submit accounts of their expenditure after the elections.

The Election Commission ultimately drew up a very strict model code of conduct. Parties could no longer take voters to polling stations; they were required to obtain the authorities' permission before setting up camps where they traditionally helped voters find the candidates of their choice on facsimiles of the ballot paper, which, admittedly, is sometimes festooned with a hundred-odd names!

To economize, the parties no longer printed copies of voters' lists on which citizens could find their name before entering the polling station. The 1996 elections, unlike the preceding ones, were no longer marked by innumerable rallies, a plethora of posters, and the use of blaring mobile loudspeakers or video vans that one was accustomed to; the parties went back to door-to-door campaigning. While this newly introduced discipline cut back on the festive aspect of the elections, it also reduced the funding needs of parties, which was expected to impact the degree of corruption.

T.N. Seshan's popularity, especially in urban areas, stemmed from his efforts to bring an increasingly decried political class to heel. In 1994, a survey of 2240 people (1620 dwellers of the six largest Indian cities and 620 villagers) revealed that Seshan's name was familiar among two-thirds of the citizens interviewed (30 per cent of the rural population), who felt that he was motivated to root out corruption rather than put himself in the limelight.[16] Nonetheless, a relative majority considered that he possessed too much power, a sign that a part of the public was aware of the risk that one man's growing power could pose for democracy.

The trajectory of the Election Commission under T.N. Seshan shows that the effectiveness of institutions is highly dependent upon the personalities at their helm. The same institution may have very different attitudes if its chief is strong or weak, disinterested or preparing for his next (post-retirement?) office. Certainly, some institutions will be better equipped than others to resist pressure, but the character of its leader always plays a major role.

The Election Commission is a case in point because it is exposed to political pressure. But other institutions are in a similar situation,

like the Reserve Bank of India or even the Supreme Court, as evident
from the eras, respectively, of Raghuram Rajan and Justice Aziz
Mushabber Ahmadi, who initiated a phase of 'judicial activism'.
Interestingly, when these personalities leave the scene, their legacy
remains for some time, creating a form of path dependency,[17] but
equally strong men or women are needed for perpetuating a sense
of the professional duty that is likely to fulfil the office's mission.
There's no bureaucracy, there are only men and women.

V

Participation Revolution with Voter Education

S.Y. Quraishi

'Democracy cannot succeed unless those who express their choice are prepared to choose wisely. The real safeguard of democracy, therefore, is education.'

—Franklin D. Roosevelt

Democracy is all about participation of citizens in self-governance, which begins with the electoral process—from registration as voters, turning out on poll day, to voting without fear and contesting elections on a level playing field. But most election management bodies (EMBs) neglect the educational aspect, concentrating only on the managerial and regulatory aspects of conducting elections. There is very little effort to inform and motivate voters to participate and get their fair share in a democracy. Many consider voter education beyond the ambit of an EMB, putting all responsibility on educationists, politicians and the media. In such a scenario, low participation and turnout are natural.

Voter apathy has been our major concern over the years, youth and urban turnout being particularly low. In some constituencies of politically hyperactive states, such as Bihar and UP, even the rural voter turnout is disappointing. While disturbed areas such as Anantnag and Baramulla in Jammu and Kashmir have understandably suffered from low voter turnout (5.01 per cent and 5.37 per cent respectively in 1989), even districts such as Singhbhum in Bihar (1971, 15.83 per cent), Koraput and Bhanjanagar in Odisha (1962, 11.58 per cent and 11.72 per cent respectively) and Tarn Taran and Sangrur in Punjab (1992, 8.91 per cent and 10.35 per cent respectively) have required targeted intervention to bring voters to polling booths.[1] Until recently, low turnout was a problem even in metros and large cities where the educated and economically well-off people abstained and then boasted about never voting.

'Bad officials are elected by good citizens who do not vote.'
—George Jean Nathan

Although voter outreach was a concern of the Commission from the very beginning, efforts were rather perfunctory, until the ECI decided to take the problem head on, with the introduction of the Systematic Voters' Education and Electoral Participation (SVEEP),[2] which was started as a division called IEC (information, education and communication).

Increasing Voter Participation

The theme that the ECI adopted in celebrating its diamond jubilee in 2010 was 'Greater Participation for a Stronger Democracy'.[3] Hence, the SVEEP division rolled out comprehensive community outreach and multimedia campaigns to get all citizens to participate in the electoral process. The aim was to fill up all possible gaps in information, motivation and facilitation. Now, before every election, the ECI carries out a survey of knowledge, attitude, behaviour and practices (KABP) of voters before launching targeted interventions. In 2011–13, around thirteen states conducted KABP surveys.[4] Post the national elections in 2014, the ECI engaged the Tata Institute of Social Sciences for consolidating survey findings and recommendations. The major findings were ignorance about eligibility, registration process and services, inherent cynicism and contempt for politicians, fear of violence and lack of infrastructural facilities. We had to find answers for all these.

One must hasten to add here that despite the shortfall in participation, we were not looking at the easy but questionable option of compulsory voting. That does not go with the democratic tenet of freedom. Besides, it would not be feasible in India where over 300 million enrolled voters do not vote for various reasons. The demonstrably increasing participation of voters has proved the success of non-coercive methods for encouraging voter participation and turnout through targeted education. We cannot, after all, start 300 million legal suits! Imagine the burden of court cases that could spill out of the exercise of compulsory voting. If you look at the few countries that have resorted to this measure, they are not exactly smiling. Australia is one glaring example.[5]

One of the biggest constraints on the citizens' desire to come out and vote was the fear of violence at polling stations. The Commission, therefore, decided to launch a big information campaign regarding the steps it was taking for the safety of the voters, like vulnerability mapping of all districts to find out areas that suffered from threat and intimidation by criminals, and a series of measures to ensure peace. Peaceful elections led to increasingly large participation, especially of women, who are usually the first victims of any violence. The communication of special confidence-building measures for women appealed to them enormously. As a direct result of these efforts, their turnout went up from 55.8 per cent in 2009 to 65.6 per cent in 2014—a jump of nearly ten percentage points as against eight for men.[6]

The youth were the next important target. As many as 25,000 youth ambassadors were appointed in universities, colleges and school campuses before the 2014 elections.[7] Their role was clearly defined and included identification of students and teachers and non-teaching staff for voter registration, guidance for filling up forms, coordinating with the electoral machinery for approval of applications, and co-curricular activities and core team activities for voter awareness.

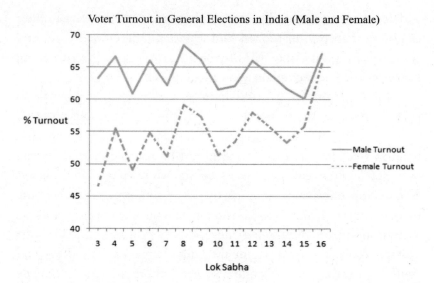

Voter Turnout in General Elections in India (Male and Female)

Lok Sabha

Source: The Election Commission of India

Special measures such as the provision of ramps and Braille for people with disability, and the recognition of transgenders as the third gender were widely publicized and were greatly advantageous. I would like to add here at least one shortcoming—undertrials and convicts cannot vote in our elections. Under Section 62(5) of the Representation of People Act, 1951, individuals in lawful police custody and those serving prison sentences cannot vote. Only those under preventive detention can vote through postal ballots. The Supreme Court has observed that prisoners cannot claim equal rights due to their conduct.[8] To me this appears to be a faulty stand on two counts: one, it amounts to conviction without trial and a punishment over and above what is prescribed in the Indian Penal Code. Two, it is taking away an important right from the prisoners regardless of the gravity of the offence committed.

A seven-member panel was constituted by the ECI in April 2016 to explore prisoner voting, and it received several representations that prisoners should not be disenfranchised.[9] No decision has been taken yet. I think it goes against the ethos of an inclusive democratic process to deny them this basic right. There are nearly 400,000 prisoners in Indian jails, 70 per cent of whom are under trial.[10]

Till convicted, they are deemed to be innocent. Taking away their fundamental rights of liberty, movement, occupation and dignity besides the right to vote is grossly unfair. Even logistically, it is not difficult to enfranchise them. All it will take are postal ballots.

Initiating SVEEP

The SVEEP initiative has evolved in three broad stages. In the first phase (2009–13), gaps were identified in voter turnout and stagnations around 55–60 per cent (national elections) were acknowledged, leaving out millions of eligible voters from making a political choice. This phase covered roughly seventeen elections to state assemblies and three revisions of the electoral rolls based on levels of urbanization, illiteracy, security and logistics.

The second phase (2013–14) involved strengthening and building on a strong foundation through planned strategies. These steps included identification of 10 per cent of the lowest turnout polling stations, poll station-wise analysis, interventions and implementation, followed by monitoring and evaluation. Content development was undertaken for voter outreach for the literate, the neo-literate and the illiterate. Thus, the supply side of the SVEEP was emphasized.

The communication efforts were aimed at three broad goals: increasing electoral participation through voter registration and turnout, increasing qualitative participation by ethical and informed voting, and continuous education of electoral processes.

The above two stages have returned impressive dividends in terms of higher turnout in each of the state elections, including reaching new records in some states. Some remarkable examples include Goa (15.91 per cent increase over 2008 in 2013), Gujarat (19.29 per cent over 2007 in 2012), Jharkhand (16.61 per cent over 2009 in 2012), Odisha (12.79 per cent over 2009 in 2014) and Uttar Pradesh (29.24 per cent over 2006 in 2011). Among women voters, the jump was phenomenal. Noteworthy are Goa (20.3 per cent over 2007 in 2012), Gujarat (21.89 per cent over 2007 in 2012), Jharkhand (22.87 per cent over 2009 in 2014) and

Uttar Pradesh (a whopping 43.8 per cent over 2007 in 2012).[11] The combined efforts of the first two stages of the initiative culminated in the highest ever turnout (66.38 per cent) in the 2014 general elections.[12] Many states crossed the 80 per cent threshold, including Assam (79.8 per cent), Lakshadweep (86.6 per cent), Nagaland (87.8 per cent), Tripura (84.7 per cent) and West Bengal (82.2 per cent).[13]

National Voters Day

As we know, India's demographic dividend is its economic strength, but it also has the potential of being its political strength, if voter apathy among the youth is reduced. Every year, a staggering 4 per cent of the population in the eighteen–nineteen age group becomes eligible for voting. The potential of these is, however, far from realized, as reflected in the low registration and turnout of young voters. Keeping this in mind, as a historic and unique measure, the Commission declared 25 January, its foundation day, as the National Voters Day (NVD) from 2011, with the avowed purpose to increase the enrolment of voters, especially the newly eligible ones. From 2013, every NVD was given a theme, each centred on participation (see Table 1).

Table 1

Themes of National Voters Day (2013–18)

Year	Theme
2013	Inclusion
2014	Ethical Voting
2015	Easy Registration, Easy Correction
2016	Inclusive and Qualitative Electoral Participation
2017	Empowering Young and Future Voters
2018	Accessible Elections

In its first year, 17 million new voters were added to the electoral rolls, including 5.2 million newly eligible and registered youth. They were given their voter ID cards at more than 800,000 polling stations on the first National Voters Day. This could well be billed as the largest exercise of youth empowerment on a single day, anywhere in the world. The national-level event was inaugurated by the President of India where chief election commissioners of over thirty-five countries were present.

The second NVD in 2012 received even more dramatic results, when a total of 38 million additional enrolments took place, of which 11 million were newly eligible youngsters. In the four years between 2009 and 2014, the NVDs registered over 100 million new voters. This is like adding a South Africa and South Korea combined, or three Canadas, or four Australias, or ten Portugals or twenty Finlands![14]

In subsequent years, voter registration, especially among the youth, shot up from 10 per cent to 15 per cent to a phenomenal 80 per cent in almost all state assembly elections, and a much higher turnout was recorded.[15] Impressed with its astounding success, several countries of the world adopted this model of National Voters Day.

An awareness campaign for ethical voting without falling for bribes and inducements is the core of the ECI's efforts, with every participant in the NVD programme administered a pledge for voting without fail and ethically. (See box below.) . This had a substantial impact on voter turnout. The theme for National Voters Day 2013 was 'Ethical Voting' to promote quality electoral participation with administration of voter's pledges and with messages such as 'Vote without Note' and 'Vote with Conscience'.

National Voters Day Pledge

'We, the citizens of India, having abiding faith in democracy, hereby pledge to uphold the democratic traditions of our country and the dignity of free, fair and peaceful elections, and to vote in every election fearlessly and without being influenced by considerations of religion, race, caste, community, language or any inducement.'

The third phase of SVEEP has been going on since 2015. A more robust planning has been undertaken this time, with electoral education being made a part of academic curricula through initiatives such as literacy clubs for secondary and senior secondary schools and colleges. Increased attention is being paid to voters who are absent from their constituency such as service voters, NRIs, migrants and the marginalized, besides the youth and urbanites whose apathy continues to linger. Registration counters are set up in weekly village markets and minor forest-produce collection centres for registration of migrants, especially labourers and homeless people.

The revolutionary potential of information and communications technology tools is being exploited for awareness campaigns through social media. There is a toll-free helpline for addressing queries. Poll-day reminders are sent through SMSs, radio, television, social media and public-address systems. The ECI has partnered with the social networking giant Facebook to launch a slew of initiatives to encourage voter registration. The #JetSetVote campaign was launched in 2017 in partnership with Facebook and Youth ki Awaaz to create a community of first-time voters for information dissemination on voting rights.

The first nationwide voter registration campaign was rolled out from 1–4 July 2017 in thirteen languages. Those who turned eighteen received a Facebook newsfeed message wishing them a happy birthday and reminding them to register to vote on the ECI's website. The seven episodes of the National Election Quiz 2017–18, which were shared on Facebook's 'Government and Politics' page, were aimed at creating awareness. All those who will turn eighteen years and above on 25 January will receive a reminder on their newsfeed to take a National Voters Day pledge.

For bringing in our defence personnel, nodal officers from the armed forces have been appointed for facilitating enrolment. The intranet of the armed forces is employed for electoral awareness among them. Electoral literacy has been included in the curriculum of soldiers and officers. A special drive is undertaken for service personnel utilizing Army Day that falls on 15 January every year. The service personnel are engaged with the NVD celebrations as well.[16]

Embassy and defence personnel posted abroad have been sensitized about their voting rights. Despite these measures, the turnout among the defence personnel continues to be low. For skill development initiatives of the Ministry of External Affairs, literacy modules have been prepared regarding voter education of diplomats posted abroad. Their turnout also continues to be dismal. For other overseas electors, interactive guides have been published under the SVEEP initiative. An overseas elector can be any citizen of India of eighteen years or above who is absent from the country owing to education, employment and other reasons, and is not otherwise disqualified.

Creative Strategies

A successful strategy from the beginning has been to enlist eminent national and regional icons to endorse the ECI's initiatives for encouraging voter participation. These include icons such as former president A.P.J. Abdul Kalam, M.S. Dhoni (cricketer), Aamir Khan (Bollywood actor), Prahlad Singh Tipaniya (folk singer), Cheteshwar Pujara (cricketer), Gopinath Muthukad (magician), and Abhinav Bindra (shooter), among others. The first female personalities to support the ECI's initiatives were M.C. Mary Kom (boxing) and Saina Nehwal (badminton) in 2012. Since then, professionals such as Apurvi Chandela (shooter), Dipa Karmakar (gymnastics), Ankita Raina (tennis), Kiran Parmar (kabaddi) and Daxa Patel (Bharatanatyam) have motivated women to realize their political power and cast their vote.[17] They complemented the efforts of folk singers Malini Awasthy and Sharda Devi from UP and Bihar respectively.

The comprehensive efforts of SVEEP have consistently paid off. A look at the size of the electorate in the general elections in 2014 is fairly indicative. Not only was the registration high, so was the turnout. Women outnumbered men in more than half the states. In UP, the performance was extraordinary—a whopping 30 per cent increase in voter turnout, especially of women (45 per cent).

Increasing awareness among sex workers such as Amina Begum from Chandni Chowk, who first started voting in 2008, puts to shame several well-to-do people in our society. They are aware that the fate of their children's education and welfare is linked with the outcomes at the ballot and hence, they are spreading awareness among their colleagues. Many newly registered voters have the enthusiasm of new converts and any obstacles pale in comparison to their firmness of will. When the SVEEP team of Amreli district made the documentary, 'A Fistful of Salt', the salt workers of 98 Rajula assembly constituency in Gujarat pledged on the salt that they would cast their vote and never miss an election. Many stories of homeless men and women eager to cast their ballots are matched only by those of persons with disability and the elderly who have never missed one opportunity to make themselves count.[18] Having no hands is not a weakness for these brave people; they vote with their mouth and their feet, their heart and their soul, all in the spirit of never taking democracy for granted. This really puts to shame the so-called educated urbanites who proudly trumpet that they've never voted in their life.

The overwhelming public response inspired the Commission to bring out a volume comprising 101 human-interest stories related to voter enthusiasm in elections.[19] Citizens now recognize the value of the vote, and bravely express their belief in it despite adverse circumstances. There are proud electors on wheelchairs casting their votes, patients in hospitals suffering from terminal illnesses anxious to reach the polling stations, homemakers coming out to participate in the festival of democracy.

During the diamond jubilee celebrations in 2010–11, the Commission had articulated its vision in the following words: 'Elections that are completely free of crime and abuse of money, based on a perfect electoral roll and with full participation of voters.'

The SVEEP programme has made a singular contribution in the fulfilment of this vision.

> 'Elections belong to the people. It's their decision. If they decide to turn their back on the fire and burn their behinds, then they will just have to sit on their blisters.'
>
> —Abraham Lincoln

VI

The Election Commission as Producer of Political Data

Gilles Verniers

B esides its role of conducting elections, the Election Commission of India is also one of the most important providers of public data in the country. In order to fulfil its multiple missions, the ECI must rely on empirical evidence on voters and constituencies, electoral campaigns and political parties, public safety and electoral fraud, and election results. In order to assert and guarantee its independence, it must also produce itself most of the data that it needs.

Over the years, the role of the ECI has greatly expanded, including new practices and rules in the administration of voters, candidates and parties (McMillan 2012). The Commission has also introduced new divisions and programmes aimed at increasing voters' participation; it frequently submits electoral reforms proposals to the Government of India (Quraishi 2014). Producing data enables the Commission to fulfil its role of conducting elections with the transparency required in any healthy democracy.

Some of the data the Election Commission produces is public information, such as electoral rolls or statistical reports on elections, including the Form 20 data (polling booth data). Other data produced by the Commission is not made public, due to its sensitive character or due to its internal utility for the ECI. The Election Commission must be able to rely on confidential information regarding public safety.

Because of the sensitive nature of some of its data, the role of the ECI as producer of data has been an object of intense debate and at times, controversy. Recent attacks on the reliability of EVMs and suspicions of voter manipulation through data reinforce the necessity to maintain high standards of data production and management.

After surveying various types of data produced and/or used by the ECI, this chapter underlines how the availability of public political data can and does enhance scientific research on Indian elections and, by extension, on India's democracy. This chapter also discusses the ethical dilemmas posed by the exigency of transparency and calls for the adoption of a thoughtful transparency position that combines the protection of citizens' interests without impeding scientific research on elections.

Voters' Data

In a masterly account of the making of India's democracy, Ornit Shani resurrected the fact that Indians became voters before they became citizens (Shani 2017). In the immediate aftermath of the Partition, the Constituent Assembly Secretariat was tasked with registering all Indian adults into the country's first electoral roll. This role was quickly passed on to the Election Commission, who is the sole responsible authority for the maintenance and cleaning of the electoral roll. As time passed, the task has proven to be increasingly complex, due to the ever-expanding size of the electorate—from 172 million registered voters in 1952 to 814 million registered voters in 2014 (Jensenius and Verniers, 2017) and due to increased internal migration, which makes the tracing of individual voters exceedingly complicated.

Maintaining clean and comprehensive electoral rolls is a fundamental task of the ECI, since all forms of exclusion or omission from the list amount to disenfranchisement of citizens. For decades, a gap in participation between men and women persisted, due to a gap in voter registration of men and women (Quraishi 2014).

In 2010, under the initiative of the CEC, the Commission decided to set up a new division dedicated to voters' education— the SVEEP division—with the purpose of increasing the rate of registration of the adult population. In order to identify the gaps, it ordered surveys conducted by an external agency, named KABP, to locate and understand the various barriers to registration, both physical and psychological.

The Commission analyzed these survey results against census and various population data, including the gender ratio, the elector-population ratio and the age cohort of voters, to identify and target vulnerable groups, or groups whose turnout has historically lagged behind.[1] The Commission then organized campaigns and registration camps targeting young urban voters, voters in reserved constituencies, and more particularly women. It enrolled star campaigners, singers, actors and cricket players to mobilize citizens to register.

The ECI used those findings to make the voting process more inclusive. For instance, and based on the KABP findings, the ECI made provisions to facilitate women voting, including providing toilet facilities near polling booths, securing further polling booths by detailing instructions on how to set up an ideal polling booth.[2] During the 2012 elections, the ECI introduced yet another innovation, which consisted in letting two women vote for every man in the queue, in order to speed up the process of voting for women, who continue to perform domestic duties on the day of election. These efforts paid off. Between 2009 and 2014, 34 million women voters were added to the electorate, to the effect that women now outvote men in seventeen states (Verniers and Quraishi 2017).

Since 2014, the ECI has collaborated with Google to facilitate and manage the online registration of voters, to allow enrolled voters to easily check their information, including address under which they are registered and to provide to voters directions to their attributed polling station. In both cases, the use of data and the recourse to web technologies enable the Commission to pursue its mission to make Indian elections as inclusive as possible.

Candidates' Data

Since the 1996 elections, the Election Commission exerts great scrutiny on candidates standing for elections. In the mid-1990s, the then CEC, T.N. Seshan, started the practice of collecting data on candidates and potential local troublemakers, criminal elements, in a campaign against the criminalization of politics (McMillan 2012).

A 2002 Supreme Court order supported that effort and mandated that every candidate to a state or national election sign an affidavit containing detailed information of assets, household composition, education and occupational background, as well as their criminal record.[3] The Election Commission makes that data public by publishing scans of those affidavits and, in recent years, by providing profile summaries of candidates through mobile apps.

The task of digitizing and analyzing the content of these affidavits is undertaken by the Association for Democratic Reforms (ADR), a civil society organization dedicated to promoting electoral probity in India.

Constituency Data

The deployment of a vast electoral machinery requires a sound understanding of the territory on which elections are held. The ECI collects a large amount of data on each constituency, including population and voters' data, data on polling booth location (polling booth mapping) as well as data on public safety.

Since the mid-1990s, holding elections require mobilizing large numbers of security personnel, who are deployed according to a complex empirical assessment of vulnerabilities and risk. The ECI gathers data from various police sources to construct a constituency vulnerability index, which helps decide the areas that require more policing during the campaign and on election day. This index includes data on crime, the presence of notorious criminal elements, past incidences of electoral fraud or violence (booth capturing or riots), evidence or indications of electoral anomalies such as unusual turnout or candidate performance.[4] Nowadays, this information is geocoded and can be transmitted easily to state election commissions as well as to electoral agents on the ground.

Electoral Campaign Data

Electoral campaigns are closely monitored by the Election Commission. All political rallies are registered, subject to authorization. Candidates' expenditures are monitored through video-surveillance and auditing. Raids are conducted to seize illegal sops and props, including cash, liquor, saris and other goods distributed by parties.

With the help of web technologies, the ECI can collect detailed data on electoral fraud and violations of the Code of Conduct[5] and can issue notices and sanctions rapidly. In most states, this data is now produced in real time, through digital platforms and mobile applications.

Election Results

The Election Commission produces detailed accounts and reports on election results. On counting day, the data is uploaded in real time on a dedicated website. The data is cleaned, analysed, and organized in the form of statistical reports that are uploaded on the ECI website several months after the conclusion of an election.[6]

These reports contain constituency-level data on voter registration and participation, the performance of individual candidates, the performance of parties, women candidates, and various forms of voting (postal, proxies and overseas voting).

Soon after the conclusion of an election, the Election Commission also publishes polling booth-level data. While the election reports are available in Excel format since 2005 (for state elections; general elections data has been available in Excel format 1998 onwards), the polling booth data is uploaded in a 'raw' form, PDFs and scanned documents, with varied formats between states and often within states. As such, polling booth data is not immediately usable, although it can be browsed online and crawled with the help of data-cleaning software.

A Scholar's Treasure Trove

All this data constitutes a treasure trove for students of Indian elections. Sound and reliable political data is essential for the conduct of empirical research on Indian politics. Most studies on Indian elections have relied on the ECI's election reports. The National Election Surveys (NES) conducted since 1967 by Lokniti at the Centre for Study of Developing Societies are all backed by ECI data.[7]

More recently, scholars have started combining ECI data with other datasets, either existing or specifically assembled. For her doctoral thesis and book on the effects of reservations, Francesca Jensenius digitized and expanded the ECI reports and combined their content with census data (Jensenius 2013; Jensenius 2017) The ECI data is now hosted, updated and made accessible by the Trivedi Centre for Political Data, at Ashoka University (Jensenius and Verniers 2017).[8]

The affidavits provided by the ECI have enabled the development of a new field of empirical studies of crime and politics. Milan Vaishnav conducted the first comprehensive examination of the data in his doctoral dissertation and subsequent book (Vaishnav 2017). Rikhil Bhavnani has used the assets data to ascertain the links between electoral performance and personal enrichment of elected representatives (Bhavnani 2011). Sam Asher and Paul Novosad have combined ECI reports and economic data to study the effect of political representation on local economic growth and activity (Asher and Novosad 2016).

The availability of polling booth (form 20) data enables social scientists to study electoral processes at the most granular level, enabling a microanalysis of politics at an unprecedented scale (there were more than 9 lakh polling booths deployed during the 2014 general election).

Any dataset that has a constituency identifier can be combined with ECI data. Linking election data to lower-level administrative units, such as sub-districts or villages, can also be done manually or by using GIS maps, opening new and vast avenues for research (Jensenius and Verniers 2017).

Scholars have, however, only been able to use a fraction of the data that the ECI possesses. For a number of reasons, from the sensitive character of the data to the simple unwillingness to provide access to it, the Election Commission has important data that is not yet in the public domain, or available to research scholars: voters' registration data, data on electoral fraud and violations, SVEEP and KABP data, and campaign data. The Election Commission also does not provide authoritative electoral maps, which forces scholars and journalists to work with various commercial or open source maps that might be of dubious quality.

In some cases, the lid posed on certain data is justified. Advertising in advance which area will get more security deployment would be self-defeating. In other cases, it stems from a lack of initiative and capacity. The ECI is a small institution, which employs barely 400 officers in Delhi. Amazingly, it does not have a proper statistical division.[9]

That being said, the ECI has made considerable progress in the diffusion of data and more particularly in paying attention to the quality and usability of the data it publishes. It has undertaken a complete digitization of its archives and has started using data visualization suites for the display of elections results. Recent CECs have been far more open to researchers than their predecessors have, which has considerably helped the production of new research on Indian elections.

The Case for Thoughtful Transparency

While the availability of detailed political data in open access offers opportunities to parties, scholars, journalists and citizens, it also causes a number of ethical dilemmas, linked to its possible misuse.

The argument for transparency is strong. First, citizens ought to be informed about who runs for election, and they should have easy access to the source of election results. Second, the sanctity of the electoral process relies on the trust citizens have for the Election Commission. Transparency is a necessary condition for building that trust. Third, making the data public ensures that it is not exploited by political and commercial interests in an exclusive manner. Too many individuals and organizations are already in the business of monetizing public information that ought to be freely accessible. If anything, making more data public would give these entities incentives to add value to the data that they are currently selling.

At the same time, the possibilities of misuse and abuse are real, particularly when it comes to voters' data. Candidates and political parties are known to have used polling booth data to identify sub-localities, villages and *basti*s that voted for them in a previous election. This gives them incentives and means to take retributive or even punitive measures against those who did not vote 'the right way' (Verniers 2016). Electoral rolls have also been used in the past to discriminate between intended beneficiaries of public schemes, according to the past electoral behaviour of their locality.

Parties and candidates can also use the electoral roll to micro-target individual voters for political communication, or, more nefariously, to target individuals in the context of communal riots (Bhushan 2002, Human Rights Watch, 2002). The intensive data work done by political parties to 'map' the electorate is currently done in a legal void when it comes to data protection or the protection of privacy.

Since the act of voting in India is often a collective act, the protection granted to guarantee the individual voter's secrecy should be extended to localities as well.[10]

A solution exists, in the form of a totalizer, a system that mixes results across localities, making micro-targeting of voters difficult, if not impossible. The ECI has repeatedly requested the implementation of a totalizer but has so far faced resistance from parties and the government, who rely on this very data for their electoral strategies (Press Trust of India 2015).[11]

The ECI has to perform a permanent balancing act between the demands for transparency and the imperative to protect voters and the elections. In the case of electoral rolls, for instance, the ECI does not provide online photos of voters, which are however printed on the forms (in a post stamp format).[12] Nowadays, with the availability of crawling tools, some of these protective measures are not particularly effective.

Not all the data that the ECI sits on falls under the category of sensitive. Research scholars, policymakers and journalists could put to great use the survey data that the ECI has collected over the years. In fact, the job of disseminating political data can be complemented by external organizations, who may do it for advocacy or for research purposes.

In 2011, the ECI set up the India International Institute of Democracy and Elections (IIIDEM), under the aegis of the then CEC, S.Y. Quraishi. One of the mandates of IIIDEM is to exploit the rich data the ECI possesses to further the expertise and understanding of Indian elections. For long confined to a floor of the ECI building, this body has essentially been used to train election officers, from India and a number of other countries. It has so far lacked the capacity to function as a proper data division of the ECI.

This institution should have the vocation of handling and disseminating data produced by the ECI, enabling the Commission to focus on its primary mission, which is to organize and conduct elections. The IIIDEM could also partner with universities and scholars, and even provide access to some of the more sensitive data under guarantee of anonymization. With the IIIDEM, the Election Commission has a rare opportunity to create a unique institution that can foster both public transparency and research. It could form the institutional base for a model of thoughtful transparency that keeps balancing and protecting various legitimate interests around political data in India.

The Election Commission is guided by two objectives that can be at times contradictory. On the one hand, the Commission must ensure the free and fair character of elections, as well as reduce as much as it can the possibilities of electoral fraud and manipulation. On the other, it must submit itself to standards of transparency that government bodies in India are not accustomed to, in order to maintain the trust that citizens have in the electoral process. This effort towards transparency can at times be self-defeating, as some of the data released by the ECI can be used by political actors to unduly manipulate or exert coercion on voters. Solutions exist, however, and the ECI has the institutional autonomy and capacity to effectively balance legitimate 'interests that are in fact more complementary than contradictory'.

References

Asher, Sam, and Paul Novosad. 2017. Politicians and Local Economic Growth: Evidence from India. *American Economic Journal: Applied Economics* 1.

Bhavnani, Rikhil. 2011. Corruption Among Indian Politicians: Evidence from Unusual Data. 1–47.

Bhushan, Ranjit. 2002. 'Thy Hand, Great Anarch', *Outlook*.

Gilmartin, David. 2009. One Day's Sultan: T.N. Seshan and Indian democracy. *Contributions to Indian Sociology* 43(2): 247–84.

Human Rights Watch. 2002. We Have No Orders to Save You. Human Rights Watch Reports 14: 68.

Jaffrelot, Christophe. 2007. 'Voting in India': Electoral Symbols, the Party System and the Collective Citizen. In *Cultures of Voting*, eds. Romain Bertrand, Jean-Louis Briquet and Peter Pels, pp. 78–99. London: Hurst and Publisher.

Jaffrelot, Christophe, Kumar, Sanjay and Verniers, Gilles. 2017. The Indian Assembly Legislators and Candidates Caste Dataset 1952–today, TCPD Dataset.

Jensenius, Francesca Refsum. 2013. *Power, Performance and Bias: Evaluating the Electoral Quotas for Scheduled Castes in India*. PhD diss., University of California, Berkeley.

Jensenius, Francesca Refsum. 2017. *Social Justice through Inclusion: the Consequences of Electoral Quotas in India*. New York: Oxford University Press.

Jensenius, Francesca Refsum, and Gilles Verniers. 2017. Studying Indian Politics with Large-scale Data: Indian Election Data 1961–Today. *Studies in Indian Politics* 5(2): 269–75.

McMillan, Alistair. 2012. The Election Commission of India and the Regulation and Administration of Electoral Politics. *Election Law Journal* 11(2): 187–201.

PTI. 2015. EC for new machine to enhance voter secrecy. *The Hindu*.

Quraishi, Shahabuddin Yaqoob. 2014. *An Undocumented Wonder: the Great Indian Election*. New Delhi: Rainlight, Rupa Publications.

Shani, Ornit. 2017. *How India Became Democratic: Citizenship and the Making of the Universal Franchise*. Cambridge: Cambridge University Press.

Singh, Divya. 2017. *Safer Elections and Women Turnout: Evidence from India.* Columbia University.

Vaishnav, Milan. 2017. *When Crime Pays: Money and Muscle in Indian Politics.* New Haven: Yale University Press.

Verniers, Gilles. 2016. *The localization of caste politics in Uttar Pradesh after Mandal and Mandir: Reconfiguration of identity politics and party-elite linkages.* PhD thesis, Sciences Po, Paris.

Verniers, Gilles, and S. Y. Quraishi. 2017. The Lawmakers We Need. *Indian Express.*

VII

Indian Elections: Lessons for and from Nepal

Ila Sharma

Two countries in the South Asia region that are closest to each other in terms of not only culture, religion and historical ties, but also the electoral system, are Nepal and India.

Common historical, social and political contexts, and cultural, ethnic and religious affinities in South Asia make it essential that they work together to strengthen democratic values and norms through electoral processes and to design even better mechanisms to deliver free and fair elections. Similar challenges and struggles in achieving electoral excellence bind the election management bodies of the region together. This relationship became institutionalized in the form of a regional establishment for cooperation among the South Asian Association for Regional Cooperation (SAARC) countries in New Delhi in 2010 called the Forum for the Election Management Bodies of South Asia (FEMBoSA).[1]

The Election Commission of Nepal (ECN) has actively participated in various trainings and events held by the Election Commission of India, especially on National Voters Day of India, celebrated on 25 January every year. This provides the ECN an opportunity not only to interact with the largest democracy of the world, but also with several others invited by India to discuss issues of electoral reforms and best practices. India has thus become a hub of global experience-sharing. Inspired by the Indian experience of creating awareness among voters, particularly the young, to take part in the electoral process, Nepal has started to mark its own National Voters Day, albeit with a different name—Election Day—on 7 Falgun (the eleventh month of the Nepali calendar) that falls in mid-February.

The Election Commission of Nepal has benefited from the Indian experience through these interactions as well as from frequent trainings at the India International Institute of Democracy and Election Management (IIIDEM), a one-of-a-kind institution set up by the ECI.[2] This institute has been a useful forum for Nepal and for other countries, particularly SAARC members, to train their officers. IIIDEM conducts training for SAARC nations on various aspects of election management, such as capacity-building of stakeholders, code of conduct, voter inclusion and registration so that EMBs of the regional bloc can effectively shoulder their responsibilities.

With the ECI being the largest election machine in the world and one that conducts elections almost perpetually, there are many good practices in India, from policy level to operational level, from which other EMBs can learn. My visit ahead of the third phase of the Kolkata Lok Sabha election on 29 April 2014 with a fourteen-member Nepalese electoral delegation was an overwhelming experience in terms of scale and management. I was struck by how efficiently the randomization of polling stations and polling personnel was done and as an ultimate test of ensuring electoral neutrality, the idea stayed with me. During the elections to the House of Representatives in 2017 in Nepal, the ECN also piloted randomization.

Many of the good practices in India's elections are a result of experience and the sheer magnitude of the event. Among them is the use of technological advancements, a media monitoring system, an electoral expense regulation system, etc., that may be emulated in the region as these good practices are some of the many reasons behind the successful conduct of elections across India.

Nepal has successfully piloted electronic voting machines from India in two Constituent Assembly elections (in 2008 and 2013). However, EVMs were not used in the 2017 general elections, as there was not enough time for adequate procurement and appropriate trainings.

The election commissions in both Nepal and India have been envisaged as independent constitutional bodies. Both their functions include quasi-judicial, civic engagement and advocacy, management and administration, code of conduct and regulatory responsibilities.[3]

Unlike India, where the ECI has steadily consolidated its position ever since its creation in 1950, the ECN has had a chequered history. Set up in 1951,[4] Nepal's Election Commission started playing a greater role in its national life after the 1990s when the country overthrew the autocratic panchayat era with what was known as called a people's movement and established constitutional monarchy. Since the first general elections of 1959, Nepal has seen five national-level parliamentary elections under a multi-party political system. The latest such election was to the Constituent Assembly in April 2008, held after sweeping political changes were brought about by the second popular movement of 2006.

The interim constitution of 2007 was a provisional arrangement until a Constituent Assembly could write a proper constitution that would address the aspirations and interests of all sections of people, as an instrument to guide the nation towards social justice, equal access and inclusion.[5] The new Constitution of Nepal, 2015, declared Nepal a federal democratic republic with three levels of government—the federal, the state and the local.[6]

Nations that are small in size, transition democracies and emerging from a conflict, can sometimes be role models in many ways. As opposed to transformation in larger and mature democracies, it is easier to bring about changes in countries where democracy is yet to mature. And their small size makes the implementation of changes more efficient. Nepal is going through a similar phenomenon where changes are swift, radical and unpredictable. One such area is the political participation of women, which has increased phenomenally.

Women's Participation

Demographically, Nepal has more women (51 per cent) than men (49 per cent). But in the general elections of 2017, the percentage of women voters (49 per cent) was less than that of men (51 per cent). This is a sign that women are still not as politically aware. However, in terms of representation, women have a very respectable seat on the table due to constitutional and legal provisions, beside the country's commitment to the Convention on the Elimination of All Forms of Discrimination Against Women (CEDAW). Combined with treaty obligations, the rising expectations and aspirations of the people led to Nepal formulating a progressive and forward-looking constitution in 2015.

This constitution ensures that there is at least one woman member and one Dalit woman member in each ward, which means the presence of at least 40 per cent women in the local governments. Further, the Election Commission proposed that political parties must ensure that they field at least 50 per cent women candidates between chairperson and deputy chairpersons of local levels, which include rural municipalities, municipalities, sub-metropolis and metropolis. As a result of these elections held under the new constitution, the country has 41 per cent women in powerful local governments, 34 per cent in provincial assemblies, 33 per cent in the House of Representatives, and 33 per cent in the National Assembly.[7] In 96 per cent of local-level units, the elected head is a man, however, in 95 per cent of local-level units, the deputy is now a woman. The constitution provides that between the president and the vice-president of the country, one must be a woman.[8] Consequently, Nepal also has a woman president, Bidhya Devi Bhandari, who was recently re-elected in March 2018.[9]

The Election Commission has always believed in proportional participation of women in the entire electoral process. The Commission believes that women should be represented proportionately, not only as voters and candidates but also in election management and security. It is not always possible to do so in choosing its officers as the percentage of women in the civil service pool is very low. The ECN tries to make up for this by securing reservations for women wherever possible. This is why the ECN deploys at least 50 per cent women among volunteers in polling stations and asks the home ministry to hire 50 per cent women as temporary security personnel. The Election Commission has also reduced the candidacy nomination fee by half for women candidates. Separate queues for women voters are arranged and instructions given to polling staff and security to be sensitive to needs of people with disability, pregnant women and new mothers. In every election, some polling centres are managed by women as a confidence-building exercise for women voters.

The ECN has tried to ensure a gender equality and social inclusion (GESI) perspective in all legal framework, including in its internal operation. As mentioned earlier, the Commission prepares the initial drafts of laws and has always promoted greater participation of women in laws related to political parties and other electoral ones.[10] The ECN passed a gender and inclusion policy in September 2013.[11] There is a high level GESI committee chaired by a commissioner as well as an operational unit that develops GESI strategic and action plans, ensures gender responsive budgeting and conducts an annual review of gender and inclusion in policies and programmes.

Today, Nepal's federal parliament is by far the most inclusive legislative body in South Asia. With 33.5 per cent members of parliament being women, Nepal should climb to the thirty-third spot out of 193 in the global ranking of women in parliament, somewhere between Switzerland and Austria. This has been achieved by a combination of factors: a progressive constitution, legislation that tries to capture the constitutional spirit, and the role of civil society at large, including the media (see Table 1).

Table 1

Women's Representation in Five Elections

Elections	Total seat	Elected	Percentage
General Elections 1991	205	7	3.4
General Elections 1994	205	7	3.4
General Elections 1999	205	12	5.9
Constituent Assembly Elections 2008	575	191	33.2
Constituent Assembly Elections 2013	575	172	29.9
General Elections 2017	275	90	32.7

Source: The Election Commission of Nepal

Inclusion through Proportional Representation

The most prominent distinction between Nepal and India's electoral systems is the proportional representation (PR) system, which Nepal follows and India is still debating on. Like India, Nepal has a bi-cameral parliament with a House of Representatives (the lower house) and a National Assembly (the upper house). But the election system is a bit different. The House of Representatives has 275 members; 165 elected from single-member constituencies by the first-past-the-post (FPTP) criterion and 110 elected through proportional representation where the whole country is considered one constituency and voters vote for political parties.[12] The National assembly of the Federal Parliament has fifty-nine members and the election is through a single transferable vote.

Table 2
Inclusion in House of Representatives through PR

S. No.	Clusters	Percentage
1	Dalit	13.8
2	Adhibasi Janajati	28.7
3	Khas Arya	31.2
4	Madhesi	15.3
5	Tharu	6.6
6	Muslim	4.4
7	Backward Area	4.3

Note: 50 per cent of women in every cluster and minimum number of candidates for PR is 10 per cent of total seats.

Source: The Election Commission of Nepal

Nepal, in fact, is cited as a good example of political inclusion because of its laws being drafted in compliance with the reformist spirit of its new constitution by adopting a mixed or parallel electoral system. In the PR electoral system, the entire country is considered a single constituency and candidates are elected from different political parties based on votes secured by those parties. For this purpose, political parties are required to submit their 'closed rank lists' of candidates to the Election Commission within the time frame specified by the Commission. Such lists ensure proportional representation of groups, such as women, Dalits, indigenous tribes, backward regions, Madhesis, Khas–Aarya, on the basis of the percentage of their population as prescribed in the constitution. The system requires all political parties to prepare their closed list in such a way as to incorporate at least 50 per cent women candidates.[13]

Inclusion in Local Government

As there is a three-tier system of government in Nepal, it is important that inclusion is ensured at all three levels. While the ECN conducts local-level government elections in Nepal, in India the ECI is not involved with local bodies' elections.[14]

While the proportional representation system has enabled women's participation, there is a need to create the right environment for more women to be elected to top positions. The Election Commission of Nepal, for many years, has stressed that the internal committees of political parties should also be proportionally represented. Article 169C of the Constitution of Nepal, 2015, stipulates that parties should ensure inclusive representation in their executive committees at all levels in a way that will reflect the diversity of the country. But in a heterogeneous society, low political awareness and the need to further strengthen laws in relation to local governments have hindered the participation of women in local government institutions.

One particularity of the local elections is that the seats reserved for Dalits were all taken from the seats reserved for women as per the constitution, so the representation of Dalit women at the local level is relatively high, and the representation of Dalit men is low. As a result, 41 per cent of elected local representatives are women, a total of 14,353 women in a very powerful local government, which is a major advancement for Nepal. In this, India compares favourably, as at the local government level, the Panchayati Raj Act, 1992, provides one-third reservation for women. Several progressive states have increased it to 50 per cent. But as far as state and national legislatures are concerned, there is no reservation for women. Consequently, they are very poorly represented, at only around 10 per cent across India.

Simultaneous Elections

Nepal has practiced simultaneous elections successfully, though not by design but due to compulsion of constitutional deadline. The legislative elections that were held in Nepal in two phases, on 26 November and 7 December 2017, to elect the 275 members of the lower house of the Federal Parliament of Nepal, were held alongside the first provincial elections for the seven provincial assemblies. They went off smoothly with the voters showing none of the expected confusion. Here, probably, India has a lesson to learn from its smaller neighbour.

Autonomy of Commissioners

The biggest strength of the Election Commission of Nepal in terms of its autonomy has been the process of the appointment and removal provided for in the interim constitution of 2007 as well as the new constitution of 2015. According to Article 245 of the new constitution, the Election Commission consists of five election commissioners, one of whom is the chief election commissioner, who acts as the chairperson.[15] All the commissioners are appointed for a term of six years or up to the age of sixty-five, whichever is earlier, by the president on the recommendation of the Constitutional Council. The Constitutional Council consists of the prime minister, the chief justice, the speakers of both houses, leader of the opposition and deputy speaker of the House of Representatives.

The eligibility for a chief election commissioner and other election commissioners is that they must hold a bachelor's degree, must not belong to a political party immediately before their appointment, must have attained the age of forty-five and must possess a high moral character. Interestingly, in India, no qualifications are prescribed and the appointment is done by the government of the day at its discretion, making commissioners vulnerable to accusations of partisanship. Not surprisingly, there has been a long pending demand that these appointments be made through a collegium.

As for removal, the election commissioners in Nepal can be removed by a resolution of impeachment under Article 101 of the constitution, or by the recommendation to the president by the Constitutional Council if he or she is deemed unfit to discharge their duties due to physical or mental illness or in case of their death.

In India, too, they can be removed as per the procedure for Supreme Court judges, namely impeachment by Parliament after an inquiry by the Supreme Court.

Drafting Electoral Laws

The ECN is distinguished by some extra functions from the ECI, one of them being legislative, as the ECN also carries out the responsibility of drafting bills related to electoral laws. The Election Commission of Nepal prepares the draft bills of electoral laws that are forwarded through the home ministry, the liaison ministry, to the ministry of law and then to the government. After appropriate review by the ministry of law, the draft bills are discussed in the State Affairs Committee and other Parliamentary Committees. After extensive discussions, these bills are tabled and passed by Parliament.

Other Areas of learning

Nepal took small steps but could not do effective media monitoring in the most recent election in 2017 due to a shortage of staff. Similarly, it fell short of expenditure control. New electoral laws have fixed the ceiling of the amount that the candidates and political parties can spend during elections but there was widespread criticism of candidates spending way above the permissible limit. The ECN needs to devise more effective strategies in the next elections to force the candidates and political parties to strictly adhere to campaign expense laws. In this area, it can learn a lot from the ECI that has made considerable headway.

Training and Capacity-Building

The ECN signed an MoU with the ECI for assistance in capacity-building of electoral staff.[16] This is one critical area of cooperation between the two ECs, where Nepal can benefit from the long experience and greater resources of its senior counterpart, though the ECI is also struggling with the problem.

Reforms have been a continuous process for the Election Commission of Nepal, which believes in excelling in every election and works according to a Five-Year Strategic Plan since 2009, extending the use of information technology and advocating for other substantive reforms consistently.

Nepal's electoral laws are more than sufficient to help the ECN conduct elections in a free, fair and impartial manner. The ECN, however, needs to strictly enforce a code of conduct during elections as well as the campaign finance law. The ECN also needs to lobby MPs to amend electoral laws that could give the polls panel powers to announce election dates, like its Indian counterpart. Vesting this power in the government gives an unfair advantage to the ruling party.

It would be fair to conclude that though there is a lot in common between the electoral systems of the two countries, and the learnings from the senior partner have greatly benefited Nepal, yet there are significant aspects where Nepal can teach a thing or two to its bigger neighbour.

VIII

Indian Contribution to Bhutan's First Parliamentary Elections

Dasho Kunzang Wangdi

The Kingdom of Bhutan has evolved into a society where age-old values and customs combine flawlessly with many beneficial elements of modernity. Nowhere is this more apparent than in the journey of evolution from monarchy to democracy. Bhutan has travelled a long path to a unified nation through increasing freedom and public participation in good governance to the full-fledged democracy it is today.

The transformation of Bhutan began at a time when it was uninfluenced by the outside world. It gradually transformed from a feudalistic society to a sovereign nation, and became a part of as part of the United Nations.

The political reforms achieved significant momentum with the delegation of power to the people and the introduction of a formal representative form of government with the establishment of the erstwhile National Assembly in 1953. The introduction of the principle of collective responsibility and a decision-making body to incorporate the opinions of the people into their governance was a timely move.

The will and wisdom of Bhutan's monarchs helped it to flourish into a constitutional democracy underpinned by its continued successful economic and social development.

In its quest to evolve internally into a more modern and enlightened state, cultivate its external relationships, exercise caution in accepting political and financial support from the outside world to advance its development strategies, India, which is Bhutan's closest neighbour, serves as an outlet for trade and is a global partner. This special relationship was consolidated by the historic visit of Pandit Jawaharlal Nehru to Bhutan in 1958, an epoch-making event in the relations between our two countries.

The initiation of Bhutan's five-year plans, beginning in 1961, with financial and technical assistance from the people and Government of India, allowed the country to plan its national goals strategically.

A New Era

Druk Gyalpo Jigme Singye Wangchuck at the young age of seventeen envisioned the future of the Kingdom of Bhutan in democracy. A series of policy reforms that His Majesty introduced culminated in transforming Bhutan into a democratic constitutional monarchy in the year 2008 with its first parliamentary elections.

His Majesty commanded the drafting of Bhutan's constitution in 2001. This royal decree not only provided a historic and unprecedented opportunity but also posed great challenges in taking the kingdom towards a democratic system of governance.

On 29 December 2005, His Majesty commanded that parliamentary elections be held in Bhutan in 2008—the centenary year of the Wangchuck Dynasty. In this connection, it was further commanded that the Election Commission be established to conduct free and fair democratic elections.

So, a democratic constitutional monarchy was ushered in with the conduct of elections to the National Council and National Assembly in December 2007 and March 2008 respectively.

Even as these sweeping reforms happened, the social fabric of Bhutan was kept neatly woven by its time-tested values and age-old culture. The overall vision for the transformation of power from the throne to the people was thus successfully completed.

Learning from India

With no experience or professional background, the Election Commission of Bhutan (ECB) ventured fearlessly into its mission in 2006. The year 2008 was not far, and we had to learn about elections and put in place a working electoral system capable of successfully conducting parliamentary elections in a matter of two years. It seemed like asking for a miracle.

Bhutan and India, although with obvious contrasts in size and strength, continue to share one of the closest relationships among nations, setting an excellent example to the global community. If we had to learn anything about managing and conducting elections, we had to look no further than India, which has successfully managed electoral activities over the span of several decades. India, being the world's largest democracy, has had unwavering success in conducting democratic elections (with over 834 million voters in 2014, making it the largest in the world and more than all the voters in the European Union and the USA combined). The task of deploying thousands of officers and millions of EVMs and other materials to 930,000 polling stations (as of the 2014 Lok Sabha elections) and conducting elections of unquestioned integrity is a major accomplishment for any democratic nation.

Immediately after its establishment, the ECB was invited by the Election Commission of India to visit the country and study its electoral system and conduct of elections. Having had time only for cursory readings of the draft constitution and the draft election bill, all the members of the infant Election Commission visited India. First-hand exposure to the Indian election machinery was a godsend of a crash course.

An orientation to the Indian experience proved truly worthwhile and helped in making a good beginning for the ECB. One of the biggest impacts made was the decision to use EVMs, a very practical and user-friendly voting device that had revolutionized Indian elections, for Bhutanese elections for the very first time!

As an exchange visit, B.B. Tandon, then chief election commissioner of India, visited Bhutan in May 2006 during which a Memorandum of Understanding (MoU) was signed between the two electoral management bodies of India and Bhutan. With this, Bhutan and India embarked on a new era of friendship as Bhutan moved toward adopting a democratic system of governance. Bhutan will continue to receive guidance from India's experience in the field of conducting and managing democratic elections.

The MoU helped strengthen our respective democratic institutions with the exchange of technical know-how, expertise and information for mutual benefit, as well as consultation and cooperation in the field of electoral management and administration.

Under this arrangement, the ECB could field a number of delegations to observe various elections and provide to its staff and election officers first-hand experience of how elections are being conducted in India. Such observational visits have been effective in helping Bhutanese election officials understand what their jobs entail towards ensuring free and fair elections.

The secrecy of the vote is fundamental to a free and fair election, the sanctity or the violation of which could ultimately determine the election's outcome. It, thus, became essential for the ECB to choose the right electoral system and technology. Hence, the decision to use the Indian EVM over the conventional ballot paper method and even sophisticated computer systems used in other countries was a crucial one.

Bhutan received the Indian EVMs as a gift from the people and the Government of India, which was a fitting gesture for Bhutan's embrace of democracy.

The EVMs played a big role in the conduct of the very first parliamentary elections in Bhutan and ensured smooth and efficient voting. It also enabled the declaration of the results on the day of the poll. The simplicity and ease of use of the EVMs, their portability and convenience of setting up in any environment, and the speed and reliability in counting, instilled trust and confidence in the Bhutanese people and helped the stakeholders to accept the outcome. Two nationwide rounds of mock parliamentary elections were conducted in 2007 to familiarize voters and officials alike with the EVMs as well as educating them on machines of the electoral process. The Indian EVMs helped the Bhutanese elections to become a modern yet simple system from the very beginning.

The Bhutanese voter photo identity card (VPIC) was also modelled on the Indian EPIC and is another example of Bhutan learning from the Indian experience. The VPIC has curtailed possible abuses of voting arising out of impersonation. The smooth and orderly conduct of the first parliamentary elections could be attributed to the VPIC. Learning from this experience, the ECB has upgraded the voter identification system for future elections to use biometric technology.

Bhutan's first parliamentary elections were closely observed at the highest level led by a team of officials comprising N. Gopalaswami, the then Indian chief election commissioner, Shyam Saran and Salman Haidar, former foreign secretaries of India, and at the field level by a team led by the chief electoral officers of Tamil Nadu.

Modern, Successful Elections

Also, learning from the Indian experience, the application of information and communication technologies assured that the first parliamentary elections in Bhutan were modern and up to the standard, as reported by international election observers. These technologies strengthened the capacity of the ECB to monitor and coordinate the entire exercise. From the visits (in 2009 to the Lok Sabha elections of India and in October–November 2010 to the legislative assembly election in Bihar), the monitoring of the conduct of polls through live web-casts, use of Short Messaging Service (SMS) and other mobile phone technologies and services,

ECB managed to enhance electoral service delivery and helped disseminate crucial electoral information.

With each observation visit made to India, the ECB continues to learn newer ways of incorporating and innovating use of information and communications technologies in the conduct of Bhutanese elections.

A notable Indian experience replicated in the conduct of local government elections in Bhutan (January–June 2011) deployed 'micro election observers'. Such close scrutiny helped ensure that the conduct of elections was free, fair and democratic in every sense.

The learning from the Indian experience was valuable to the successful conduct of the first parliamentary elections in Bhutan, which were described as being at par with international standards of conducting elections. The outcome was received well by the international community. The learnings from the Indian experience continue to guide and transform the conduct of Bhutanese elections. India also financed the construction of an office building, which is called the Democracy House, an edifice that proudly stands testimony to Indo-Bhutan cooperation.

As a young and evolving democracy, the ECB looks up to India, the world's largest democracy, with admiration, a keen sense of learning and hope to share lessons from our own experiments.

Jai Bhutan. Jai Bharat.

PART THREE

People and Perspectives

I

Civil Society in Elections in India

Jagdeep S. Chhokar

What Is Civil Society?

Civil society is a nebulous concept. It can, and often does, mean different things to different people in different contexts. The simplest description of civil society, perhaps, is that it consists of non-governmental organizations and groups, which are sometimes called 'non-state actors'. Occasionally, it is called the 'third sector', in contrast to the government and the business (profit-making) sector. This also implies 'not-for-profit' as one of the defining characteristics of civil society. However, this characterization has somewhat got blurred in recent years with the rise of what is called 'social entrepreneurship'.

According to the Centre for Civil Society, UCLA School of Public Policy and Social Research, civil society refers to the set of institutions, organizations and behaviour situated between the state, the business world, and the family.[1] Specifically, this includes voluntary and non-profit organizations of many different kinds, philanthropic institutions, social and political movements, other forms of social participation and engagement and the values and cultural patterns associated with them. It therefore includes 'intermediary institutions' such as professional associations, religious groups, labour unions, and citizen advocacy organizations that give voice to various sectors of society.

The World Bank uses the term civil society 'to refer to the wide array of non-governmental and not-for-profit organizations that have a presence in public life, expressing the interests and values of their members or others, based on ethical, cultural, political, scientific, religious or philanthropic considerations.' Civil Society Organizations (CSOs) therefore include a wide array of organizations: community groups, non-governmental organizations (NGOs), labour unions, indigenous groups, charitable organizations, faith-based organizations, professional associations, and foundations.[2] Perhaps the most succinct description of civil society is 'private action for public good'.

Civil Society in India

The tradition of 'private action for public good' in India is ancient. Its origins can possibly be found in the emergence of charitable and philanthropic organizations set up to support spiritual and religious activities. This was done mainly by the ruling classes and the elite mercantile classes.

Civil society does not seem to have had much of a role in elections in independent India during the early years, unless political parties are considered a part of it. Since the primary purpose of political parties is considered to be to contest elections,[3] it stands to reason that political parties are left out of consideration as part of civil society.

Of course, there have been instances of political parties being formed by organizations that, by themselves, may well be considered to be 'civil society' organizations. Two prominent examples of this phenomenon are Shiromani Akali Dal (SAD) and Bharatiya Janata Party (BJP). SAD was 'established in December 1920 to help guide the quasi-militant Akali movement of the early 1920s, in which Sikhs demanded and (through the Sikh Gurdwaras Act of 1925) won from the ruling British authorities in India control over the gurdwaras (Sikh houses of worship)'.[4]

The BJP traces its lineage to Rashtriya Swayamsevak Sangh (RSS), which was 'founded on 27 September 1925' by Keshav Baliram

Hedgewar, who was 'inspired by public service and nationalism' of several persons. 'The name "Rashtriya Swayamsevak Sangh" was formally announced in April 1926.'[5] It was during 1950–51 that 'RSS felt the need to nurture an independent political entity with a distinct, nationalist identity'. It can thus be inferred that this was the impulse for Syama Prasad Mukherjee to form Bharatiya Jana Sangh (BJS) as a political party in October 1951. BJS was part of the government formed by Janata Party, an 'experiment (which) failed within thirty months' and this 'led to the emergence of BJP' in January 1980.[6]

Another case of a civil society movement morphing into a political party is that of Aam Aadmi Party (AAP). The civil society movement, India Against Corruption (IAC), began in early 2011 with the avowed purpose of fighting widespread and big-ticket corruption prevalent in the political and bureaucratic establishments. As the IAC ran its course without much concrete success, it culminated in the formation of Aam Aadmi Party in October 2012.

Some civil society members have also contested elections from panchayat and local bodies, all the way to state assemblies and the Lok Sabha. The success rates have been very low, actually dismal, though there have been some notable successes at the panchayat level.

Initial Civil Society Involvement in Elections

The first known instance of civil society playing a role in elections was in August 1974 when Jayaprakash Narayan set up a committee on electoral reform on behalf of citizens for democracy, consisting of Justice V.M. Tarkunde, M.R. Masani, K.D. Desai, and E.P.W. Da Costa as convener. This committee gave its report in February 1975 but it did not get enough exposure due to the imposition of the Emergency on 25 June 1975.[7]

After the Emergency was lifted on 21 March 1977, Narayan appointed another committee on 13 August 1977 called the Committee on Election Expenses, which comprised Justice Tarkunde, Masani, P.G. Mavalankar, Surendra Mohan, and Desai as member–secretary. The terms of reference of this committee were:

a) To examine and report upon the feasibility of the government defraying the election expenses of candidates in the Lok Sabha and state assembly elections;
b) the manner in which the government may defray such expenses, the security if any to be furnished by candidates, and other incidental matters; and
c) the desirability of making it compulsory for the voters to cast their votes in these elections.[8]

The committee submitted its report on 19 March 1978, suggesting that some 'facilities should be made available at government expense to every candidate in Lok Sabha and state assembly election' to subsidize their election expenses indirectly, in kind. Examples of the facilities proposed included the provision of a fixed number of copies of electoral rolls, free air time on radio for broadcasting publicity material, free printing of posters and other 'propaganda material'.

The committee also made some very progressive recommendations, such as all parties being 'required by law to keep accounts duly audited and *open to public inspection*', things that are yet to be implemented!

On the issue of compulsory voting, the committee adopted a very practical stand, saying:

> It appears to us that compulsory voting may be resented by the voters and may on balance prove to be counter-productive. It is desirable that compliance with the duty to cast one's vote should be brought about by persuasion and political education, rather than by compulsion.

Not surprisingly, the recommendations of what came to be popularly known as the Tarkunde Committee Report did not find favour with the then and subsequent governments except for providing some facilities to candidates and parties at the time of the election, at government cost. This was actually done not as a follow-up of the Tarkunde Committee Report but on the recommendation of a committee appointed later by the government in 1988—the Indrajit Gupta Committee.

There was a kind of a lull after the Tarkunde Committee until the early 1990s. That decade saw four major committees, all formed by the government:

a) Goswami Committee on electoral reforms (1990)[9]
b) Vohra Committee Report (1993)[10]
c) Indrajit Gupta Committee on state funding of elections (1998)[11]
d) 170th report of the Law Commission of India on reform of the electoral laws (1999)[12]

The involvement of civil society in the above committees was minimal, if at all. The Vohra Committee, for example, does not mention any involvement of any non-governmental persons or agencies. The Law Commission of India, on the other hand, did try to involve persons outside the government. It says:

> The working paper prepared by the Law Commission was communicated to all the recognized political parties, both at the national and state level, the houses of Parliament, the state legislatures, to the high courts, bar associations, Election Commission, prominent media personalities, associations and organizations interested in electoral reform and many other public-minded persons . . . In addition to circulating the working paper, the Law Commission also held four seminars to elicit informed opinions and views of the political parties and the responsible members of the public.[13]

The Beginning

It can be said that the 170th report of the Law Commission was the harbinger of the involvement of civil society in elections in a very significant way. It was this report that, in part, caused a civil society organization, Association for Democratic Reforms[14] (ADR), to file a public-interest litigation (PIL) in the Delhi High Court on 2 December 1999, asking the court to:

(i)   direct the respondents to implement the relevant recommendations of the Law Commission given in its 170th report,

(ii) direct respondent No. 1 to amend the relevant provision of law to implement the said recommendations,

(iii) direct respondent No. 2 to make it mandatory for every candidate to provide the relevant information by amending Form 2A to 2E prescribed by Conduct of Election Rules 1961 relating to filing of nominations and making it penal in the event any of the said disclosures are found to be inaccurate or incorrect making the said candidate if elected liable to be disqualified,

(iv) issue an appropriate writ order or direction directing Respondent No. 2 to put together the information on criminality of all candidates for an election and make this information available to the public, and print and electronic media for wide dissemination,

(v)   pass any other or further orders as may be deemed fit and proper in the circumstances of the case.[15]

After several hearings, Delhi High Court announced its decision on 2 November 2000, granting the petition and directing:

[. . .] the Election Commission (to) secure to the voters the following information pertaining to each of the candidates standing for election to the Parliament and to the State Legislatures and the parties they represent:

1. Whether the candidate is accused of any offence(s) punishable with imprisonment? If so, the details thereof.
2. Assets possessed by a candidate, his or her spouse and dependent relations.

3. Facts giving insight to candidate's competence, capacity and suitability for acting as parliamentarian or legislator including details of his/her educational qualifications.

4. Information which the Election Commission considers necessary for judging the capacity and capability of the political party fielding the candidate for election to Parliament or the State Legislature.[16]

The above decision of Delhi High Court was, for some reason, not acceptable to the government of the day and, therefore, the Union of India filed a Special Leave Petition (SLP) in the Supreme Court (SC) against Delhi High Court's judgment. Several political parties joined the SLP as interveners in support of the government. The SC described the reason for the SLP as:

> Short but important question involved in these matters is—in a nation wedded to republican and democratic form of Government, where election as a Member of Parliament or as a Member of Legislative Assembly is of utmost importance for governance of the country, whether, before casting votes, voters have a right to know relevant particulars of their candidates? Further connected question is—whether the High Court had jurisdiction to issue directions, as stated below, in a writ petition filed under Article 226 of the Constitution of India?[17]

The judgment[18] of the SC upheld the judgment of Delhi High Court and ordered as follows:

> The Election Commission is directed to call for information on affidavit by issuing necessary order in exercise of its power under Article 324 of the Constitution of India from each candidate seeking election to Parliament or State Legislature as a necessary part of his nomination paper, furnishing therein, information on the following aspects in relation to his/her candidature:

1. Whether the candidate is convicted/acquitted/discharged of any criminal offence in the past—if any, whether he is punished with imprisonment or fine?
2. Prior to six months of filing of nomination, whether the candidate is accused in any pending case, of any offence punishable with imprisonment for two years or more, and in which charge is framed or cognizance is taken by the Court of law. If so, the details thereof.
3. The assets (immovable, movable, bank balances etc.) of a candidate and of his/her spouse and that of dependants.
4. Liabilities, if any, particularly whether there are any overdues of any public financial institution or Government dues.
5. The educational qualifications of the candidate.

The SC further said, 'Hence, the norms and modalities to carry out and give effect to the aforesaid directions should be drawn up properly by the Election Commission as early as possible and in any case within two months.'

When the Election Commission implemented the SC decision, it disturbed the entire political establishment. An all-party meeting was called by the then law minister, K. Jana Krishnamurthi, which was attended by representatives from twenty-two political parties. It was *unanimously* resolved that the SC decision would not be allowed to be implemented and the Representation of the People Act, 1951 (RPA), would be amended in that very session of Parliament to ensure that the SC's decision was rendered ineffective. A draft bill to amend the RPA was prepared in seven days but it could not be introduced in Lok Sabha as it was adjourned sine die due to some controversies.

Some speculation surfaced that the government of the day was planning to issue an ordinance.[19] In a remarkable civil society action, thirty people representing civil society organizations from different parts of the country met the president, A.P.J. Abdul Kalam, and briefed him on the background of the proposed ordinance and also pointed out to him that certain sections of the ordinance were likely to be unconstitutional, and he should, therefore, exercise due caution before signing it if it was sent to him.

Sure enough, the cabinet did send the ordinance to the president for signature. The obvious conclusion that follows from this is that the cabinet was convinced that 'circumstances exist(ed) which render(ed) it necessary for him (the President) to take immediate action'.

The president did not sign the draft ordinance and 'returned' it. The draft ordinance was sent to the president again, in the same form. Actually, it was carried personally to him by the then attorney general. Since it had been sent a second time exactly in the same form, the president signed it, or more precisely, had to sign it under the existing convention. The ordinance became law and the Supreme Court judgment stood nullified.[20]

The ordinance and the consequential legislation were challenged in the Supreme Court for being unconstitutional. The Supreme Court, in a landmark judgment[21] delivered on 13 March 2002, declared the offending parts of the ordinance and the consequential act 'to be illegal, null and void'.

Further Developments

This episode has been described in some detail, as this is, arguably, the first instance of civil society taking an active role in the electoral process of the country. This has been followed by several efforts by civil society actors (individual persons and organizations) to influence, positively, the holding of elections in the country. Some of the prominent examples are:

a) *Lily Thomas and Lok Prahari judgments*[22] (July 2013) which struck down Section 8(4) of the Representation of the People Act, 1951, for being unconstitutional, thus barring convicted MLAs and MPs from continuing in the legislature and contesting elections. Section 8(4) had provided special privilege to MPs/MLAs to hold office even after conviction

if an appeal had been filed in a higher court within a span of
three months.

b) *NOTA judgment*[23] (September 2013) which directed the
Election Commission to provide a button on the EVMs,
labelled NOTA (none of the above) so that a voter who did
not wish to vote for any of the candidates on the ballot, could
exercise her/his choice.

c) *No blanks in the affidavit judgment*[24] (September 2013) in
the Resurgence India case that ruled that the candidate must
'explicitly remark as "NIL" or "Not Applicable" or "Not known"
in the columns and not to leave the particulars blank'.

d) *Declaration of the source of income and assets judgment*[25] (February
2018) in the Lok Prahari case, which directed candidates
contesting elections to declare the sources of their assets as
well as their spouses' and dependants', as part of their election
affidavits, saying 'non-disclosure of assets and sources of income
of self, spouse and dependants by a candidate would amount to
undue influence and thereby, corruption and as such election of
such a candidate can be declared null and void'.

In addition to the above judicial interventions, civil society
organizations have also been active in disseminating information
about candidates and political parties, to assist voters to make an
informed choice while casting their vote. A prime example of this
is the website http://myneta.info/ maintained by the National
Election Watch (https://adrindia.org/content/national-election-
watch), another civil society initiative. This website carries scanned
copies of election affidavits of all candidates who have contested
Parliament or state assembly elections since 2003, numbering over
one lakh.

There are many civil society organizations and groups working
on election-related issues such as Common Cause,[26] Mazdoor
Kisan Shakti Sangathan (MKSS),[27] Commonwealth Human Rights
Initiative (CHRI),[28] and Forum for Electoral Integrity. These and
several other individuals, groups and organizations, which can be

characterized as being part of civil society, work on a variety of issues that have a bearing on elections.

Civil society organizations have also worked, in many ways, to support the correct actions of the Election Commission. One documented case is of the Tamil Nadu assembly elections in 2011[29] in which eight PILs were 'filed in Madras High Court by interested parties', to frustrate the Election Commission's efforts to stop the distribution of illicit cash to entice voters to vote for particular candidates. Madras High Court stopped the Election Commission from taking intrusive measures through an interim order. 'A few counter petitions were also filed by NGOs . . . in favour of the EC's actions and opposing the interim order of the High Court.' The interim order was subsequently set aside and the EC's actions were upheld.

In conclusion, it can be said that civil society has played an increasingly important role in elections in India over the last couple of decades. The efforts of civil society actors have been diffused, with minimal coordination. Attempts have at times been made to initiate coordinated and concerted actions but such attempts have met with limited success. Perhaps it is the fundamental nature of civil society to be diffused. What can be said without any doubt is that civil society has been playing an increasingly larger role in elections in India, hopefully, for the betterment of democracy in the country.

II

Women Vote 'Yes' to Empowerment

Naina Lal Kidwai

Sarojini Naidu, Annie Besant, Vijaya Lakshmi Pandit, Aruna Asaf Ali, Bhikaiji Cama and Sucheta Kriplani are just some of the women who stand proudly alongside the male leaders of India's struggle for independence. These women were not a minority, and the vast multitudes of freedom fighters included millions of men and women.

In fact, Mahatma Gandhi and Jawaharlal Nehru had once remarked, 'When the history of India's fight for Independence comes to be written, the sacrifice made by the women of India will occupy the foremost place. When most of the menfolk were in prison, then a remarkable thing happened. Our women came forward and took charge of the struggle. Women had always been there of course but now there was an avalanche of them, which took not only the British Government but their own menfolk by surprise.'[1]

Universal Suffrage

However, the fact is that India was not unique in the important role played by women in society. After all they constituted half the population, but it certainly was a rarity among nations, because it granted women equal voting and representation rights from the very beginning. In other nations, the women's suffrage movement was a long and arduous struggle. For example, much older democracies like the United Kingdom and the United States gave voting rights to women only in 1918 and 1920 respectively. This is despite the fact that the Isle of Man within the British Isles was the first country to give voting rights to women in 1881, and New Zealand became the first self-governing British colony to do the same in 1893. In fact, some women in colonies like Massachusetts and New Jersey[2] in the US had been voting since 1776.

The United Nations introduced voting rights for women into international law only in 1948.

It is generally believed that these 'equal rights' developments for women in the UK, US and later in the UN were an acknowledgement of their contribution to the countries and the world during the first and second world wars when they stepped forward to drive their countries' production and economies while the men were away at war.

As seen from the above examples, India is indeed fortunate that when it became an independent nation, it had broad-minded leaders who readily acknowledged the vital role played by women in the freedom struggle. They also recognized the fact that gender equality is critical to the development of every nation. It would have been a travesty of justice if women had been excluded from building the nation they had helped create.

The truth is that this freedom of choice—to exercise one's right, to fulfil one's duty as a citizen to participate in the political process and elect one's representative—is a fundamental right and a determinant of what one gets in return for civil society.

Policy Impact

Former UN secretary-general Kofi Annan has said, 'When women thrive, all of society benefits, and succeeding generations are given a better start in life.'[3] I could not agree more with this statement. For the past few years, I have worked closely with NGOs and associations and have seen first-hand the positive impact of women's empowerment. I have also seen that in rural areas, economic development is largely driven by women through self-help groups and by individual contribution to household incomes.

Several studies have revealed that women in general are more responsive to issues of human development. Women suffer more than men due to lack of education, health, hygiene, sanitation, drinking water, nutrition, and so on. They are also more engaged in issues around their children. As a result, women are normally more concerned about these issues. Thus, it is not enough for them to just vote, but to represent this large population and to ensure a shift in the focus of the political agenda towards human and social development.

In this endeavour, the process can begin with women's participation in elected bodies at the grassroots level—village panchayats, for instance. Some headway has already been made in this area. Some states, such as Bihar, Uttarakhand, Himachal Pradesh, Kerala, Madhya Pradesh, Rajasthan and Chhattisgarh, have 50 per cent reservation for women and have made the administration more gender-sensitive. Today fourteen states have 50–58 per cent representation of women. Jharkhand leads the way with 59 per cent followed by Rajasthan and Uttarakhand at 58 per cent. In Uttar Pradesh, the percentage of women is 34 per cent among sarpanches, in Odisha 58 per cent with Manipur at just 7 per cent. In an interesting twist, Bihar has seen the spouses of women heads of panchayats styling themselves as 'mukhiyapatis'. This is a symbolic yet significant role reversal. However, women in state legislatures at the all-India level is a dismal 9 per cent of state assembly members and 5 per cent of state council members

This increasing role of women in administration will be critical in drawing attention to, and resolving the problems and needs of, the disadvantaged. Their participation becomes even more vital in the context of the adoption of development strategies that are favourable and beneficial to women. We need to develop special programmes to meet the special requirements of women in urban or rural areas.

To give them their due, political parties in the last few years have begun to accept women's concerns in their programmes, as reflected in their election manifestos, speeches and slogans. Many NGOs and organizations working for the upliftment of women, especially the poor, have also actively participated in the process and have led to the recognition of women as an important constituency, and this has resulted in their entry into the decision-making process.

True Empowerment

Once this process gains momentum and women begin to play a more active role in the political process with increasing representation, with or without reservation, we will see an acceleration in the pace of social development across all levels of society. As I mentioned earlier, I have witnessed first-hand the impact of economic empowerment of women in society—the confidence that their own financial independence gives them. I have also seen the tremendous work being done by institutions like Self-Employed Women's Association (SEWA) and Mann Deshi, to name only a couple among many more in this field. There are several others like them working across the country.

However, women's groups working at the grassroots level are small and scattered and have diverse ways of empowering women. There aren't enough infrastructural or networking facilities available that could bring them together, allow them to share best practices and strengthen them. It is therefore also important to create unity between women's groups, organizations and individuals involved with women's empowerment. They need to adopt a common strategy, have a common vision, and be able to bring about necessary changes in policies and structures.

As of January 2017, the global participation rate in national level parliaments was at 23 per cent. In India, there are sixty-six women MPs out of 543, a mere 12.5 per cent of the strength. In the current Union government Council of Ministers (October 2018), six out of twenty-six (23 per cent) cabinet members are women and two out of thirty-eight (5.3 per cent) are ministers of state. The Rajya Sabha too has only around 12.7 per cent women representation.[4]

Clearly, while we have come a long way in India, we have a long way to go.

III

A View from the Poor Woman Voter's Window

Ela R. Bhatt

Elections in India have been always historic, in one way or another, and seven decades of work of the Election Commission is worth celebrating. And celebrated these elections are, by our elected leaders, political parties, administration, media, academics, and many others in many ways and at many levels. They all have their views, valuable and valid. But, perhaps, let me suggest, that these elections are not viewed, at least in any major or ongoing way, from the window of poor women voters.

This is odd. Because at least half of India's voters have been and continue to remain poor and half of these poor voters are women, working and raising families. Poor and working women have played a major role in every election, yet we know little about their views. So, let us look at the seven decades of elections in India from their window. Or, shall I say 'windows', as there are so many of them? I have spent most of the past four decades with these poor and working women, of whom 1.5 million are now members of the Self-Employed Women's Association (SEWA). I have found that SEWA sisters' views are well-defined, worth watching from their window, and worth sharing here.

Marginalized Voters

The view from their window shows that a majority of India's voters are poor and this fact is often missed by most election watchers. The huge cost to the public exchequer of holding elections is repeatedly and loudly pointed out. But the cost, calculated and real, of elections to the poor is not only not mentioned, but is also not accounted for even in rough estimates. What does an election cost our poor? In terms of money? Time? Social stress? Political pressure? How much time—and therefore income—do poor women let go of (they do not get paid for not working on an election day as do the salaried class) to vote? This view of the economic contribution of poor women to the election process and therefore to our democracy has remained shut out from most of our windows.

Similarly, advances in election methods, including electronic voting machines, are our nation's pride, but the fact that poor and illiterate women voters have learned how to use such machines and voted wisely to nurture and grow our democracy are seldom discussed. Sure, there is bogus voting, voting as per husband's order, and so on. Yet a large number of women have understood the process, meaning, technology and spirit of elections, have put faith in elections over guns or bribes, and nurtured democracy from election to election. From poor women voters's windows, we do not see any celebration of these women's unshakeable faith in democracy.

We hear that elections slow down economic growth, divide social structures and politicize development. But we have found that in fact the poor, in particular the women, actually love elections, the process and the outcome. They see them as empowering and can distinguish their remarkable potential to bring about change. SEWA's 1.5 million sisters elect their *agevan* every three years, and 300 agevans elect their executive committee called *karobari*, the general secretary and the president. SEWA co-operative bank elects its board members. SEWA rural marketing, RUDI, elects its office-bearers. SEWA social security (insurance company) elects its board of directors. As many as 110 primary co-operatives elect their own board and most of them distribute dividends, every year.

Almost all institutions of the SEWA sisters are run on democratic elections. But this election process has not slowed down the economic growth of their coops, or divided self-help groups, or politicized the SEWA movement so far. The SEWA sisters have internalized the spirit and empowering process of the national elections, over four decades, to make their own lives and their own institutions run by elections, and hence the democratic spirit. Voting has changed their views on how life should be run, how India should be run. Their windows show that when we invest in explaining elections, their spirit and process, democracy deepens among the poor and the women. When I ask my sisters what is most important in an election, they hardly ever say 'vote', though they vote in high numbers even in elections in various SEWA organizations. They say it is understanding 'the other's view'.

There is hardly any politicizing or sense of victory or loss among SEWA sisters. The focus of the elections is on choosing someone to get a specific agenda carried out. This might be about bringing water to a village or building a toilet in a slum or deciding new loan programmes for green jobs or paying insurance or investing in eco-friendly textiles. Most elections are based on mutual agreement, often by consensus among SEWA sisters. Now this is not unique to SEWA. I find this interest and understanding of elections in so many self-help groups across India, in so many NGOs, in working with women. So what we also should celebrate is the mainstreaming of the election spirit in our poor and women citizens. Elections are not about one winning over the other, as we have done as a nation. The purpose of an election, in the end, is to build a common understanding (not same or singular) among diverse views and that is what our voters have understood, but not our leaders or parties yet.

Implementation of Manifestos

Now let us view the present elections from these windows. How do our sisters understand elections in India and what do they want?

What I am about to explain is discussed by our sisters in almost every Lok Sabha election-related meeting in SEWA. To start with, women want to first know what the candidate has done and not what he or she promises to do. Sisters in SEWA want the election to focus on results and not on manifestos. This also means that women want their priorities addressed and do not care so much for the party candidate. Who represents them takes a second seat to the result achieved for them.

'Our focus on who gets elected—rich–poor, man–woman, Dalit–Muslim–Adivasi, Gujarati–Bihari—is wrong,' SEWA sisters often say. 'This is what is taught by our leaders but when they select candidates or ministers they keep these labels in mind,' the sisters lament. 'We should have elections based on subjects of priority like a job for every youth, a water tap in every urban home, *pucca* walls in every rural house, child daycare for every working mother, affordable food, accessible financial services, health insurance, free transport for rural students, and, deforestation, corruption, war, seat in the UN Security Council, whichever,' they add in SEWA discussions. Let each party come to women to say not what the new manifesto will be, but what the last manifesto achieved. Let the Election Commission make past performance on manifesto a criterion for accepting candidacy. As a result, the elected party candidates will aim at results and not new ideas to sell new dreams or promises. The newly elected government will ask experts and institutions to plan ways to make the manifesto operational, and the machinery will deliver accordingly. 'And then, after two years, midway, we will ask our elected member to report their performance to us, and, we will make suggestions, criticism, reform,' our sisters say. 'And assist our elected members if they need help for better performance.' In other words, the SEWA sisters want to vote on results and not representation.

I agree with their vision. True, we have not focused on what we do with our manifestos. Election manifestos have become more of a public relations blurb, to attract attention and make noise, but not always to be delivered. Though I must add that more and more attention is being given to these manifestos in recent years. We need to reestablish their importance in the election process, not only by the voters, but also by the Election Commission. Past performance by the candidate on his manifesto must be made public by the Election Commission for each candidate. In essence, candidates must be voted for according to their manifestos and what they achieved from them. Sure, new candidates and new parties will be able to swim ahead the first time, but voters will soon catch up. This is the view of the present elections from these windows.

An Agenda for Elections

Now let us view the future from these windows. Perhaps upcoming elections in the coming decade will be most significant, not so much for their outcomes, but more for the fluidity, simultaneous division of the electorate on the basis of religion, never-ending fragmentation on the basis of caste and sub-caste, separation on the basis of location and region, inter- and intra-party dynamic groupings, and the yet unknown role of many new political forces, such as Maoist citizens.

It is hard to predict how much of a say civil society will have on setting the agenda as hired public relations, advertisement, and marketing firms lead and launch most of the agenda items based on opinion surveys and focus group feedbacks. Civil society has made notable initiatives over the past decade or so to influence the election agenda, but it is far from enough.

And what do we see in future from these windows? We see the need to reclaim and influence the election process and agenda, mainly comprising four items.

One is the democratization of economic gains. Many citizens understand that India is taking enormous strides in its macroeconomic development indicators over the past years. Our SEWA sisters have also understood this; sometimes they too get the benefits. The time is overdue when this growth is designed for a larger number of business interests—small businesses, street vendors, traders and microenterprise—across big and small towns in India. Not only government plans and projects but also the election process itself must push issues of the poor woman who sells vegetables on a city street or makes packages for food products in her home. Similarly, in the rural and agriculture sectors, women farmers to young food processors must benefit from this growth. The time has come to help these poor women demand the benefits of economic growth, including the rise in land markets around cities and ports and economic zones. This windfall is mainly for the men and the non-poor. It must be shared more directly and justly with local entrepreneurs and businesses in a time-bound manner. The fastest possible democratic distribution of economic growth has to be a part of election agendas.

The second item for the election agenda in the coming decade is re-establishing the faith of all citizens in governance. The past few years have seen rapid growth and unprecedented turmoil, boundaries have been reclaimed, real and imagined, feared and fought, across social, economic and political spheres. Rapid and top-down growth is notorious worldwide for causing such a need for reclamation. The relations between the state and civil society have seen many difficulties and gaps. In many cases, the corporate sector has stepped in to perform civil society functions, such as celebrating Navaratri *utsav*s or running health or school facilities, often with effective performance but ineffective protection of public interest. Contesting political parties must expand citizens' faith in police, judiciary, courts, policy-making and the delivery system.

The third election agenda is having a larger say by citizens over budgetary allocations. Budgets decide what and where growth takes place. Elected leaders, often with corporate engines, have made use of public budgets to give momentum to economic growth in India. This growth is riding on two unequal wheels, as it were—one of a sophisticatedly engineered car and the other of a handcart. The car is the financial market and the handcart is the employment sector. Enhancing social sector expenditure and effective revenue collection from fast growth sectors may lead to equal-size wheels. The social sector should not be handed over to the private sector or thrown large amounts of money at. However, social sector costs must be proportionately funded from rising private sector revenue.

The fourth item would be accelerated social inclusion of citizens in growth. This relates to the first item I mentioned above. India is committed to rapid economic 'growth with inclusion' in its Eleventh Plan period. Now, India must show ways of making both rapid and sustainable economic growth that particularly includes women workers, Dalits, minorities and casual labour. India has emerging basic, social and institutional infrastructure to ensure that honest and hard labour by marginalized citizens is rewarded as much as well-planned financial investments. If direct foreign investment in stock markets is assured high returns, then why cannot direct honest labour invested by our poor and women be assured the highest returns?

Importantly, the Election Commission must not allow political parties to shortchange the future of India out of either the arrogance of achievement or the frustration of helplessness. The Election Commission must be with poor and working women voters to reclaim elections as a democratic way of living in an India that we all love.

I was wondering with the SEWA sisters if this view from their windows matters when other windows matter, when other windows are larger, taller, brighter, and set in more powerful buildings and mansions. As always, again, they said, 'Our window is small and simple but there are so many windows.'

IV

A Foreign Correspondent's Coverage of Elections

Mark Tully

Looking back at my coverage of Indian elections, I am reminded of one of the most colourful Indian politicians I have known in my long career here spanning forty years—the stalwart of Haryana politics, Chaudhary Devi Lal. During the 1980 general elections, I went to see Chaudhary sahib on the day he and other leaders of the Janata Party were discussing their manifesto. He was obviously in a bad mood so I asked him what the matter was. 'I don't like this table work,' he growled. 'All day sitting around having discussions.'

'But the discussions were surely very important,' I said. 'You were deciding on the manifesto and what should be included in it.'

'Fool!' Devi Lal shot back, 'I can't tell you how many elections I have fought but I can assure you I have never read a single manifesto!'

Of Aya Rams–Gaya Rams and 'Rigging'

I can't remember how many elections I have covered, but I can say I never read the manifestos that carefully. Some might say that's a terrible admission, but I would reply that I can never remember a time when the voters I met as I travelled around India during election campaigns seemed concerned about manifestos. They might well have been struck by one or two big-ticket promises like free electricity for farmers, or free mid-day meals for schoolchildren, but they didn't need to read manifestos to take those on board. Voters, especially in the villages, were interested in working out which candidate would do the most for them, and that seems fair enough to me. Often, a voter would say of a sitting candidate, 'I am not going to vote for him because he didn't do my work,' or, 'that candidate is from my caste so he might help me.'

This presents a problem to those reporting for foreign media, because with personalities counting so much more than principles, it is difficult to report election campaigns without mentioning lots of names and getting entangled in the complications of India's ever-changing political scene. To understand an election in India, it is necessary to know the movements of the 'Aya Ram–Gaya Rams', as party hoppers popularly came to be known. Then there is the tortuous history of the parties themselves with their splits and broken alliances. But a foreign editor wants an election to have parties neatly divided into Left-wing and Right-wing. When it comes to names, the editor thinks readers only want to be faced with those they know well.

I was very privileged because I reported elections for the BBC World Service as well as the services broadcasting to British audiences. The world service included services that broadcast in Indian languages—Hindi, Bengali, Urdu and Tamil. My dispatches were translated into these languages so the reports I sent were heard by a large audience who were very interested in detailed coverage of election campaigns.

The audiences were large because I was broadcasting in the seventies and the eighties, the heydays of radio. Cheap transistor sets, capable of receiving shortwave transmissions, had arrived by then and boosted audiences for radio. There was virtually no competition from television in India. The only Indian broadcaster was All India Radio and listeners often used to tell me scornfully that they didn't trust its bulletins because they were 'government news'. Foreign radio stations, broadcasting on shortwave, were the only alternative and, fortunately, the most popular of those was the BBC.

It was because I had a dedicated audience that my coverage of elections was more detailed than most foreign correspondents'. I would travel extensively during election campaigns asking voters their opinions. I always remember two opinions I got on one of my first forays into the countryside in an Uttar Pradesh election. A labourer repairing a road said to me, 'What does it matter who I vote for? Whoever I do choose will put my vote in his stomach.' In a village, whose MLA was the chief minister, dissatisfied voters complained, 'If he can't provide us with kerosene during an election campaign when he's seeking our votes, what hope do we have of getting it afterwards if we do vote for him?' One of the most common complaints I used to hear was about MPs and MLAs who during the election campaign promised to care for their constituencies, but after being elected were not seen until they next came to ask for votes.

After the coverage of the campaign came polling and, of course, the question of rigging. On the day before polling in the 1980 general election, I was sitting in the house of a former MP in Muzaffarpur, Bihar. Every now and then, an excited supporter would arrive and report that the opposition candidate's men had captured another polling station. There was a constituency where I was so confident there would be rigging that I sent the distinguished British psephologist, David Butler, there to witness it. The next day an article appeared in the London *Times* in which Butler said, in shocked tones, 'I have seen vote-stealing for the first time.' After polling came the results, which, considering the scale of the operation and the lack of communications technology in those days, came through remarkably quickly.

Rigging is a much less common phenomenon nowadays because of the measures taken by successive chief election commissioners. However, moving police around the country to provide the security the commissioners regard as necessary has made elections much longer, which means it's harder for foreign journalists to keep up the momentum of their coverage. Because of the restrictions on loudspeakers, wall painting and other traditional means of campaigning, elections are also less colourful, which is an added problem, especially for television journalists.

'Authentic News'

Elections did demonstrate the extent of the BBC's audience and the trust voters had in its coverage. Indian columnist and journalist Saeed Naqvi tells the story of asking an elderly villager in UP which party was the strongest. The villager replied, 'Don't ask me now, wait until I have heard the BBC.' On several occasions, I was accosted by angry candidates who wanted to know why the BBC had said their opponent was winning. I had difficulty in convincing them that the BBC did not forecast results of individual constituencies. What had happened was that the candidates' opponents had tried to boost their claims by invoking the name of the BBC because they knew that it had a widespread reputation for authenticity. The phrase 'authentic news' was often used to describe BBC bulletins. Once while traveling during an election, a television journalist from Britain and his Indian producer came across a villager who was disappointed to discover that the journalist was not Mark Tully. When the producer, who was doubling as an interpreter, told the journalist what the villager had asked, he shot back, angrily, 'Tell him I am much more famous.' Many other less vain foreign journalists used to tell me they had been asked whether they were Mark Tully.

My prominence was not due to any particular journalistic talent or skills. I became so widely known because my dispatches were broadcast daily on all Indian language services of the BBC. But that was just a matter of being in the right place, India, at the right time, the heyday of radio. Any other BBC journalist in my position would have become just as renowned. I must also add that the BBC would never have won such a wide reputation for authenticity if it hadn't been for my colleagues in the Delhi office, particularly Satish Jacob, and the local journalists known as 'stringers' in state capitals and elsewhere who reported for us.

Then there were the broadcasters in the Indian language services who translated and read my dispatches, and the editors who edited these back in London. They kept a very close eye on my reporting and often put me right. I well remember one reprimand I was given by a strict editor during a UP assembly election. I had visited villages where a candidate who was a former feudal landlord was campaigning. To demonstrate his democratic credentials, he had said to me, 'I have never asked anyone to touch my feet.' In reporting this remark, which added colour to my story, I said I had been 'campaigning with the candidate', which could have been interpreted as I had been campaigning for him. After the rocket I received, I never made that mistake again. The BBC World Service's election coverage was certainly not a one-man-band.

In the seventies, we, who were involved in the BBC World Service election coverage, had to be cautious to retain our reputation for authenticity. It would have been severely damaged had we forecast the result of an election and got it wrong, which was more than possible, but at the same time we had to give some indication of the way elections were going. So I, at least, tended to hedge my bets. Time and again, I would be interviewed by those I was interviewing. They would ask, 'Which way do you think the wind is blowing?' The only election in which I was able to give a confident answer to that question was the 1977 general election, which was held while the state of Emergency was still in force. Then, wherever I travelled in northern India, I could feel the gale that would sweep Indira Gandhi out of power blowing. It was amazing how sudden that gale was and how short-lived. Reporting the next general election, less than three years later, there was no gale sweeping Indira Gandhi back to power, but I did feel a wind blowing in her favour because the split in the Janata party had left her opponents in disarray. As psephology advanced in India, we were able to pass the buck by quoting the results of the surveys that were published.

Changing India

In recent years, the influence of foreign radio broadcasters like the BBC has declined. That is not the fault of today's BBC correspondents. Indian television's many channels now provide independent coverage of elections, although radio is, for some inexplicable reason, still chained to the government. Private radio stations are not allowed to broadcast news and current affairs, which remain a monopoly of All India Radio. The Indian language press has expanded too. So listeners and readers don't have to rely on the BBC or other foreign broadcasters to get an alternative to government news. Nevertheless, as a viewer and listener, I find that the BBC still takes a great interest in the general elections. After all, which editor can resist covering a story with the headline 'The World's Biggest Election', especially when it comes with the unfolding of another episode in the true-to-life serial starring perhaps the world's longest-lasting political dynasty, now that the Kennedys have gone.

There is one major change that has taken place over the last twenty years in news and current affairs broadcasting—improvements in technology. In the seventies and the eighties, I had to either rely on the telephone or book a line. That involved going to the nearest All India Radio station. The quality of the telephone call, even when boosted by the best technology available at that time, was often so poor that my dispatches had to be read in the studio rather than broadcast in my voice. Booking a line was a cumbersome procedure. On many occasions, even after I'd shouted until I was hoarse, 'Can you hear me, this is Mark Tully, can you hear me?' there was no reply; the line did not materialize. Nowadays, the ubiquitous satellite phone means correspondents can broadcast from anywhere. Mind you, there is a downside to this. Because it is so easy to broadcast live from the location of a story, the television viewer today is forever watching overexcited correspondents dramatizing their stories by flapping their hands in all directions, and ad-libbing. Correspondents being interviewed by presenters have become a substitute for carefully crafted television dispatches with a script in which the words match the pictures.

There has been a decline in British newspaper coverage of Indian elections. Shortly after I arrived in India, the London *Times* correspondent, Neville Maxwell's editor gave him the space to write a series of articles with the title 'India's Disintegrating Democracy'. The articles went down in history because looking forward to the 1967 general election, Maxwell prophesied it would 'surely be' India's last general election. That just shows the dangers of forecasting the outcome of Indian elections.

It's unlikely that a British correspondent of today would be given the space Maxwell was. The British press is now so commercialized that the power to decide what goes into the paper no longer rests with the editor alone. The circulation and advertising managers have their say because they are paid to know which stories will sell papers. Unfortunately, they don't rate foreign news very highly and so even an election has to fight hard to get into a paper. The 2010 Bihar assembly election caused a considerable stir in India because the sweeping victory of the incumbent chief minister, Nitish Kumar, seemed to confirm that at last a state renowned for bad governance had found a politician who could provide efficient administration. But a British foreign correspondent based in Delhi told me he had found it difficult to get one story about the Bihar election into his paper.

India is changing too. This change may well revive international interest in elections here. When I first covered elections, India was seen internationally as a land of irredeemable poverty. In television news and current affairs, vultures regularly featured as symbols of this poverty. I remember once pointing out to a meeting of senior BBC editors that the peacock and not the vulture was the national bird of India. But now the pendulum has swung the other way and the leitmotif of foreign reporting on India is 'the country with the potential to become an economic superpower'. The West is seen as waning and Asia as rising. India, with its size and its young population, is forecast to be one of the two giants of new Asia, alongside China.

This view of the present and the vision of the future is already influencing the foreign financial press to take a greater interest in all things Indian, including elections. If, as most economists seem to think is likely, the Indian economy continues to grow at its present rapid rate, then surely the interest of the international media as a whole will grow too. Elections will hopefully be seen as celebrations of the success of democracy after long years of struggle during which the Western media often wondered whether it would succeed.

V

A Modern Miracle

Kabir Bedi

India is a land of miracles. Not many people remember that the country narrowly escaped disintegration into a mosaic of smaller nations on the verge of its independence in 1947. The British had decided to slice out two large chunks of India, east and west, to appease the Muslim separatists who had clamoured for the creation of Pakistan. They also planned to return power, not to a united India, but to the 565 rajas and maharajas from whom they had taken it in the first place. What made India's unification possible was the collective will of the people. They had been promised a democracy by the heroes who led them to freedom—Mahatma Gandhi, Jawaharlal Nehru, Vallabhbhai Patel, Bal Gangadhar Tilak, Abul Kalam Azad and others—so they made unification their first priority.

Most of the royals would have gladly accepted the power that would have been given back to them by the British. But Sardar Patel's iron-fisted negotiations, sweetened with plum privy purses, ensured that most of them acceded to the newly born nation in time for India's historic 'stroke of midnight'. The two remaining holdouts, Kashmir and Hyderabad, showed how explosive the situation would have been if all or many of the others had not signed on. But the royals realized that the nationalistic fervour of the country would not allow it. Though India has an amazing diversity—of customs, castes and creeds, cuisines, clothes, complexions, countless languages and whatever else you can codify—most Indians wanted to make democracy the foundation of their future governance. Despite all those who feared its death at birth, one of the great miracles of modern India has been its success as a vibrant democracy.

Many had prophesied that in a poor, largely uneducated country like India, in 1947, democracy would be subverted, sabotaged, or shaped by a powerful few. (In fact, that's what happened to our neighbours, Pakistan and Burma, and a host of African nations.) But India proved them wrong. It showed that being uneducated did not mean being unintelligent.

Democracy: A Continuing Journey

If we look back at all the changes in national governments since 1947, even the most urbane, sophisticated person would have to admire the collective judgement of the Indian voter. Every political party in power was removed when it failed to deliver, when it didn't respond to people's expectations, or when it ran out of ideas and leaders. The striking differences between all those who have been our prime ministers, even our presidents, vividly personify the success of India's multi-level democracy. We have shown the world the extraordinary wisdom of ordinary Indian people.

Democracy, as we all know, is far from perfect. Perfection is a goal for which we strive, and in striving lies our glory. Democracy is a continuous journey to find the truest expression of the human heart and mind. It has proved its superiority over all other political philosophies by its ability to give voice to the individual, as well as the collective instincts of a vastly diverse people. As Thomas Mann said, 'Democracy dignifies the human being, it respects humanity.'[1] Above all, it gives us the sacred right to freely choose, or throw out, our rulers.

People often complain of what's wrong with the government of the day. It's a national pastime in almost every country. As Rodney Dangerfield says, 'Many people know how to rule the country. But they're too busy driving taxis.'[2] The truth is that the effectiveness of a democracy depends on 'the active, intelligent fulfilment of individual civic duty'[3]. And one of the prime duties of citizenship is taking the trouble to stand in line and vote. Countless patriots died to give us that right, and we should celebrate by asserting it.

The Biggest Exercise on Planet Earth

Getting people to vote is only half the problem. The other is the nightmarish logistics of making sure that they *can* vote. The numbers and statistics of our elections are overwhelming. I learnt what an awesome task it was from an earlier chief election commissioner of India, S.Y. Quraishi, a good friend from our days at St Stephens College, Delhi University. It reminded me of a Bob Hope joke about the Cold War when Russia was a classic Communist state. 'Who says the Russians don't have TVs? Every home in Russia has a TV. The only difference is *you* don't watch *it*, *it* watches *you*.'[4]

Imagine how many people the Russian state would have had to employ if they actually did that! That should give you some idea of the sheer scale of the organization over which India's Election Commission presides. But there's one major difference. Theoretically, it's not that difficult to watch millions of people from the comfort of large government offices. But the Election Commission's teams have to physically travel to every locality in the country. *They* come to *you*. Imagine what that takes in a country of over a billion people, with 716 million voters in the 2009 general elections.[5] That's more than double the population of America or the whole of Europe put together! It's the biggest exercise of democracy on planet earth. And the EC is ultimately accountable for every voting booth, every ballot form, every voting officer, and ensuring the safety and privacy of every single voter. I'm in awe of what they must do, election after election. A billion things could go wrong.

The Election Commission is supported by 11 million intrepid personnel across the country. From snowbound Himalayan ranges to the vast Rajasthan desert, to the smallest islands of the Arabian Sea and the Bay of Bengal, no voter is without an easily reachable polling booth. Whether in teeming mega cities or the tiniest of hamlets, everyone can vote if they wish to do so. Violent insurgencies, fires, floods, or earthquakes, nothing derails the work of the Election Commission. There are ruthless people who do try to sabotage the system to win by any means. Only a few succeed. In the broader historical perspective of India's successful national and state elections, such malpractices seem no more than tragic footnotes.

India's journey to independence and democracy was a painful struggle that lasted for decades. Both my parents, Baba Bedi and Freda Bedi, were freedom fighters, imprisoned by the British for many years. During those tumultuous years, my mother, a hand-picked Gandhian *satyagrahi*, also wrote nursery rhymes meant for Indian children. *Rhymes for Ranga*,[6] published in 2010, includes a poem that gives us a rare insight into the passion that infused their cause:

'Dawn of Freedom'

Mother, see how the bird flies,
Joyful, full of song.
I want to be like that, Mother,
How long will it be, how long?

Son, as the river is flowing
From the mountain to the sea,
As to his hive, unthinking,
Travels the honeybee.

So India is marching
Straight to her Freedom Day,
And nobody shall stop her
And nothing bar the way.

And you shall be free as the bird is
Free as the air, my son!

The bars of your cage will be broken,
Your journey just begun.

Beginning that journey didn't mean India's struggles had ended. Winning freedom and democracy aren't enough. Maintaining them is a battle that never ends. If 'eternal vigilance is the price of freedom', then the election commissioners of India personify that vigilance. They are constant guardians of our acclaimed democracy. The Election Commission is one of the greatest success stories of modern India. I salute its inspiring service to the nation. Jai Hind!

VI

Bollywood Goes to the Polls

Meghnad Desai

Hindustani cinema (Bollywood as it is now called) has an unenviable reputation of dealing in simple, oft-told stories dressed up in music, dances, colourful costumes with caricatures rather than characters. No one in Bollywood would deny these strictures as its success over the hundred years since the first film was made by D.G. Phalke has been sustained by this formula.

Yet this reputation is only partially deserved. Bollywood has succeeded because it manages to tell the nation's story even as the nation changes. It reflects the changing vicissitudes of the nation deftly—in society, in politics and in the attitudes of different generations—while at the same time using its well-worn formula. Dilip Kumar, the iconic star of the 1945–70 period, played the simple rural youth in films like *Mela* (1947), *Naya Daur* (1957) and *Ganga Jamuna* (1960) within a span of fifteen years, but the characters he played go from a simpering lost soul with no control over his destiny to a man challenging the system as it threatens to make him redundant to a rebellious and wronged fighter for justice. Each film had romance, good music, dances, villains and comics, and yet they mirrored changing perceptions of rural India. Social reform, economic trouble, political turmoil, everything was included in these stories.[1]

Cinema in other Indian languages has, of course, been much more explicitly political. C.N. Annadurai and M. Karunanidhi were both successful screenplay writers for Tamil cinema, and used it to spread the case for the DMK. M.G. Ramachandran played many characters with an explicit political message, as did Sivaji Ganesan. The same can be repeated for Bengali, Malayalam and Marathi films. Hindustani films have not been shy of discussing political themes though they have seldom championed a single party or ideology. They have taken a middle road of consensus and rarely raised the hackles of one or another side in any argument. In this brief essay, I want to explore some Hindustani films, which take up political, even electoral themes explicitly.

The list of films with an overt political theme is quite long indeed. Politics can cover elections, stories about injustice and corruption, guerrilla wars as in the case of Naxalites, etc. Bimal Roy's *Udayer Pathe*, which was remade in Hindi as *Hamrahi* (1946), Dilip Kumar's 1964 film *Leader*, *Aandhi*, Tapan Sinha's *Sagina Mahato*, Prakash Jha's *Rajneeti*, Shyam Benegal's *Welcome to Sajjanpur* and *Well Done Abba* can all be said to deal with politics. The early stage of the Naxalite struggle in which many middle-class young men and women made many sacrifices is captured in *Hazaar Chaurasi ki Maa* and *Hazaaron Khwaishein Aisi*. Political corruption is dealt with much more widely, for example, in *Maqbool*, *Sarkar*, and *Kanoon Apna Apna*. Politicians are almost invariably portrayed as corrupt and, on the make, breaking the law with impunity and bullying their subordinates.

Three Films with a Political Theme

I want to take up three films that have overtly political and electoral aspects to their plot. They span almost fifty years. By accident, they also reflect the lives of three major figures in Indian politics—Jawaharlal Nehru, Indira Gandhi and Sonia Gandhi—not explicitly, of course, but by implication.

In the 1964 Dilip Kumar film, *Leader*, Motilal plays a character, Aacharya, whose pronouncements reflect Nehru. He is shown as a revered senior leader rather than as a prime minister, but the parallel is unmistakable. His critics oppose him for advocating some boundary adjustment with a neighbouring country, which echoes the Berubari settlement with East Pakistan that Nehru was much criticized for. Aacharya's critics are strident and reflect the orthodox Hindu nationalist forces that the film sees as the main danger facing India. The subsequent story revolves around the murder of Aacharya, and Vijay Khanna (Dilip Kumar)'s, the hero, quest for his killers.

The quest takes him to a princely state where, by the film's portrayal, reactionary feudal elements gather. There is the usual mayhem with the heroine, Princess Sunita (Vyjayanthimala), being tortured and so on. But finally the villains are caught as the chase climaxes in Bombay at a mass rally. It is Dussehra and a giant effigy of Ravana is burned even as the villain tries to escape by hiding behind it.

The political association is similarly clear in *Aandhi*, in which Suchitra Sen plays Aarti Devi, a party leader fighting an election under stressful circumstances. She is visiting her constituency for what seems to be a crucial re-election. She is surprised and charmed to discover that the hotel where she is staying has been exceptionally thoughtful about her preferences. It transpires that her long-estranged husband (Sanjeev Kumar) is the hotel's manager. After a while they meet up and realize that despite the pressures that drew them part, they continue to share a lot of affection for each other and for their daughter. Aarti Devi's meeting with a 'strange man' is exploited by the Opposition candidate to besmirch her reputation. There is a lot of criticism. She is then forced to assert the truth about her private life and acknowledge that the man she has been meeting in secret is indeed her husband and the father of her daughter.

With an election at the centre of a film at a time when Indira Gandhi's 1974 election had been challenged in a court of law, *Aandhi* obviously points to a contemporary theme. Suchitra Sen models her appearance and her gestures on Indira Gandhi without the film at any stage acknowledging that this is the case. It fooled nobody, certainly not Indira Gandhi. Made in 1975, the film could not be released as Indira Gandhi was prime minister. She had also just lost the case against her election in the Allahabad High Court and as a consequence imposed Emergency. The film was only released in 1977 after Indira Gandhi's defeat, when the Janata government gave it licence.

The third and most recent film that was released in 2010 is *Rajneeti*, which models its story on the epic Mahabharata. There are several layers to the story, which spans generations. Chief Minister Ramnath Rai's daughter, Bharti Rai (Nikhila Trikha) is a Left-wing rebel and has an affair with Bhaskar Sanyal (Naseeruddin Shah) who is modelled after a Naxalite leader. She is married off to Chandan Pratap after having borne an illegitimate child to Bhaskar. The child is floated down the river Ganga, only to be found by the chauffeur who serves Bharti's in-laws' family. Chandan Pratap inherits the leadership of the party when his older brother, Bhanu Pratap, has a stroke. But Bhanu Pratap's son, Veerendra (Manoj Bajpai), resents this and has him assassinated. Bharti's younger son, Samar (Ranbir Kapoor), is about to go back to the USA to resume his studies but stays behind when his father is murdered. He becomes the shrewd manipulator behind the scenes, helping his older brother, Prithvi (Arjun Rampal), grab leadership of the party. Prithvi is tricked by Veerendra who now has Bharti's illegitimate son, Sooraj (Ajay Devgn), as his henchman. Samar rescues Prithvi and brings him back into the political game, but just as he is about to win an election, Prithvi is murdered. A twist at the end brings his widow Indu (Katrina Kaif) to the top position. The way in which Katrina Kaif is dressed and the way she acts is reminiscent of Sonia Gandhi, though this was vehemently denied by the filmmakers.

Politics from 1964 to 2010

The three films thus span three generations of the Nehru–Gandhi family–Jawaharlal, Indira and Rajiv/Sonia. They all have an electoral theme, though *Leader* does so by implication while the other two are explicit. *Rajneeti* even manages to mention the Election Commission when the nomination papers of Veerendra's candidates are rejected by the Commission because they are photocopies, and not original documents. The final shoot-out is staged by the hero, Samar, who entices his rivals to a disused factory by spreading the rumour that he is manipulating electronic voting machines for his party. It is clear that no manipulation of the EVMs is going on. Sooraj even tries to warn Veerendra that this may be a trap but Veerendra refuses to listen. The EVMs have been under some scrutiny amidst allegations that they can be tampered with. *Rajneeti* thus is spot on with a contemporary story.

The three films—*Leader*, *Aandhi* and *Rajneeti*—span the period from 1964 to 2010 during which India has remained a vibrant democracy in which elections have taken place with exemplary regularity. Whatever the power struggle, it is conducted in the context of elections that have to be won and cannot be manipulated. Having said that, the films portray some disturbing incidents. One is violence. *Aandhi* does not have any violence except for disruption of meetings, but both *Leader* and *Rajneeti* have political assassinations at their core. *Rajneeti* abounds in political violence. Chandan Pratap is shot in his car by a passing motorcycle rider. Bhanu Pratap's son, Veerendra, who is clearly a villain, is shot by Samar towards the end. Samar also manages to pin down the likely suspect involved in his father's murder, Babu Lal, and blows him up with a remote-controlled car bomb. Prithvi takes revenge on a police superintendent who had framed him in a rape allegation by clubbing him to death. Prithvi himself is blown up by a remotely controlled car bomb. Sooraj, who is the illegitimate and unacknowledged older brother of Prithvi and Samar, is the evil genius who helps Veerendra conduct the assassinations. He is also gunned down by Samar. It is almost as if we were watching an Indian version of the *Godfather*!

The depiction of politics in films has decidedly become much more violent in the twenty-first century as compared to the 1960s. There is no doubt as to who the killer is in the new century, unlike the 1960s, where the killer had to be tracked down. Killers are no longer sinister, shadowy figures; they are rival politicians. Murders are committed with impunity, and, indeed, with immunity from the law. If we go back as far as *Hamrahi*, the disruption of a meeting that is being addressed by the idealistic hero is the only 'violent' incident. The deterioration in Indian political morality from the idealistic days of *Hamrahi* to the cynical power struggles of *Rajneeti* is no fantasy; it very much reflects the lows in Indian politics.

At the same time, the politics portrayed is increasingly emptied of ideology. In *Leader*, the villain is not only the feudal order but also an ideology, unabashedly identified as the Jan Sangh's. The hero, Dilip Kumar, is relentlessly denouncing this ideology, and when he wins, in the climax a burning effigy of the ten-headed Ravana is shown, using a Ramayana image to denounce the champions of Hindutva. In *Aandhi*, there does not seem to be an ideological division that is as sharp. The focus is on the bad morals of the rival candidate, who uses underhand methods to spy on and disgrace the heroine. Yet Lallu Lal (Om Prakash), the heroine's political agent, is as amoral as they come as he bribes spectators at the rival's meeting to throw eggs. But he is devoted to his leader and very upset when she threatens to quit politics since she cannot bear the innuendo about her marital life. Her politics is personal.

By the time we get to *Rajneeti*, there seems to be no political ideology at all. The issue is personal rivalry for power in which real issues like Dalit representation are cynically exploited to maintain one side or another in power. Raising money for a political campaign by fair means or foul becomes a major pursuit. The marriage of Indu with Prithvi is arranged by her father, who is shown at the outset to benefit in his income tax affairs thanks to his access to the political dynasty of Bhanu Pratap. Which is why he makes it clear that he does not want his daughter to marry Samar though she may love him, and that he would finance Prithvi's campaign only if his daughter marries the potential chief minister. In an echo of past political struggles, a Left-wing ideologue is introduced at the outset as a 'good' person (Naseeruddin Shah playing Bhaskar Sanyal). The contrast with what happens later in the film is stark since the naïve idealism of Bhaskar has no place in today's politics. At the end, his lover, Bharti, the mother of Prithvi and Samar, acknowledges Sooraj as her son, but there is no attempt to bring Bhaskar back in the story. Had this been done, we might have seen some re-injection of old idealism in the story.

The way women are portrayed also changes but is not much better. *Leader* has Vyjayanthimala playing Princess Sunita. She is associated with the murdered leader but plays a purely decorative, apolitical role in the remainder of the film. In *Aandhi*, the woman is at the centre of the story, and her public life in politics being combined with her private life is at the centre of the story. By the time of *Rajneeti*, two women are at the core of the story though the men occupy centre stage. The mother who bears Sooraj starts as a radical, independent woman defying her corrupt politician father. Her baby is taken from her before she has even had a chance to see him. She then marries into a political dynasty and bears two more sons and is an active witness to the carnage. Prithvi is propositioned by a woman eager to have a seat nomination and explicitly offers herself for the favour. This then leads to the rape charge against him. Indu is introduced as a spoiled young woman who matures into a grown-up, understanding woman when she is married off to the man she does not love in the beginning but whom she comes to love. When her husband dies, she has to take up the family's political mantle. This is shown as manipulative but yet somehow a logical way of retaining power within the dynasty. The women have minds of their own but face more powerful forces, which overwhelm them. Indu triumphs at the end in a sense, even though she has been put in her current position as a result of a game of power in which she started out as a pawn. The film ends with the news that she is carrying Prithvi's child. She has thus performed her duty and provided an heir for the dynasty.

Integrity of the Electoral Process

Through all this mayhem, the integrity of the election process is seldom in doubt. The Election Commission gets a mention in *Rajneeti* almost factually as not allowing a certain practice—

nominations from one faction of the party—which is accepted unquestioningly by even the so-called bad guys. The conduct of elections is shown to be perfectly sound and routine. The rumour of EVMs being manipulated is just a ruse to entice the villain to his death. Sooraj, the Dalit leader and the relatively modern one, doubts that such manipulation can be done but he is overruled by Veerendra, who cannot believe he has lost the election by honest means. In *Sajjanpur* as well, the election is fairly conducted where the transgender candidate wins. The conduct of the election is not impugned in any way in the midst of some bizarre and very comic goings-on.

Aandhi has no mention of the Election Commission but an election is at the heart of the entire story. The election campaign is portrayed in it replete with noise and loud humour and chaos. Both sides indulge in poking fun at the other even scurrilously in case of the heroine's rival who spreads rumours about her. *Rajneeti* has some footage of election campaigns but the tone is much more serious. Power can be got by winning elections but the business of elections is no longer just fun; it is a matter of life and death. An election campaign is seen as being akin to those European festivals where for one day, the clown (or the voter) becomes the king.

Yet, at the end, politics is a game played by the protagonists and their rivals. It is an elite game where the *demos* (the people) are just a backdrop. It is manipulated by Lallu Lal, the party agent, who bribes people to throw eggs at the rival candidate or to follow the hero Veerendra Khanna as he is chasing the villains. They come as vote-bank representatives in *Rajneeti*, to donate money, or insist on their sectional demands. But even so they are pawns in a larger game between politicians. That is perhaps the nature of Indian democracy. It is also perhaps the only way Bollywood can tell a political story where the crowd is just the chorus and it is the leading actors who front the screen. But then, they also attract the same mob who come and pay good money at the box office.

VII

The Business of Elections

Ratan Tata

There was no dearth of sceptics when, in 1950, India's founding fathers chose parliamentary democracy based on universal adult suffrage as the country's mode of governance. After seven decades, however, nobody doubts that democracy has embedded itself into the Indian polity so deeply that it is difficult to imagine that it can ever be uprooted.

During this period, India has had sixteen general elections, four of these in one decade—the 1990s—apart from the nearly 400 rounds of elections to state assemblies. The government has been voted out as many as seven times in the last ten Lok Sabha elections, but at no time was there even a shred of doubt that the transfer of power would happen seamlessly.

A Credible Commission

India's record in political participation is just as commendable, with the voting percentage notching around 60 per cent, impressive by global standards. Moreover, electoral participation has become deeper and wider, with the percentage of voting seeing a steady increase from among the poorer sections and rural areas. If voter apathy has grown anywhere, it is among the urban well-off.

Conducting elections in India is not for the faint-hearted. India's electorate for the general elections of May 2014 totalled 834 million, with close to 930,000 polling stations spread across diverse geographic and climatic zones. Conducting a general election calls for the marshalling of nearly 10 million polling and police personnel over a time period in excess of a month.

Making all this possible is the Election Commission of India, a body of 300 odd professionals, headed by a three-member team of election commissioners with one chief election commissioner. The Commission gets noticed mostly for the conduct of elections but this constitutional body's role is central to a host of issues that are key to determining the democratic temper of the country.

It is the uncontested view among the country's intelligentsia that the Election Commission has discharged its responsibilities with competence and dignity. It is among the few organs of the Indian establishment that has grown in lustre and credibility over the years, earning the reputation of being impartial and above partisan politics. To be sure, being a constitutional office has assured it of insurance against interference by the political executive. But equally important is the fact that many of the chief election commissioners have been persons of outstanding integrity and competence.

The high standing that the Election Commission enjoys among the people of the country is a matter of great assurance for all Indians concerned about the good health of India's democracy. This includes the Indian industry, which has an equal stake in India's democracy as any other section of society and, consequently, a responsibility to contribute to the strengthening of its roots and branches.

Industry and Politics

India's business community and its political executive have had a long and eventful association, right from the early days of India's independence movement. The pioneers of Indian industry, men like Jamsetji Tata and Walchand Hirachand, were fervent nationalists. Gandhiji's association with the houses of Bajaj and Birla is well-known.

Jawaharlal Nehru and J.R.D. Tata did not always think alike on key economic issues but shared a high degree of mutual respect. Indian industry was happy to be the key financier of the Indian National Congress through the independence movement.

In contrast, Indian industry's association with the political executive in post-independence India has not been quite as driven by the same degree of selfless national interest, in tandem with deterioration in the moral fabric of politics. As politics became increasingly financed by unaccounted money, business became the natural source for black money as the biggest beneficiary of the 'Licence-permit' Raj. As the power of government discretion grew, unscrupulous businesspersons joined the ranks of vested interests who sought to tailor the exercise of government discretion to further their own narrow objectives.

Easing of government controls from the 1980s did little to introduce transparency in money flows between industry and political parties. Laws on official donations to political parties from companies did several flip-flops till it was settled by changes in the Companies Act, placing a limit of 5 per cent on the average profit over three years as the maximum that could be extended to political parties. The limit was later increased to 7.5 per cent and eventually removed altogether in 2018.

It has been gratifying to see how various initiatives by the Election Commission in recent decades have changed the tone and tenor of the conduct of elections. The time for electioneering has been compressed from three weeks to two weeks. Gone are the use of posters and hoardings and the rampant debasement of walls for election slogans. A liberal increase in the number of election observers, coupled with increased vigil by the local bureaucracy with greater empowerment, cooperation and coordination among both sets of officials, has meant a sharper vigil on all overt expenses and curbs on malpractices. These are some of the most important changes that are evident to all.

The contrast between elections in Bihar even a decade ago and now is perhaps the best testimony of the positive changes in the conduct of elections. There was a time when elections in Bihar were a long series of events of 'booth capturing' and pitched battles between political factions resulting in scores of deaths. In contrast, the elections held in November 2010 barely saw any violence. Other than a few incidents instigated by Maoists, electoral malpractices, booth capturing and rigging of ballot boxes is simply not in evidence.

Cost of Campaigning

At the same time, I recognize that the corrupting influence of the role of money in our politics has only grown over time even as many improvements have been embedded in the conduct of elections. Only a naive person would believe that in Lok Sabha elections, or state assembly elections, candidates adhere to the spirit of limits on election expenses (even today at an unrealistic Rs 70,00,000 per Lok Sabha seat). Thanks to the heightened vigil by election observers, the expenses that can be traced to either candidates or parties are now accounted for to a greater degree. But the scope of abuse of money power in persuading voters by holding out inducements that leave no trace has, I understand, only increased. What should be overt election expenses, because of greater vigil, have become covert.

As campaign costs have spiralled, elections have become even more expensive affairs at all levels, right down to the modest Panchayat elections. Indian political parties, usually at each other's throats on most national issues, have united in giving themselves a legal loophole, which allows expenses incurred by parties on candidates' election to be virtually limitless and untrammelled. Political ability is often an amalgamation of right credentials (family, caste or community) and access to funds. A sterling record of services to the people comes lower down the eligibility rung. The increasing presence of criminal elements, in parties virtually across the spectrum, among the elected people's representative is another cause for despair.

We may be advised to look at other developments to hope for a more responsive and cleaner future of politics in India. In several recent elections, it has become increasingly apparent that the politics of a development orientation can indeed score over other, baser motivations. At one time, voter preferences used to oscillate between competing parties and incumbency was seen as a mill around the ruling parties' necks. In the last few elections to state assemblies, however, we have seen that performance that has genuinely improved the lives of the people has conquered the incumbency. Partisan appeal, to either communities or castes, would often sway voters but we are now seeing the primacy of inclusiveness coming to the fore.

The Election Commission is only an enabling body whose impact is circumscribed by the laws enacted by Parliament in the Representation of People Act, 1951. There can be little doubt that the Commission has done the country proud. But it is the people's representatives who write the laws that can address areas of concern in the arena of Indian politics. It is for all responsible citizens, including industry, to pressure the political class to do this expeditiously and comprehensively starting with the structuring of state funding for elections.

PART FOUR

The Path Ahead

I

Decoding Electoral Politics in India

Pramod Kumar

Elections constitute the core of democratic polity. Free and fair elections provide legitimacy to the political system to transform people's lives for the better. In this sense, electoral management becomes pivotal. The role, outlook, approach, response and instruments of the Election Commission of India, which is assigned the task to manage elections, have largely influenced the outcome of elections and, in turn, made democracy worthwhile. There has been a qualitative improvement in election management. Interestingly, election management has significantly improved since 1990, ever since the Election Commission started playing a proactive role.

Participatory and Competitive

Elections have become relatively more participatory, competitive, and entail the likelihood of a change in government. In terms of participation, the number of registered voters has increased from 173 million in 1951 to 834 million in the 2014 Lok Sabha elections. However, voter turnout has been fluctuating depending on the political climate. As compared to other functional and genuine democracies, voter turnout is fairly high and representative in India. Out of sixteen Lok Sabha elections, in eight elections, it was less than 60 per cent and in the remaining elections it was above 60 per cent,

with the highest turnout of 66.4 per cent in the 2014 elections
(Election Commission of India data 1951 to 2014). A relatively high
turnout has been possible, besides ideological factors, due to electoral
reforms like awareness campaigns for voters, efficient polling booth
management leading to elimination of rigging and booth capturing,
increasing accessibility, and so on. To illustrate, the poorer sections,
scheduled castes and scheduled tribes, minorities and women were
either not allowed to go to polling booths and their votes were
forged or they were threatened to vote for a particular candidate.
The vulnerability mapping undertaken by the Election Commission
proved to be effective in checking these practices.

Another qualitative shift in elections is that these have become
more competitive. For instance, elections have been transformed from
single party dominance to multi-party contests leading to a crowding
of electoral space. In 2014, six national political parties and thirty-nine
state/regional parties were in contest. And most importantly, since
1951, the effective number of political parties by votes and seats has
multiplied. In 1951, the effective number of parties by votes was 4.53,
which increased to 6.92 in 2014. The effective number of parties by
seats was 1.80 in 1951, which increased to 3.45 in 2014 (see Table 1).
Uncontested seats too have come to nil in the 2014 elections from ten
in 1951 elections. This clearly shows that there is a positive movement
leading to multiplication of choices for the voters. Elections, in a way,
perform an effective choice maximization function.

Table 1
Effective Number of Parties in Lower House Elections
(by votes and seats)

S. No.	Year	Effective Number of Parties (Votes)	Effective Number of Parties (Seats)
1	1951	4.53	1.80
2	1957	3.98	1.76

S. No.	Year	Effective Number of Parties (Votes)	Effective Number of Parties (Seats)
3	1962	4.40	1.85
4	1967	5.19	3.16
5	1971	4.63	2.12
6	1977	3.40	2.63
7	1980	4.25	2.28
8	1984	3.99	1.69
9	1989	4.80	4.35
10	1991	5.10	3.70
11	1996	7.11	5.83
12	1998	6.91	5.28
13	1999	6.74	5.87
14	2004	7.60	6.50
15	2009	7.98	5.01
16	2014	6.92	3.45

Note: Data for 2014, calculated by the author.

Source: E. Sridharan (2014), 'Why Are Multi-Party Minority Governments Viable in India? Theory and Comparison'; p. 35–70; in E. Sridharan (ed.), *Coalition Politics in India: Selected Issues at the Centre and the States* (New Delhi: Academic Foundation).

Electoral architecture represents a shift from single party dominance to a coalition of multi-parties; a monolith nation-building project to a more diversity-sensitive party system, and has created conditions for greater accessibility for people irrespective of their gender, religion, caste and class affiliations. On gender, 39 per cent of the women registered went to the polls in 1957. The number shot up to 66 per cent in the 2014 elections. Not only this, women votes polled in 1957 were 38 per cent of the total votes polled, and increased to 47 per cent in 2014 elections (see Table 2). Representation of Muslims in Lok Sabha too increased from 2 per cent in 1951 to 6 per cent in 2009.

Table 2

Gender-wise Participation in Lok Sabha Elections from 1951–2014

Election Year	Votes polled over total votes polled (percentage)		Gender-wise registered voters over votes polled (male/female) (percentage)	
	Men	Women	Men	Women
1951	–	–	–	–
1957	61.7	38.3	–	38.8
1962	60.2	39.8	63.31	46.6
1967	56.6	43.4	66.63	55.5
1971	57.7	42.3	60.90	49.1
1977	56.4	43.6	65.62	54.9
1980	56.9	43.1	62.16	51.2
1984	55.6	44.4	68.17	58.6
1989	56.1	43.9	66.13	57.3
1991	57.0	43.0	61.58	51.3
1996	56.0	44.0	62.06	53.4
1998	55.6	44.4	65.86	57.7
1999	55.7	44.3	63.96	55.6
2004	55.6	44.4	61.66	53.6
2009	54.2	45.8	60.20	55.8
2014	53.0	47.0	67.09	65.6

Note: Data on participation of women is not available for 1951 elections.

Source: Computed from statistical reports of Lok Sabha Elections for the year 2009, 2004, 1999, 1998, 1996, 1992, 1991, 1989, 1985, 1984, 1980, 1977, 1971, 1967, 1962, 1957, 1951,

Eci.nic.in/ci_main1/ElectionStatistics.aspx, accessed on 5 August 2014.

For 2014: Registered electors, votes polled over total votes polled and votes polled over registered electors are computed from statistics given in eci.nin.in/eci_main1/GE2014/STATE_WISE_TURNOUT.htm, accessed on 3 August 2014.

Elections have catapulted regional political parties to political centre stage and provided articulation to their aspirations in the political discourse. To illustrate, in 1951, national political parties polled 76 per cent votes and other state parties, 8 per cent. In the 2014 Lok Sabha elections, the votes polled for national political parties declined to 61 per cent while for regional parties, it increased to 28 per cent (see Table 3). As a result, the electoral process not only created an environment for competitive politics, but also increased the likelihood of change in government.

Table 3

Percentage of Votes Polled in Lok Sabha Elections in India
(1951–2014)
(Recognized National and State Parties)*

Lok Sabha	Year	Types of Parties			
		Recognized National Parties		Recognized State Parties	
		No. of Parties	Vote %	No. of Parties	Vote %
1	1951	14	76.00	39	8.10
2	1957	4	73.08	11	7.60
3	1962	6	78.50	11	9.28
4	1967	7	76.13	14	9.69
5	1971	8	77.84	17	10.17
6	1977	5	84.67	15	8.80
7	1980	6	85.07	19	7.69
8	1984	7	79.80	17	11.56
9	1989	8	79.33	20	9.28

* If a political party is treated as a recognized political party in four or more states, it shall be known as a 'national party'. If a political party is treated as a recognized political party in less than four states, it should be known as a 'state party'. Please see the criteria for recognition on Election Commission of India website.

Lok Sabha	Year	Types of Parties			
		Recognized National Parties		Recognized State Parties	
		No. of Parties	Vote %	No. of Parties	Vote %
10	1991	9	80.65	27	12.98
11	1996	8	69.08	30	22.43
12	1998	7	67.98	30	18.79
13	1999	7	67.11	40	26.93
14	2004	6	62.89	51	28.90
15	2009	7	63.58	34	23.60
16	2014	6	60.70	39	27.74

Note: Data from 1951 to 2004 taken from statistical reports of Election Commission of India.

Note: Data for 2009 and 2014 calculated.

One-party dominance was clearly visible till the eighth Lok Sabha, with the Congress party forming all the governments except in 1977. And since 1989, the general elections have shown that the Indian polity has become more competitive and experienced, with change in government composition regularly.

Electoral politics has come of age. It has become more participatory, representative and competitive, while at the same time becoming a battle of false claims and empty promises, of political leaders presenting themselves as representatives of the common man and servants of the privileged, trivializing real issues and basing their appeal on a modelled image.

Decoding Electoral Messaging

The gap between promises and performance has become a hallmark of elections in India. Until the 1980s, promises like 'Garibi Hatao', i.e. poverty eradication, social justice for all and a fight against authoritarianism were made. However, post mid-1980s, 'justice for all' was replaced by justice for the backward, Dalits and minorities, and so on. In the 1990s, a near consensus on market reforms and neo-liberal global economy among the major political parties and actors was reached, notwithstanding the occasional noises about 'Swadeshi'. This was seen in the election manifestos of the Congress and the Bharatiya Janata Party, which reinforced each other on economic reforms.

Therefore, it is essential to decode claims and counterclaims of leaders in the electoral fray. This can be done at various levels. One, to what extent do the political parties represent national concerns—like decisive leadership to liberate the country from land speculators, illicit businessmen, crony capitalists, extortion, loot, price rise or inflation, unemployment, poverty and inequalities. Given the consensus amongst political parties on a neoliberal path of development and, in the absence of any alternative vision, it may not be possible to eliminate poverty, inequalities and unemployment.

Political parties, however, are not expected to confess, particularly at the time of elections, that they have ceased to govern. When the market is allowed to govern, the government becomes powerless to effect any radical change. Proponents of market reform have no plans for those who do not have the resources and income to buy even two square meals a day. The signals are that those who cannot pay for their food have no right to survive. Poorer sections of society are therefore reduced to mere victims, beneficiaries, clients and recipients. In this dichotomous relationship, the state is seen as the 'dole giver' and the people as the 'dole receiver'. In other words, a patron–client relationship defines the conditions for electoral discourse.

Major political parties have not cared to analyse the causes and ways to reduce prices, and simultaneously raise the purchasing capacity of the poor. Also, they are silent on formulating policies for food security. These parties have not cared to ponder over why a large section of the poor are finding it difficult to afford two meals a day; and how pauperization and land alienation have become a major electoral issue.

There is no alternative available in elections to bring about a shift in the nature of development. Overtly the content of economic reforms appears to: (a) reduce employment in the public sector and allow market forces to generate or curtail employment in private sector; (b) encourage people to participate in self-help groups and launch small businesses in the face of intense competition; (c) tell people to mind their own health and give subsidies to private hospitals; and (d) teach them to pay for life-saving services even if they do not have the opportunities to earn a livelihood.

Populism and Doles

Political parties tend to address people's miseries with occasional doles at election time. The voters are promised these doles as entitlements or populist patronage without reversing other activities such as the process of privatization of education, public health, and so on. In line with the overall approach, political parties use a cocktail of doles and promises containing something for everyone—'menu-festos' rather than manifestos—with menu cards for farmers, traders, students, Dalits, industrialists, women, and so on.

Leaders in the electoral fray seem to cover every possible local concern of their constituents, ranging from creating new jobs, committing to improving living standards of workers, young and old, the rich and the poor, and especially the aspiring middle class, making the country safe for women, changing by-laws to please one and all, managing traffic by building over- and under- bridges, et al. In the background of the enormous gap between such promises and actual performance, the style of governance and local issues becomes the main concern during elections.

In this sense, elections have become a ritual of democracy. They have failed to make democracy distributive and justice-oriented. They use the popular screen to make their politics appear pro-people. To provide content to this, serious issues are reduced to doles rather than the right of the electorate.

If politicians are to be believed, elections are a matter of *atta-dal* subsidies, freebies, *shagun* at the time of marriage, and enticements such as foreign tours for government employees. And if you have pretensions of being psephologically literate, then you may believe the pollsters that elections are a matter of incumbency levels and popularity ratings—that too of leaders and not parties, with vote swings emerging from individual candidates. But can elections be absolved from the reality of people's fight for mere survival, demand for dignity in governance and protection from abuse?

Identity vs Secular Politics

Political parties have vacillated between religious and caste identities and their claims to build a secular polity. In the 2014 elections, Nehruvian institutional secularism was replaced by a unified conception of indigenous (Hindu) nationhood, thus negating the politics of 'appeasement' of minorities. And regional, caste and tribal identities are increasingly invoked to expand electoral constituencies.

The overall approach has been to employ a cocktail of civilizational symbols with a Hindutva flavour. Slogans like 'development for all', were presented as universal, purer and more unadulterated, located in caste, religion, gender and ethnicity. There has been a selective appropriation of universal symbols like Ganga (river), Geeta (scripture), Navratras (ritual), etc., to provide content to (Hindu) civilizational symbols as inclusive. These symbols were garnished with religiosity, for instance, the cleaning of the rivers Ganga and Yamuna was called 'purification' as these were holy rivers. Further, these (Hindu) civilizational symbols were located in regions. They were regionalized and referred to as, for instance, Haryana as land of Lord Krishna, Gujarat as the land of Som Nath, Uttar Pradesh as the land of Ram Rajya, and so on. These catch-all symbols not only blur structural realities of caste and religion, but also the appropriation of some symbols like the cow has also led to polarization in society.

Virtually immune to the fault lines of Indian reality, like secular-communal, socialism-state welfare capitalism, it has reduced the elections to only a fight against corruption, reminiscent of Nehruvian pronouncement of 'hanging the corrupt to the nearest lamp-post'. The main feature of an economic reforms agenda is an increase in the quantum of corruption, and political parties do not fail to make it an election issue. But none of them address the core issue—why corruption? In the name of outsourcing public resources to bring about efficiency under the banner of PPP, it has perpetuated massive loot of the public resources. There is no major debate for changing these policies.

Corruption as an Issue

Even when the country was ruled by leaders with impeccable integrity and honesty, scams kept on multiplying and the lamp posts continued to wait in attendance. While the government led by Prime Minister Manmohan Singh consisted of some of the best minds, it saw some of the worst scams and corruption. Further, poverty, discrimination and inequalities have multiplied and even the political and economic sovereignty of the country seem to have been compromised by some honest political leaders.

So, what is the lesson? Although individual honesty is an essential virtue for every human activity, it is not a core value. A legitimate question then arises, for what purpose is individual integrity used to bring about systemic transformation or reinforce the status quo?

Another distinct feature is that with a discredited political class, there is competition among political parties to poach singers, comedians, journalists, human rights activists and so on to bolster their credibility. Earlier these celebrities were called in to gather crowds for politicians; now many of them have transformed themselves into politicians. Not only this, to connect with the people, professional managers are also hired. Elections are being treated as events, where voters have to be 'managed.' This has liberated political parties from holding any ideological position.

Real issues like the challenge posed by the WTO agreement to small and marginal farmers, decline in the social development index with the status of women being the lowest in India, an increasing non-productive youth population, unemployment, and so forth thus remain outside the realm of electoral politics. Anti-incumbency becomes a saviour by providing parties rotational preference.

Besides anti-incumbency that provides a safe passage to issueless politics, the winnability criteria allows faceless politicians to find entry into political management. In the course of the selection of candidates, political parties use this novel criterion. It does not matter whether a candidate is with or without a criminal record, has or does not have the capacity to do pro-people work. But if he has the capacity to manipulate votes and is himself 'manageable', there is every chance of his being selected. Above all, the money a candidate can invest with the hope of recovering it at a later date is a major deciding factor. This is symptomatic of the erosion of the ideological support base of political parties.

Notwithstanding issues like quality of candidates, absence of real issues in election campaigns, trivialization of promises, reducing manifestos to menu-festos, leader disconnect with the people, etc., elections have become integral to the accepted political culture in India. There is a visible engagement of citizens with the electoral process as any violation of holding of free and fair elections does invite strong protest from the people now.

The debates on electoral reforms have become a regular feature and in turn have made democracy healthier. By creating more conducive conditions, especially for people on the margins, the electoral process has become more participatory, empowering people to change governments or effect change.

II

Elections, Exit Polls and the Electronic Media[1]

Rahul Verma

To err is human, and to err again and again is to be a pollster in India.[2] The inability of pollsters to make accurate forecasts in the recent past has added to the criticism of polls becoming election night *tamasha* that attempts to forecast a complex election based on a few thousand voters. Some have suggested eliminating televised coverage of election forecasting since it is nothing more than 'a circus in town' while others have called for a blanket ban on election polls. It is business as usual—political parties winning in the polls agree with the findings and those trailing question the motive of the pollsters and label election forecasting a 'fraud science'. Despite all these criticisms, one thing is clear: that opinion polls will continue to happen. So, it would be helpful to understand the strengths and limitations of opinion polls. When and why do they go wrong? And what positive things do they offer despite their failures to predict the outcome?

There is no doubt that much of the controversy related to election polling and forecasting in the public domain is less about the methodological challenges that survey research is confronted with, and more to do with three perceptions. First, opinion polls are often wrong in forecasting the result and so why do them in the first place. Second, many argue that they sway voters' preferences, create a '*hawa*' (bandwagon effect) in favour of a particular party or sometimes create 'sympathy' for another party (the underdog effect).[3] Third, some argue that political parties use 'paid surveys' to influence voters and subvert the process of electing a government by fair means. In the past, parties used to commission surveys to select 'winnable' candidates and make their campaign strategy, but now they have resorted to using survey findings in a way that has become an impediment in conducting free and fair elections. [4]

Thus, regulating the release of election forecasts has become a critical issue for the Election Commission of India. Due to security concerns and logistical requirements, national and many state elections are spread over a month. The possibilities of opinion polls inducing a momentum effect (parties that perform well in initial phases tend to do well in later phases as well) has been argued as a rationale to ban the release of such polls before the last phase of an election ends.[5] While a specific regulation on the release of findings between phases is justifiable, the idea of putting a blanket ban on opinion polls is, frankly, naïve.

Opinion polls are not the only source of information that voters depend on in forming expectations about the election. Even if the telecast of opinion polls is banned, in the age of social media, it is impossible to regulate users or commentators sitting in television studios from making predictions about election outcomes. More than the worries about influencing voters' preferences, there is another issue at hand: even if election-related polls were to be banned or contained, can those in policy-making, in the election campaign design world and in academia, do without the data that is generated from them?[6]

This essay briefly discusses the typology of election-related surveys, reviews the status of opinion polls from a historical perspective, and addresses some of the criticisms levelled against election polling in India.

Three Types of Election Surveys

It is important to distinguish between election polls that are conducted just for the purpose of forecasting and polls that gather large amounts of data to study overall trends in both society and polity.[7] Election-related surveys fit into three broad categories. Pre-polls are conducted a few weeks before the formal election process begins and at best, can inform us about trends, with a caveat that the results would hold only if the trend continues. It is not surprising that pre-poll estimates rarely match actual results given the volatility of political preferences and the fact that a significant portion of electorates make up their mind very close to voting day. However, that does not mean pre-polls are a futile exercise, for they provide the baseline to measure the change and they become even more useful while conducting the analysis after the results are known. They help in making a credible interpretation of the trends that ultimately shape the verdict.

Post-polls are conducted between the time the last ballot is cast and before the counting of votes begins. Post-polls have been better in predicting elections outcomes (better in estimating vote shares, but not so much on seats). The third and most popular type of poll is the exit poll. These are conducted on the election day outside polling stations. Our experience suggests that exit polls in India fail to collect a sample that is representative of the local population. Those who get interviewed in an exit poll tend to be more forthcoming, male, from the upper strata of India society, among many other such characteristics that skew the representativeness of samples. It is not surprising that most often exit polls fail to predict the result.

Origins and the Market of Election Polling

The first election surveys in India can be traced to 1957, before the second Lok Sabha elections, when Eric D'Costa conducted an all-India poll. The survey not only predicted the outcome but also alluded to variation in voting intentions based on various demographics such as income, religion, and region. In the 1960s, a team led by Rajni Kothari and others at the Centre for the Study of Developing Societies (CSDS), New Delhi, gave opinion polling an academic turn. In the 1980s, Prannoy Roy and his team provided a new momentum with their sophisticated analysis of the 1984, 1989 and 1991 Lok Sabha elections. Meanwhile, the election studies programme at CSDS was revived in 1995 under the auspices of the Lokniti network. The National Election Study (NES) surveys by this network of scholars was primarily conducted to undertake an in-depth analysis of voting behaviour, but as the data on voting preference was collected before the counting day, it was also used for forecasting votes and seats.

With the explosion in the number of TV news channels, a large number of firms got involved in the business of conducting election opinion polls. The entry of multinational market-research agencies such as Nielsen, TNS and GFK Mode in the 1990s gave another impetus to India's polling industry even as election forecasting remained a small part of their portfolio. This sudden mushrooming of survey research firms came with its own set of problems.[8] The biggest of these was the lack of focus on the methodology employed in election surveys.[9] Even something as basic as a dummy secret ballot, to satisfy many respondents' wish for privacy when disclosing their vote, is not standard practice for most pollsters in India.[10]

The polling industry mostly works on a cost-per-interview (CPI) model, with the current rate anywhere between Rs 100 to Rs 700. The main reason for such huge variation is that while fly-by-night operators have low overhead costs, established research firms have sizable overheads towards infrastructure and staff, among many other things, and this is reflected in cost quotations.[11] There are three main variable costs in survey research: a) large sample size offsets the travel and logistics cost and thus lower CPI, b) the number of items on the questionnaire as more items mean fewer interviews per person per day, and c) when the turnaround time is less, a firm needs to hire and train more investigators, which increases the total cost of the survey operation.

Many market-research firms in India now prefer direct recruitment and training, use GPS trackers to identify sampled locations, and have moved from the PAPI (paper and pencil interviewing) model to CAPI (computer-assisted personal interviewing). While these changes have been very helpful in conducting market research and policy evaluation studies, this model does not look economically viable for election surveys that have to be conducted in a very short time-frame on a large scale. The total engagement between a polling firm and investigators for a typical exit poll project is not more than seventy-two hours, transporting electronic devices for CAPI is expensive, and wear and tear is high. Clients often find it difficult to accept that the premium for good surveys is substantial and thus some pollsters have turned to CATI (computer-assisted telephonic interviewing) as an alternative.[12] CATI is extremely cost-effective but obtaining a representative sample in CATI is difficult and thus hugely problematic for election forecasting.[13]

Misconceptions about Election Polling

In popular imagination, the only utility of opinion polls is to be able to make exact seat forecast and thus there are several misconceptions. There are five basic issues. First, do polls really influence voting preferences, especially when they sometimes make conflicting predictions? Second, why do polls err in making accurate estimation of election results? Third, how fair is it to expect on-dot polling predictions? Fourth, can we devise an academically explainable formula for converting vote share into seats? Fifth, how do we educate voters and political parties to meaningfully interpret survey findings?

Critics of opinion polls allege that election forecasting influences voters' decision. This criticism is based on a limited understanding of how bandwagon voters behave. While some bandwagon voters may like to vote for the party or candidate who in their perception is likely to win in their constituency, some may prefer to vote for the party leading at the state level, and others may like to vote for a party leading at the national level. Most polls merely show national estimates and rarely make constituency level forecasts. Furthermore, the outreach of opinion polls is much lower than what is understood by many. Data from the 2014 NES survey shows that one-fourth of the respondents were aware of opinion polls and those aware were also regular consumers of news. With the overload of other information—prime-time newsroom discussions, field reports, op-ed columns, social media—it is difficult to estimate the independent effect of opinion polls. Moreover, most often the predictions of opinion polls are all over the place and thus it is an exaggeration to argue that they swing elections one way or the other.

While forecasting is an important aspect of election polling, the overall goals of most opinion polls are much broader. Though still imperfect, opinion polls have evolved in terms of decoding citizens' political preferences. Similarly, while political parties remain critical of surveys, especially if these surveys point to a probable outcome against their respective parties, they conduct their own in-house surveys to plan their election strategies. Polls do go wrong in forecasting results, but they go wrong for very different reasons such as not following basic minimum methodological protocols, or by design their inability to predict outliers. There is no one particular reason why polls err. Finally, unless they have been horribly off the mark in estimating vote shares, the data generated through polls is still useful for academic purposes, provided the poll was conducted following methodological protocols. In particular, the data from opinion polls has been helpful in gaining insights into some of the big questions of Indian politics.

While the design of survey instruments, modes of conducting interviews, training of investigators and budgetary resources play a large role in the quality of the final data, the timing of polls matters too. The hardest part of polling is generating a large random sample that is representative of the population. It is here that most polling agencies in India have dubious records. Except for a few, none make their methods available for public scrutiny. Further, the declining response rate (the proportion of achieved interviews vis-à-vis targeted interviews) is also worrisome, since variation in response rate skews the representativeness of the sample.[14]

Challenge of Converting Votes into Seats

The data collected through surveys is processed, sample representativeness is cross-checked and if there is any skew, it is corrected.[15] Statisticians then use mathematical models to arrive at vote estimates and seat predictions. This may sound odd, but by definition, 'estimate' and 'prediction' can only be ballpark-range figures. The demand for statistical precision from pollsters is unwarranted.[16] The whole process of generating data from the field is long, tiresome, cost-intensive and often messy. This is not something that is immediately apparent to an average person when the whole exercise is boiled down on TV screens to a few numbers. During the span of a few hours of prime-time viewing, we are thrilled and glued to our TV sets by the thought of being able to foresee the future. Anchors do not want to dampen the euphoria by lecturing viewers about 'margin of error' and how a change of a few percentage points, which often happens, will turn the results upside down.[17] As a result, the average viewer has an unrealistic expectation from election polls.

Once it becomes clear after the election results are announced that most opinion polls were wrong, there is often an outcry to ban them. The criticisms range from unfair expectations to much deeper questions that lie at the heart of various traditions of social science inquiry.[18] Supporters of opinion polls take refuge in the principle of freedom of speech and expression, whereas opponents go to the extent of questioning pollsters' motives. In the case of the latter, pollsters get labelled as having 'sold out' and the whole enterprise of election studies is equated with a set of 'palm readers' and 'astrologers'.

To be fair, pollsters in India often succeed in estimating vote shares correctly (close to the actual outcome), but they often fail in predicting seats accurately (though they get the direction of seat shares right). The data provided in tables 1 and 2 clearly show how difficult it is to correctly predict the number of seats despite getting vote shares right. For example, the Congress won 19.3 per cent votes in 2014 but could win only forty-four seats, while the BJP in

2009 won 116 seats with 18.8 per cent vote share. In some cases, parties with lower vote shares manage to win more seats due to a concentration of their votes in specific regions.

Table 1
Disproportionality in Votes and Seats in Lok Sabha Elections

Year	Congress		BJP	
	Vote (%)	Seats Won	Vote (%)	Seats Won
2009	28.6	206	18.8	116
2014	19.3	44	31.1	272

Table 2
Lower Voter Shares, but More Seats

	Winning Party	Winner Vote (%)	Winner Seats Won	Runner-up	Runner-up Vote (%)	Runner-up Seats Won
Karnataka 2008	Congress	34.6	80	BJP	33.9	110
Kerala 1996	UDF	44.4	59	LDF	42.7	78

Source: Author's analysis of data provided by the Election Commission of India

Also, political parties in India win and lose by a few percentage points. In such a scenario, even with fairly large sample surveys, if one accounts for the margin of error, statistically, often the numbers are un-differentiable. Thus, the expectation of precision is too much to ask for. Moreover, the time-series survey data collected by Lokniti-CSDS suggests that while the political preferences of a large part of Indian voters are very stable, there are enough numbers of voters who switch parties frequently.[19] This feature, combined with India's 'first past the post' electoral system with multiple parties competing and changing their pre-poll allies in every successive election, simply means that forecasting elections in India is a Herculean task. That is why psephology in India has to be as much an 'art' as it is a 'science'.[20] The data that is collected through polls must be carefully interpreted with a deep knowledge of India's diverse polity and society.

Utility of Election Polling beyond Forecasting

While election forecasting is an important aspect of polling, it is not the sole reason why many of us engage with opinion polls. Political parties and their election strategists conduct their own polls to formulate campaign plans. Of course, they are interested in knowing about the winnability of their platform or ticket, but the usefulness of survey data doesn't end there. Election strategists use data to devise campaigns, galvanize their own support base, and wean away supporters from opposition camps, in addition to locating and wooing non-partisan voters.

Critics of opinion polls must look at their utility beyond forecasting as they contribute to a nobler purpose: the production of public knowledge. Data from polls has great academic value and helps in deciphering crucial social science insights. For example, the Lokniti-CSDS data was crucial in understanding how underprivileged sections of society are participating in greater numbers in the electoral arena. These were unusual findings, given that in the Western world, voting rates were higher among privileged sections of society.

It is also true that the election studies enterprises in India and elsewhere have had their fair share of failures. There is a debate about whether surveys are the best way to capture voters' moods or preferences because a survey investigator spends far less time with a respondent than is necessary to win her confidence and gain an insight into why she votes the way she does. While this criticism is fair, alternative methods of gauging voters' moods are too narrow in their scope. For example, journalistic reports often suffer from selection bias, ranging from the choice of travel route to impressionistic accounts.

Notwithstanding methodological challenges, there are two important issues that demand some serious introspection. First, the questions posed in the survey are often too difficult for average respondents to decipher and thus a lot of these questions receive a 'no opinion' response, especially from underprivileged sections. This skews the overall results and defeats the very point of conducting a representative survey.

Second, predictions are based on what we know about how the social and political world works. Unfortunately, we have failed to produce a body of knowledge on how people vote in India on which pollsters can rely on. This is where political science departments can make a great contribution by introducing graduate-level courses on research methods; particularly survey research. This will also help a great deal in overcoming the general lacuna on how to understand the findings of a poll and what to expect and not expect from them.

Election time, by far, remains the most opportune moment to study politics and people; an instance to observe and interpret society at large. Elections are merely a window and opinion polls are one of the many tools used to peer through that window to study the political and social fabric of our society with the ultimate goal of understanding its democratic health. The unfortunate part is the shift from psephology to prophecy, which has reduced the value of these surveys to mere election-time entertainment. We hope that a clearer understanding of the tools used will help one better contextualize the results delivered.

III

Confronting the Challenge of
Money in Elections

Milan Vaishnav

One of the foundational pillars of modern democracy is vibrant
political contestation. According to one classic formulation,
contestation entails at least three features: ex ante uncertainty, ex
post irreversibility, and repeatability.[1] In other words, elections
cannot be foregone conclusions; the losers must accept defeat and
the winners must subject themselves to elections in the future
and embrace the risk that they may lose power. For seventy years
and against all odds, India has embraced robust contestation under
the framework of regular democratic elections. Today, there can
be no doubt that elections and the underlying concept of political
contestation have become deeply embedded in the social fabric of
the nation.

To say that Indian elections are contested would be an
understatement. They are not merely competitive; they can be more
aptly described as *hyper*-competitive. In the 2014 general elections,
there were 464 parties contesting elections across twenty-nine states
and seven union territories. Altogether, 8251 candidates joined the
fight for 543 parliamentary seats. Voters went to the polls in record
numbers: 66.4 per cent of the eligible voting public cast their ballots

on election day.[2] One more statistic from the last general elections also stands out: parties and candidates spent as much as $5 billion on election-related expenditures, according to one independent study. This was two-and-a-half times the $2 billion price tag the same group of researchers placed on the previous national election held in 2009.[3]

Costs of Democracy

Today in India, there is a deeply held sense that the costs of elections are exorbitant and are only getting larger. The healthy contestation embedded in Indian democracy has numerous benefits, but also carries with it costs, in the literal sense of the word. These 'costs of democracy' should be a concern—not simply because of the many ways this money could be otherwise put to use in a country where poverty, hunger, and a lack of basic amenities is so prevalent, but also because they have tangible, negative repercussions for the sanctity of democracy.

For starters, money has a powerful selection effect on the candidate pool that is willing to stand for elected office.[4] Without independent sources of wealth or access to well-heeled networks, the excessive costs of campaigning make it difficult—if not impossible—to stand for elected office. Cash-strapped parties regularly turn to self-financing candidates who will not only cover the costs of campaigning, but also pay parties for the privilege of running on their symbol. Second, the need to raise vast amounts of funds incentivizes the consummation of quid pro quos between candidates and wealthy benefactors. Campaign contributions do not often come for free; backers expect preferential treatment once their candidates are elected. Third, if candidates are required to pay for a substantial portion of their campaign costs, they are more likely to be motivated to exploit their time in office pursuing rent-seeking opportunities that will allow them to recoup their costs while building a war chest for re-election. Fourth, if the citizenry believes that elections are essentially bought and sold, the deluge of money in politics could erode the foundations of democratic legitimacy. Here, what matters is the *belief,* not simply the reality, that only the ultra-rich are viable candidates.

Regulating the flow of money into politics represents one of the foremost challenges to electoral vibrancy in India. In many respects, India has a great tool at its disposal to confront this challenge— the Election Commission of India, one of the most powerful (and respected) independent election bodies the world over. However, the ECI is fighting this fight with one hand tied behind its back. The structure of India's political economy practically invites corruption as the state remains deeply embedded in everyday economic activity more than a quarter-century following the supposed dismantling of the Licence Raj. Electoral reforms initiated by Parliament in recent years have actually made money in politics *less,* not more, transparent. While it is true that the ECI possesses unprecedented supervisory powers in conducting elections, its authorities to deal with modern methods of political finance are outmatched and outdated. It is impossible to imagine elections without money just as it is not feasible to have democracy without elections. The challenge for India in the years to come is to curb the worst excesses of money in politics, while ensuring a more level playing field for citizens who aspire to be representatives.

Rising Expenditure

There is a lack of hard data on election spending in India because so much of it is opaque, which means official reporting captures a fraction of actual expenditures. But there is a widespread belief that the costs of elections are growing at a rapid clip for at least four reasons.[5] First, population growth and the growing size of electoral constituencies mean that candidates have to spend larger sums of money on advertising, rallies, and the basic components of electioneering. Second, electoral competition has grown substantially more intense. Today, there are more parties, more candidates, and lower margins of victory in electoral contests at all levels of government. This uncertainty means that political actors struggle mightily to evaluate the marginal impact of each rupee spent campaigning. Third, popular expectations about 'handouts' distributed by office-seeking politicians have also grown in kind. From the distribution of flat-panel television sets to mixers or just plain cash, elections have become synonymous with gift-giving. Even though politicians freely admit that securing iron-clad contracts to 'buy' citizens' votes is virtually impossible, they fret that not handing out cash or other material inducements will place them at a strategic disadvantage relative to their competitors.

This backdrop of rising costs must be understood in the context of two important structural features of India's political economy.[6] The first is that the state continues to play a highly interventionist role in the economy, both directly (as a major producer of goods and services) as well as indirectly (through the issuance of licenses, permits, and other regulations). This means that politicians, and the bureaucrats who labour under their watch, can regularly trade policy and regulatory favours in exchange for bribes and campaign contributions.

Firms, for their part, prefer to provide funds anonymously so that they are not punished in the future by parties they have not supported. Furthermore, the state's regulatory powers also mean that successful politicians have myriad ways of enriching themselves by manipulating their discretionary authorities, evidenced by the fact that incumbent candidates regularly report large increases in their assets while in office.[7]

A second important contextual factor is uneven enforcement. It is extremely difficult to track cash payments or other 'black' transactions that might transpire in the course of elections. The ECI has stepped up its surveillance activities in recent years in order to ferret out such suspicious movements, but at the end of the day, its powers have limits.[8]

Stylized Facts on Political Finance

The growth in spending, combined with the state's heavy-handed approach to the economy and uneven enforcement, has led to a sub-optimal, corrupt equilibrium. This state of affairs can be characterized by a basic set of stylized facts on political finance.[9] First, there is virtually no transparency in political giving. Anonymous cash donations, which do not leave a clear paper trail, are rampant. Cash also makes it easier for parties and candidates to deliver pre-election goodies without leaving crumbs for enforcement authorities to stumble upon. Non-cash donations are becoming increasingly opaque as well, through a new mechanism introduced by the Narendra Modi government called 'electoral bonds'. Electoral bonds are bearer bonds purchased by firms or individuals from public sector banks that can be deposited with political parties in the form of a donation. An essential element of this new mechanism is the absence of disclosure: neither the donor nor the recipient must disclose the transaction, which allows the giver to protect its prized anonymity. The upside to electoral bonds is that they leave a digital paper trail (as opposed to cash), but this trail is only known to the bank and not the general public.[10]

Second, political party finances are not subject to any real scrutiny. Under the law, parties are required to submit annual audited accounts, but there is no requirement that these evaluations be subjected to rigorous, independent evaluation. As a result, party filings are openly dismissed as fabrications. Third, the ECI's regulatory authorities concerning political finance are constrained. For instance, even when candidates flout basic spending regulations (or misstate expenses on their campaign filings), the ability of the ECI to take punitive action is limited. The introduction of electoral bonds, coupled with corresponding changes that have eliminated limits on corporate giving and opened the door to foreign donors have only enhanced the Commission's burden.[11]

Agenda for Reform

Recent changes to India's political finance landscape do not boost one's optimism that India is gaining ground when it comes to regulating the torrent of money witnessed in recent years. In the first decade of the 2000s, the ECI—with support from civil society and the judiciary—did manage to marginally increase the level of transparency around political funding. With the 2003 implementation of new candidate disclosure requirements (which mandated that all aspirants to higher office release their educational, financial, and criminal backgrounds at the time of nomination) and the landmark 2005 Right to Information (RTI) Act, the needle was (slowly) moving in the direction of greater openness.[12] Recent legislative moves have cut the other way. The question is, what is the optimal path forward for cleaning up elections and maintaining the health of Indian democracy? I would submit that future reform must move on at least five fronts.[13]

First, there must be greater transparency in political contributions. At the very least, citizens must be able to find out who is making donations and to whom. The best way of ensuring full transparency is to insist on digital giving (something electoral bonds do) but ensuring that these digital payments are fully disclosed (something they do not). To go further, Parliament could legislate that donations of any amount must be linked to an individual's Aadhaar or Permanent Account Number (PAN). After all, it is ironic that politicians in India are in favour of digitizing all manner of government transactions, from real estate to welfare distribution, but have grown suspiciously silent when it comes to their own dealings.

Second, if parties and candidates are willing to adhere to greater transparency norms, there is a good argument for lifting existing candidate expenditure limits in return. At present, the spending disclosures candidates make are vulnerable to severe underreporting. For instance, candidates in India's 2014 general elections laughably declared that they spent only 58 per cent of the prescribed ceiling, on average.[14] If expenditure limits are to be relaxed—or lifted entirely—the ECI should be granted the authority to impose sanctions on candidates who fail to disclose their expenses in a timely manner.

Third, the era of political parties auditing their own books must come to an end. The law must be changed to mandate independent audits of political party finances. The Central Information Commission (CIC) ruled in 2013 that RTI is applicable to political parties, but also admitted that it has no means of enforcing compliance. Indeed, the CIC itself has turned to the Supreme Court to compel parties to follow its directive.[15] While the legal haggling over RTI will likely go on for years, Parliament could insist that political parties accept third-party audit in exchange for retaining their tax-exempt status.

Fourth, the Representation of the People Act (RPA) 1951—the law which governs most routine aspects of elections—needs a tune-up. More than sixty-five years after its passage, the entire landscape of electoral competition has changed in ways the law's drafters could not have imagined. Take the issue of 'paid news', whereby media houses collude with candidates and arrange for positive coverage (essentially, advertisements masquerading as news) in exchange for under-the-table payments.[16] Right now, paid news is not specified in the RPA as a predicate offence that could trigger disqualification. While the ECI should be pushing the envelope by referring cases for prosecution where there is blatant abuse, the body also requires enhanced legal powers to take action so that its every move is not subject to counter-litigation.

Finally, the elephant in the room whenever political finance reform is discussed is public funding. Advocates of public funding believe that the state should provide resources to parties and candidates so that they need not rely on private donations—especially large corporate donations—which facilitate corruption and cronyism. Public funding, which exists in many other democracies, can only be contemplated in India as and when parties and candidates are willing to sign up to a 'grand bargain' in which they accept reforms that constrain their behaviour. Unless political actors are willing to open up their books, agree to more robust disclosure requirements, and support better enforcement capacity, public funding should remain on the sidelines. Some members of Parliament have floated the idea of introducing matching public grants that would reward candidates who demonstrate that they can transparently collect small donations from individual supporters.[17] Such schemes must be discussed within the broader context of systemic political finance reform.

A Sisyphean Task

Advocating for reforming the manner in which money in Indian politics is regulated feels like a Sisyphean task. The practical and political obstacles are large, and the short-term rewards are few. This can hardly be grounds for retreat. For starters, a unique constellation of civil society actors, the media, academics, courts, and reformist politicians have managed to drive important changes in political finance in recent years. The entire framework of candidate disclosure—however flawed it may be—exists today because of sustained public pressure. Furthermore, the stakes are incredibly high. The space for the *aam aadmi* (common man) in today's electoral environment is shrinking, thanks to the oppressive financial requirements needed to be a viable political candidate. After one accounts for suspected criminals, dynasts, industrialists, and celebrities, there is little room for ordinary citizens to serve as the people's representatives.[18]

The silver lining in this story is that proposing, and eventually implementing, genuine political finance reform is arguably good politics. The spectacle of demonetization and its aftermath— in which the ruling Bharatiya Janata Party (BJP) turned a highly flawed anti-corruption measure into political gold—serves as a case in point.[19] Not only would genuine reform find favour with voters, it would also tap into a deep-seated frustration with the status quo that business, civil society, and even some politicians regularly express. What is missing now is a far-sighted leader who can mobilize this unique combination of strange bedfellows.

IV

How India Should Fund Its Democracy

Niranjan Sahoo

Over the last few decades, the idea of public funding of politics has received global attention. According to global democracy watchdog, International Institute for Democracy and Electoral Assistance (International IDEA), as many as 116 democracies are now offering some form of state subsidy or other to reduce the influence of money in democratic processes. Richer, mature democracies like the United States (US), United Kingdom (UK), Germany, Finland and Italy have been implementing public funding options for many years. In Asia, countries such as Japan, South Korea and Israel have adopted the public funding model for quite some time. Incidentally, Latin American countries were the initial leaders in introducing state subsidies for political parties. It was Uruguay that introduced state subsidies in the 1920s, a system which was later borrowed by Costa Rica and Argentina and now more than seven Latin American democracies have adopted it.

Why Public Funding of Politics?

As explained above, the public financing model has been put in place in major democracies for various reasons. The key reason is its anti-corruption utility. Normatively speaking, anti-corruption theorists rest their claim on intuitive and historically verifiable indicators, where election contributions in some instances, function as a kind of legalized bribery that prevents political actors from acting independently (Bradley, 1997). This is the key reason why analysts push for public financing of elections to mitigate 'the importance of private money' by keeping 'the big money out of politics'. Public finance can help protect the political process from direct, quid pro quo kickbacks or corruption. State funding for them is an affirmative, rather than just a restrictive system that seeks to prevent corruption, promotes diversity among candidates and acts as public service for the entire society rather than just the donors.

This is not to deny the original theoretical assumption for public financing to well-known political philosophers John Rawls and Ronald Dworkin. For them, public funding aspires to establish an 'equalizing influence'—an effort that goes to ensure that certain powerful groups or individuals do not exercise undue influence in the electoral processes. According to this school of thought, political equality demands the concept of 'equal political influence', meaning no citizen can have more power over political processes than others (Sahoo, 2017).

In addition, there is a public-interest argument in favour of campaign finance regulation and public financing of elections as they benefit democracy and serve public interest (Beange, 2012). The public-interest rationale claims its roots to John Locke and his seminal *Second Treatise of Government* (1689). Locke argued that 'when we say that public office is a public trust with fiduciary obligations we mean that elected representatives assume the role of trustees, with the duty of acting for the sole benefit of the citizens who elected them. And that, in turn, means they must not allow their decisions to be influenced by anything other than the welfare of the citizenry they have undertaken to serve'. (Shrugman, 1997).

Its contemporary proponents claim political parties in democracies as the critical link between citizens and the state and in doing so they serve vital public interest. According to Dawson (1997), one of the original proponents of the public-interest theory, political parties promote activities such as efficacy in arousing interest, educating for democracy, simplifying the task of the voter, constituting an alternative government-in-waiting and minimizing transitional delays following an election in which the incumbent party is ousted. Therefore, given political parties and elected representatives hold 'trustee' positions for the electorate, it would be fair for the state to fund their activities. Further, according to this school, if managed well, public funding can vitally improve legislative politics and the quality of democracy. Elected representatives need to keep their eyes on their jobs than spend time on 'relentless pursuits of contributions, sometimes from illegal ways' (Sample, 2013). To this view, it would be a failure of representation when candidates spend a great amount of time on the task of fundraising (Balsi, 1994). Thus, for democracy's good health, the state has an important interest in representatives avoiding such behaviour.

There are three broad observations that clearly come out of the discussion on theoretical positioning of public financing of elections. First, the anti-corruption argument and keeping 'big money out of politics' demands the state take appropriate steps to address the political finance challenges facing political parties and candidates. Second, public financing is necessary to 'equalize influence' and promote competition (create a level playing field for parties and candidates with less resources vis-à-vis parties and candidates with ex ante equality). Third, strong public-interest rationale demands public financing of elections as they benefit democracy and serve the common good. In the context of India, it is pertinent to understand the context of reforms in different cases, and the differences in the systems introduced in the various countries.

The Global Experience

How do these assumptions measure up in terms of actual evidence? The evidence emerging from global experience raises plenty of doubts over the effectiveness of public financing. On the key objective of bringing down electoral expenditure and reducing the role of private money, most pointers from global experience indicate a picture that is far from rosy. For instance, countries like Italy, Israel, and Finland that embraced public funding in previous decades are yet to witness any visible reduction in election expenditures. Similarly, in the case of the US, election expenditure continues to soar. The Obama years witnessed two of the most expensive presidential elections. Only a handful of countries, including Germany and Japan, have been able to reduce their poll expenditures to a reasonable extent. Yet, successes in these countries have come largely through strict transparency and disclosure norms, elaborate regulatory mechanisms, and public scrutiny of expenditures by parties and candidates.

With regard to checking the growing plutocratic influence on party finance and corruption, the results are not very encouraging either (Sahoo, 2017). For instance, in the cases of Israel and the US, as noted above, public subsidies have not reduced the reliance on big private donations. Similarly, in several Latin American countries, particularly Brazil, Argentina, Colombia, Ecuador and Costa Rica, public subsidies have proved rather ineffective in limiting the role of business in political financing. Therefore, public subsidies in this case failed to replace the need to attract private donations, but were an additional source of income for the parties.

There are a few successful examples, though. Take the case of Canada. The North American country that introduced public subsidies as a part of a whole set of reforms, including spending ceilings and tax incentives for smaller contributions, has been able to reduce the role of interested money in party financing. In Sweden, generous public subsidies, which far exceed private donations, and minimal state intervention in party affairs, have been successful in reducing the temptation for parties to seek anonymous interested money. In both these cases, it is necessary to understand that other factors were also responsible for the resultant effect than the mere introduction of public financing.

Has public funding helped motivate new entrants and promote electoral competition? The jury is still out on this, so to speak. The evidence from global experiences suggests that the fostering of competition is a function of how public subsidies are distributed. In countries like Russia, it has been used to stifle political competition and promote authoritarianism. In fact, the 2001 public funding law in Russia has led to a situation where it is almost impossible to challenge the ruling party (Golosov, 2014). Thus, it has led to the creation of a cartel. However, there is modest evidence of the opposite too globally. Many new parties have emerged in countries like Canada and Finland, where public subsidies were introduced to reduce the proliferation of parties. In some instances, particularly in the cases of Israel, Italy and Mexico, the introduction of public subsidies has brought greater competition by enabling entry of newer parties and providing smaller parties with the funds to compete with incumbents (Zamare, 2008).

This apart, there are also peculiar experiences particularly with regard to parties that have certain ideological preferences, like the Left or parties with socialist leanings. It is widely known that these entities find it increasingly difficult to compete with Right-wing parties due to the huge private funds that are readily available to the latter. In some ways, the introduction of public subsidies is helping those political entities as is evident in the case of Uruguay.

Situating the Indian Case

Notwithstanding its great strides amid mass poverty and illiteracy, India's democracy is beset by black money or illicit finances. This is evident from the fact that nearly two-thirds of political donations of registered political parties are from 'unknown' sources.[1] The associated problems related to elections largely fueled by black money are well known. To reduce the flow of illicit or black money and infuse adequate supply of 'white money' into politics, the Narendra Modi government announced a slew of reform proposals in the Finance Bill recently.[2] Noteworthy steps are to reduce cash donations from the current Rs 20,000 to Rs 2000, making tax exemption conditional to mandatory filing of income tax returns in time, and the floating of electoral bonds. While these steps notwithstanding many flaws[3] indicate the government's serious intent to address issues of illicit flows and help expand clean sources of political finance for parties, they hardly attack the structural issues surrounding political funding in India.

While the successes of democracy in a complex and large country with widespread poverty and illiteracy has earned India global respect and applause, the country's democratic process is besotted with corruption, lack of transparency and accountability. However, the most worrisome trend is the growing role of money. Arguably, the fourteenth general election was the second most expensive election after the 2012 US presidential election.[4] As per a study by the Centre for Media Studies, the figure was stated to be about Rs 30,000 crore (roughly \$5.5 billion).[5] On average (anecdotally and based their own confessions), candidates fighting Lok Sabha elections spend between Rs 5–10 crore to put up a decent campaign. Buying votes by giving cash, alcohol, drugs and so on is also common practice. The cash seized by the Election Commission of India's expenditure observers reached record levels in the last elections, with more than Rs 150 crore seized just from the southern state of Tamil Nadu.[6]

As elections become more expensive so does the burden of generating more finances on parties and candidates. Given that the ways and means to raise small contributions are more difficult and their transactional costs are still very high in India (Gowda and Sridharan, 2012), the role of 'interested money' from corporates has taken prominence (Sahoo and Chatterjee, 2014). It is well known that big political parties in India, with the exception of the Left, are liberally funded by corporate houses. For instance, among the known sources of donation, private business or corporate contribution forms a staggering 89 per cent of total donations.[7] This, coupled with the major role played by the state in the regulation of the economy, has resulted in most of the corporate money coming through illegal and undisclosed means, which in turn has resulted in the increasing role of black money in elections and other party activities. Even tax benefits have not proven good enough incentives for corporates to reveal their identity, as they fear a backlash from the parties in power (Gowda and Sridharan, 2012). Thus, cronyism and big-ticket corruption scandals have become common in India. Most part of the second tenure of the United Progressive Alliance (UPA) government was spent fighting big-ticket corruption scandals such as 2G auction and the coal scam (linked to quid pro quo decisions).[8]

While cronyism and corruption have impacted the quality of democracy and the nature of governance, the growing role of money has negatively impacted competition at the level of candidature within parties. Due to the increasing need for money, most candidates chosen by parties are individuals who can finance themselves and do not rely on party funds for campaigning. This has led to an increase of rich candidates and has also resulted in an increasing number of criminals contesting elections (Vaishnav, 2017).

Finally, given that party finances are controlled by a few dynasts and regional satraps in India, there is very limited internal democracy in parties. With the growing role of money in elections, most parties, with some exceptions, select rich candidates or ones with the ability to raise funds to fight elections. This has often led to situations where criminals self-select themselves as candidates while meritorious or talented candidates find it hard to participate in the democratic processes (Vaishnav, 2017). In short, India's democracy faces a serious credibility crisis owing to challenges surrounding political finance and every political dispensation at the federal level has burned midnight oil to reduce its eroding effects.

A number of committees appointed by successive governments in the last two decades have discussed various proposals of direct state funding of parties and elections. For instance, the report of the Goswami Committee (1990), Indrajit Gupta Committee (1998), the Second Administrative Reforms Commission (2007) and the Law Commission Report (2015) that dealt with public funding issues have advised against full state funding. Their rationale has been that prevailing economic conditions and development needs of the nation make it infeasible to fund a large democracy. Instead, they have suggested partial subsidies in kind. Whereas the Law Commission Report (1999), the Venkatachaliah Committee Report (2002) and the 2015 Law Commission Report have insisted that regulatory frameworks dealing with transparency, disclosure, auditing and submission of accounts and internal democracy of parties must precede any attempt at complete state funding. The CII taskforce Report (2012) suggested the imposition of a democracy cess of 0.2% of income to be paid by individuals and corporates to finance election expenses. Whereas, the Associate Chambers of Commerce of India (Assocham) Report (2015) proposed to set up a Rs 5000-crore government fund for elections to be disbursed over five years (Sahoo, 2017).

However, these well-intentioned efforts have largely failed to build consensus on issues of criteria, methods, and the quantum of such funding. Although state funding has been proposed by all these committees, as of now only limited indirect subsidies are provided to the political parties in India. Since 1996, parties can access free time on state-owned electronic media. But since Doordarshan and All India Radio only form a miniscule part of the advertising options for parties, this is hardly of any consequence.

The other in-kind subsidies provided to parties are in the form of free supply of copies of electoral rolls and identity slips of electors to candidates. Also, any donation to political parties is eligible for income tax deduction. However, these measures too have not had a serious dent on reducing the costs to be incurred by parties or increasing the funds available to them (Sahoo and Chatterjee, 2014). Other regulations have also largely been in vain. From no-expenditure ceilings for parties and others in support of candidates prior to 2003, to extremely low limits, has led to evasion of regulations (Gowda and Sridharan, 2012). In short, public funding has remain a non-starter over the last two decades.

Time for Public Funding

Given the nature of political finance and the increasing role of money in elections, India needs to take the option of public funding seriously. Global examples as cited in the previous section can come in handy for India. While it varies from country to country, there are established processes and practices to learn from. From a purely policy perspective, it would make sense to pay close attention to success stories. These include Sweden, Canada, and, to a lesser extent, Japan, and reveal that an effective public funding model has two elements: reduce the dependency on corporate or private money (by strict restrictions on limits, strong regulations, disclosures) and infuse white money through state funding or by incentivizing various other funding options, including tax free donations or loans, matching funds, and so on. Nonetheless, as seen from the Canadian example, success to a great degree has been achieved through strict transparency and disclosure norms, elaborate regulatory mechanisms, and public scrutiny of expenditures by parties and candidates.

India's existing system of political finance laws and institutional processes are light years away from meeting those conditionalities for state funding. India's broken political finance regime, accompanied by a lack of clear rules on transparency, disclosures, and the absence of a strong and effective regulatory agency, makes it an unsuitable candidate for public funding. Yet, these are precisely the reasons why India needs to embrace the state funding model for its politics. Given the fact that in nearly all the countries that have introduced the public financing option, this has been preceded by a regulatory regime of transparency and disclosure and a regulatory body (in many cases by empowering existing electoral commissions to go after violators), India's underdeveloped and slack political finance regime and missing regulatory body would receive a big push from the new scheme (Gowda and Sridharan, 2012; Sahoo 2017).

Second, by providing 'floor level fund' for everyone, a state fund scheme can be critical for smaller and newer political entrants. Due to various factors, India has seen a huge proliferation of political parties formed on ethnic, religious and other parochial grounds. However, due to the growing costs of elections, many of them find it difficult to put up a decent campaign. It is here that public funding of elections, especially if that is channelized through candidates, can come in handy to promote competition for candidature and bring internal democracy within parties.

In short, public funding if implemented properly, can strengthen lower levels of party units to a situation where they can demand democratization. It can therefore solve the problem of concentration of power in the hands of a few and hence dynastic politics. Importantly, if public funding is used as a lever, it can help the state secure compliance from parties on all these issues.

References

Balsi, Vincent, 'Free Speech and the Widening Gyre of Fund-Raising: Why Campaign Spending Limits May Not Violate the First Amendment After All', *Legal Review* 94 COLUM, 1994.

Beange, Pauline E, 'Canadian Campaign Finance Reform in Comparative Perspective 2000–11', PhD thesis, University of Toronto, 2012, https://tspace.library.utoronto.ca/bitstream/1807/32664/3/Beange_Pauline_E_201206_PhD_thesis.pdf.

Bradley A. Smith, *The Sirens' Song: Campaign Finance Regulation and the First Amendment*, 6 J.L. & POL'Y 1, 6 (1997).

Gowda, Rajeev and E. Sridharan, 'Reforming India's Party Financing and Election Expenditure Laws', *Election Law Journal* 11 (2012), p. 233.

Golosov, Gigorii E., 'Russia' in *Checkbook Elections: Political Finance in Comparative Perspective*, eds. Pippa Norris, Andrea Abel van Es and Lisa Fennis, 2014.

Kevin Casas-Zamora, 'Political Finance and State Funding Systems: An Overview' (Washington: International Foundation for Electoral Systems, 2008).

Marcin Walecki et al., 'Public Funding Solutions for Political Parties in Muslim-Majority Societies', IFES and USIP (2009).

Rawls, John, *Political Liberalism* (New York: Columbia University Press, 1993).

Sahoo, Niranjan, Towards Public Financing of Elections and Political Parties in India: Lessons from the Global Experiences, *ORF Occasional Paper*, 20 November 2017, https://www.orfonline. org/research/towards-public-financing-elections-political-parties-india-lessons-global-experiences/.

Vaishnav, Milan, *When Crime Pays, Money and Muscle in Indian Politics* (New Delhi: HarperCollins, 2017).

Zamara Kevin Casas, 'Political Finance and State Funding Systems: An Overview' (Washington: *International Foundation for Electoral Systems*, 2008).

Appendix I

Articles 324–29 in the Constitution of India, 1949

Article 324

Superintendence, direction and control of elections to be vested in an Election Commission.

(1) The superintendence, direction and control of the preparation of the electoral rolls for, and the conduct of, all elections to Parliament and to the Legislature of every State and of elections to the offices of President and Vice President held under this Constitution shall be vested in a Commission (referred to in this Constitution as the Election Commission).

(2) The Election Commission shall consist of the Chief Election Commissioner and such number of other Election Commissioners, if any, as the President may from time to time fix and the appointment of the Chief Election Commissioner and other Election Commissioners shall, subject to the provisions of any law made in that behalf by Parliament, be made by the President.

(3) When any other Election Commissioner is so appointed the Chief Election Commissioner shall act as the Chairman of the Election Commission.

(4) Before each general election to the House of the People and to the Legislative Assembly of each State, and before the first general election and thereafter before each biennial election to the Legislative Council of each State having such Council, the President may also appoint after consultation with the Election Commission such Regional Commissioners as he may consider necessary to assist the Election Commission in the performance of the functions conferred on the Commission by clause (1).

(5) Subject to the provisions of any law made by Parliament, the conditions of service and tenure of office of the Election Commissioners and the Regional Commissioners shall be such as the President may by rule determine; Provided that the Chief Election Commissioner shall not be removed from his office except in like manner and on the like grounds as a Judge of the Supreme Court and the conditions of service of the Chief Election Commissioner shall not be varied to his disadvantage after his appointment: Provided further that any other Election Commissioner or a Regional Commissioner shall not be removed from office except on the recommendation of the Chief Election Commissioner.

(6) The President, or the Governor of a State, shall, when so requested by the Election Commission, make available to the Election Commission or to a Regional Commissioner such staff as may be necessary for the discharge of the functions conferred on the Election Commission by clause (1).

Article 325

No person to be ineligible for inclusion in, or to claim to be included in a special, electoral roll on grounds of religion, race, caste or sex. There shall be one general electoral roll for every territorial constituency for election to either House of Parliament or to the House or either House of the Legislature of a State and no person shall be ineligible for inclusion in any such roll or claim to be included in any special electoral roll for any such constituency on grounds only of religion, race, caste, sex or any of them.

Article 326

Elections to the House of the People and to the Legislative Assemblies of States to be on the basis of adult suffrage. The elections to the House of the People and to the Legislative Assembly of every State shall be on the basis of adult suffrage; but is to say, every person who is a citizen of India and who is not less than twenty one years of age on such date as may be fixed in that behalf by or under any law made by the appropriate legislature and is not otherwise disqualified under this constitution or any law made by the appropriate Legislature on the ground of non residence, unsoundness of mind, crime or corrupt or illegal practice, shall be entitled to be registered as a voter at any such election.

Article 327

Power of Parliament to make provision with respect to elections to Legislatures. Subject to the provisions of this constitution, Parliament may from time to time by law made provision with respect to all matters relating to, or in connection with, elections to either House of Parliament or to the House or either House of the Legislature of a State including the preparation of electoral rolls, the delimitation of constituencies and all other matters necessary for securing the due constitution of such House or Houses.

Article 328

Power of Legislature of a State to make provision with respect to elections to such Legislature. Subject to the provisions of this Constitution and in so far as provision in that behalf is not made by Parliament, the Legislature of a State may from time to time bylaw make provision with respect to all matters relating to, or in connection with, the elections to the House or either House of the Legislature of the State including the preparation of electoral rolls and all other matters necessary for securing the due constitution of such House or Houses.

Article 329

Bar to interference by courts in electoral matters notwithstanding anything in this Constitution

(a) the validity of any law relating to the delimitation of constituencies or the allotment of seats to such constituencies, made or purporting to be made under Article 327 or Article 328, shall not be called in question in any court;

(b) No election to either House of Parliament or to the House or either House of the Legislature of a State shall be called in question except by an election petition presented to such authority and in such manner as may be provided for by or under any law made by the appropriate Legislature.

Appendix II

Lok Sabhas since Independence

Lok Sabha	Year	Prime Minister	Party/Coalition
1	1951	Jawaharlal Nehru	Indian National Congress
2	1957	Jawaharlal Nehru	Indian National Congress
3	1962	Jawaharlal Nehru Gulzarilal Nanda (acting) Lal Bahadur Shastri Gulzarilal Nanda Indira Gandhi	Indian National Congress
4	1967	Indira Gandhi	Indian National Congress
5	1971	Indira Gandhi	Indian National Congress

Lok Sabha	Year	Prime Minister	Party/Coalition
6	1977	Morarji Desai	Janata Party
		Charan Singh	Janata Party (Secular) with Indian National Congress
7	1980	Indira Gandhi	Indian National Congress
		Rajiv Gandhi	
8	1984	Rajiv Gandhi	Indian National Congress
9	1989	Vishwanath Pratap Singh	Janata Dal (National Front)
		Chandra Shekhar	Samajwadi Party (with Indian National Congress)
10	1991	Pamulaparti Venkata Narasimha Rao	Indian National Congress
11	1996	Atal Bihari Vajpayee	Bharatiya Janata Party
		Haradanahalli Doddegowda Deve Gowda	Janata Dal (United Front)
		Inder Kumar Gujral	Janata Dal (United Front)
12	1998	Atal Bihari Vajpayee	National Democratic Alliance
13	1999	Atal Bihari Vajpayee	National Democratic Alliance

Lok Sabha	Year	Prime Minister	Party/Coalition
14	2004	Manmohan Singh	United Progressive Alliance
15	2009	Manmohan Singh	United Progressive Alliance
16	2014	Narendra Modi	National Democratic Alliance

Appendix III

List of Chief Election Commissioners of India (1950–Present)

Name	From	To
Sukumar Sen	21 March 1950	19 December 1958
Kalyan Sundaram	20 December 1958	30 September 1967
S.P. Sen Verma	1 October 1967	30 September 1972
Nagendra Singh	1 October 1972	6 February 1973
T.S. Swaminathan	7 February 1973	17 June 1977
S.L. Shakhdar	18 June 1977	17 June 1982
R.K. Trivedi	18 June 1982	31 December 1985
R.V.S. Peri Shastri	1 January 1986	25 November 1990
V.S. Ramadevi	26 November 1990	11 December 1990
T.N. Seshan	12 December 1990	11 December 1996
M.S. Gill	12 December 1996	13 June 2001
J.M. Lyngdoh	14 June 2001	7 February 2004
T.M. Krishnamurthy	8 February 2004	15 May 2005
B.B. Tandon	16 May 2005	29 June 2006

Name	From	To
N. Gopalaswami	30 June 2006	20 April 2009
Navin Chawla	21 April 2009	29 July 2010
S.Y. Quraishi	30 July 2010	10 June 2012
V.S. Sampath	11 June 2012	15 January 2014
H.S. Brahma	16 January 2015	18 April 2015
Nasim Zaidi	19 April 2015	5 July 2017
Achal Kumar Jyoti	6 July 2017	22 January 2018
O.P. Rawat	23 January 2018	1 December 2018
Sunil Arora	2 December 2018	Incumbent

Notes

Foreword

1. 'In the happiness of the people lies the happiness of the king, their welfare is his welfare. He shall not consider as good only that which pleases him but treat as beneficial to him whatever causes happiness to all people.' Source: https://www.ndtv.com/india-news/full-text-of-pranab-mukherjees-speech-to-rss-workers-in-nagpur-1864148

Introduction

1. The written text of the speech of the thirty-sixth president of the United States, Lyndon B. Johnson, at Capitol rotunda during the signing of the Voting Rights Act, 6 August 1965, http://www.lbjlibrary.org/lyndon-baines-johnson/speeches-films/president-johnsons-special-message-to-the-congress-the-american-promise.
2. 'The Constitution of India Bill', 1895, https://cadindia.clpr.org.in/historical_constitutions/the_constitution_of_india_bill__unknown__1895__1st%20January%201895.
3. 'The Nehru Report', 1928, http://cadindia.clpr.org.in/historical_constitutions/nehru_report__motilal_nehru_1928__1st%20January%201928.
4. 'The Constitutional History of India', http://govtnic.blogspot.com/2013/11/constitutional-history-of-india-1909.html.
5. Excerpt on universal adult suffrage from Ornit Shani's path-breaking work *How India Became Democratic*, published with permission from

253

Penguin Random House India, https://theprint.in/pageturner/excerpt/universal-adult-franchise-experiment-india-democratic-history/39836/.

6. Wikipedia entry on 'Literacy in India', https://en.wikipedia.org/wiki/Literacy_in_India.

7. 'Women's Suffrage Timeline', British Library Learning, 6 February 2018, https://www.bl.uk/votes-for-women/articles/womens-suffrage-timeline.

8. 'Nineteenth Amendment to the Constitution of the United States', https://en.wikipedia.org/wiki/Nineteenth_Amendment_to_the_United_States_Constitution.
    Passed by Congress on 4 June 1919, and ratified on 18 August 1920, the nineteenth amendment granted women the right to vote.

9. Wikipedia entry on the 'Timeline of Women's Suffrage', https://en.wikipedia.org/wiki/Timeline_of_women%27s_suffrage.

10. The Women's India Association was founded thirty years before independence in 1917, and sought equal voting rights for women since its very inception. In fact, British and Indian feminists collectively published *Stree Dharma*, which analysed international news from a feminist perspective.

11. There were six articles, starting from 289. Currently they start from 324. Though the Constitution came into force on 26 January 1950, some provisions relating to citizenship, elections, provisional parliament, temporary and transitional provisions were given immediate effect on 26 November 1949.

12. 'Article 324 of the Constitution of India, 1949', https://indiankanoon.org/doc/950881/.

13. These FAQs on the official website of the Election Commission of India give us some similar interesting factoids, https://eci.nic.in/eci_main1/election-machinery.aspx.

14. 329 elections to state assemblies as of October 2013 according to the ECI website. In 2014 (8), 2015 (2), 2016 (5), 2017 (7) and 2018 (8) . . . total 359, https://eci.nic.in/eci_main1/current/Electoral%20Statisitics%20Pocket%20Book%202014.pdf, p. 72.

15. Panchayati Raj and urban local bodies were institutionalized in 1992–93 and twenty-nine subjects were transferred from the state list to these local bodies depending on consensus with the states, http://www.frontdesk.co.in/forum/showthread.php?tid=2153.

16. Milan Vaishnav, 'Understanding the Indian Voter', Carnegie Endowment for International Peace (23 June 2015), https://carnegieendowment.org/2015/06/23/understanding-indian-voter-pub-60416.

17. Amartya Sen, 'Democracy as a Universal Value', *Journal of Democracy* (1999): 3–17, https://www.unicef.org/socialpolicy/files/Democracy_as_a_Universal_Value.pdf.

Part One: Foundational Ideas

The Dialectic of Elections

1. https://timesofindia.indiatimes.com/india/85-of-indians-trust-govt-27-want-a-strong-leader-pew-survey/articleshow/61108987.cms.

Elections and Democracy: The Human Dimension

1. W.H. Morris-Jones, *The Government and Politics of India* (New York: The Eothen Press, 1967), p. 4.
2. Paul Wallace, 'Centralisation and Depoliticisation in South Asia', *Journal of Commonwealth & Comparative Politics* XVI (March 1978).
3. A similar concept labelled democratic participation is set forth by Sidney Verba and Norman H. Nie in *Participation in America: Political Democracy and Social Equality* (Chicago: University of Chicago Press, 1972) p. 47. In chapter 3, they distinguish between four modes of democratic political participation by ordinary citizens: voting, campaign activity, citizen-initiated contacts, and cooperative participation.
4. Former minister of community development, S.K. Dey, asserted that Panchayati Raj institutions had continued, 'but as skeletons devoid of soul or substance with not even an election in ten years and more in most states.' S.K. Dey, 'Rural India: A Reminder', *Tribune*, 14 May 1977.
5. 'Indira Gandhi's political Mona Lisa–like smile and her open hand symbol on posters overshadowed the publicity for her party's parliamentary candidate . . . She personally represented the idea of a strong, stable government.' Paul Wallace, 'Plebiscitary Politics in Punjab and Haryana', *Asian Survey* XX (June 1980): 617–33.
6. Paul Wallace, 'Introduction: Single Party and Strong Leadership', in *India's 2014 Elections: A Modi-Led Sweep* (New Delhi: Sage Publications, 2015), pp. 3–27.
7. Interviews in Punjab and Haryana, 1996. Paul Wallace, 'General Elections, 1996 Regional Parties Dominant in Punjab and Haryana', *Economic and*

Political Weekly XXXII, no. 46: p. 2966; Wallace, ed., *Indian Politics and the 1998 Elections: Regionalism, Hindutva and State Politics* (New Delhi, Sage Publications, 1999), pp. 21–22.

8. For a systematic analysis of the stable groups that constitute the sub-structure of politics in Haryana and Punjab, see Paul Wallace, 'The *PaaRtii* Process: Political Institutionalization in Punjab and Haryana', *Region and Nation in India* (New Delhi: Oxford & IBH, 1985), pp. 219–32.

9. Paul Wallace, 'The Regionalization of Indian Electoral Politics 1989–90: Punjab and Haryana', in Harold A. Gould and Sumit Ganguly, eds., *India Votes: Alliance Politics and Minority Governments in the Ninth and Tenth General Elections* (Boulder: Westview Press, 1993); chapter 17 describes and analyses the 1991 and 1992 elections.

10. Master Tara Singh, Congress incumbent MP from Kurukshetra, asserted that 'corruption is overrated as an issue in Haryana'. He cited a newspaper that placed Haryana fourth or fifth among Indian states on corruption with a figure of 19 per cent as compared to a high of 70 per cent. Interview in Kurukshetra on 8 May 1996.

11. Interviews in Haryana. February and March 1994, and March and May 1996.

12. Interview with Chattar Singh, department of history, Kurukshetra University, and a *Jansatta* reporter, at Kurukshetra University on 8 May 1996.

13. Interview with former Haryana home minister Mani Ram Godara in New Delhi on 25 May 1996.

14. *Tribune*, 16 June 2009.

15. Interview with Abhinav Nayar, Punjab and Haryana correspondent of *Newstimes*, in Chandigarh on 14 May 1996.

16. Paul Wallace, ed., *India's 2014 Elections: A Modi-led Sweep*, (New Delhi: Sage Publications, 2015), see especially p. 10 ff.

Law and Politics: A Brief History

1. For a brief discussion of some of the early debates on the British introduction of voting law into India, see David Gilmartin, 'Election Law and the "People" in Colonial and Postcolonial India', in Dipesh Chakrabarty, Rochona Mazumdar, and Andrew Sartori, eds., *From the Colonial to the Postcolonial: India and Pakistan in Transition* (New Delhi: Oxford University Press, 2007), pp. 55–82.

2. E.L.L. Hammond, *Indian Electioneering: A Manual Designed for the Use of Candidates, Election Agents and Officers* (Allahabad: Pioneer Press, 1920).

3. The important working of this law in the late colonial period can be tracked in the reporting of election cases, originally published in the official provincial gazettes, in election case reports. A number of India's most prominent lawyers, such as Motilal Nehru, participated in these election cases in the 1920s and the 1930s. See, among other reports of these cases, Sir Laurie Hammond, *Election Cases, India & Burma, 1920–1935* (Calcutta: Butterworth & Co., 1936) and Sudhansu Bhusan Sen and Madan Gopal Poddar, *Indian Election Cases, 1935–1951* (Bombay: N.M. Tripathi, 1951).

4. S.P. Sen Verma, *Adult Franchise* (New Delhi: Sulakhani Devi Mahajan Trust, 1971), pp. 10–11.

5. While the all-India creation of electoral rolls was thus central to the imagining of a sovereign people, as Ornit Shani has recently argued, few imagined that India's manifold social divisions would not still require powerful legal constraints if voting was to have meaning. See Ornit Shani, *How India Became Democratic: Citizenship and the Making of the Universal Franchise* (Cambridge: Cambridge University Press, 2017).

6. Grounds of 'language' were added in 1961 to the rules banning as corrupt 'the systematic appeal to vote or refrain from voting on grounds of caste, race, community or religion or the use of, or appeal to, religious and national symbols, such as the national flag and the national emblem, for the furtherance of the prospects of a candidate's election'. Election Commission of India, *Manual of Election Law* (New Delhi: Election Commission, 1997), pp. 103–04.

7. The high volume of electoral litigation in India, as compared with most other democratic electoral systems, is underscored by the cases reported in the volumes of *Election Law Reports,* which the Election Commission has digitized on its website.

8. See, for example, the case of *Moinuuddin B. Harris v. B.P. Divgi. Election Law Reports* III (1953): 248–80. In this case, an election tribunal noted the extreme practical difficulty in actually enforcing election law as written.

9. For a brief history of the Election Commission, see Ujjwal Kumar Singh, *Institutions and Democratic Governance: A Study of the Election Commission and Electoral Governance in India* (New Delhi: Nehru Memorial Museum and Library, 2004).

10. This is in marked contrast with the United States, for example, where most matters relating to the conduct of elections are left to the states.

11. Quoted in Ramachandra Guha, *India After Gandhi: The History of the World's Largest Democracy* (New York: HarperCollins, 2007), p. 156.

12. For a larger discussion of the ECI's control over party symbols, see B. Venkatesh Kumar, 'Power to Allot Symbols', *Economic and Political Weekly* 35 (16–22 September 2000): 3387–91.

13. A brief history of the model code is in Election Commission of India, *First Annual Report, 1983* (New Delhi: Election Commission, 1984), pp. 65–67. For a more recent discussion of the model code, see also K.C. Saha, *Elections Model Code of Conduct: A Reference Handbook* (New Delhi: Shipra Publications, 2005).

14. For a fuller discussion of the Election Commission during the Seshan era, see David Gilmartin, 'One Day's Sultan: T.N. Seshan and Indian Democracy', *Contributions to Indian Sociology* 43 (March–August 2009) pp. 247–84.

15. Though the government of Narasimha Rao did attempt to limit the ECI's discretion, in part by appointing two additional election commissioners (as allowed under the Constitution, a procedure that had also been tried by the previous government), this served in the end to strengthen rather than weaken the Commission's independent authority (though it was initially resisted by T.N. Seshan).

16. See *Election Commission of India v. Union of India and Others.* SC writ petition #606 of 1999. Election Commission of India, *Landmark Judgements on Election Law* 3 (New Delhi: Election Commission, 2000) pp. 35–59.

17. See *Union of India v. Harbans Singh Jalal and Others.* Election Commission of India, *Landmark Judgements on Election Law* 4 (New Delhi: Election Commission of India, 2006) pp. 394–97.

18. As one American legal scholar has recently written, 'To American observers, the degree of independence that India's Election Commission enjoys—as well as the scope of authority it enjoys in executing its responsibilities—is almost unimaginable.' Daniel P. Tokaji, 'Public Rights and Private Rights of Action: The Enforcement of Federal Election Laws', *Indiana Law Review* 44 (2010): 122.

What Is Distinctive about Indian Elections?

1. This essay is a revised version of a talk delivered at the Wissenschaftskolleg, Berlin, in 2010, as the concluding presentation at the end of a year-long fellowship.

2. Milan Vaishnav, 'Understanding the Indian Voter', Carnegie Endowment of National Peace, 23 June 2015, https://pdfs.semanticscholar.org/be1e/f2de903a7dad846a8a4da0a1b9b4bdb16559.pdf, accessed on 3 December 2018.

Why Does India Vote?

1. Election Commission of India.
2. The NOTA option is not available in Panchayat elections, the most local level of elections.

Elections Enshrine India's Democratic Pluralism

1. 'Talk with the PM' by Norman Cousins, *The Saturday Review*, 27 May 1961, pp. 10–13.

Part Two: A Tumultuous Journey

Confronting the Challenge of Money in Elections

1. See, for example, E. Sridharan and Milan Vaishnav, 'Election Commission of India', in Devesh Kapur, Pratap Bhanu Mehta and Milan Vaishnav, eds., *Rethinking Public Institutions in India* (New Delhi: Oxford University Press, 2017): 418–19; Alfred Stepan, Juan J. Linz and Yogendra Yadav, *Crafting State-Nations: India and Other Multinational Democracies* (Baltimore: Johns Hopkins University Press, 2011), p. 77; Subrata K. Mitra, *The Puzzle of India's Governance: Culture, Context and Comparative Theory* (London: Routledge, 2006), pp. 75–76; the collection of essays in David Gilmartin and Robert Moog, eds., 'Symposium: Election Law in India' in *Election Law Journal* 11 (2012): 136–266; and Mukulika Banerjee, *Why India Votes* (London: Routledge, 2014).
2. For the detailed story of the preparation of the first electoral roll under universal franchise for the first elections, see Ornit Shani, *How India Became Democratic: Citizenship and the Making of the Universal Franchise* (Cambridge: Cambridge University Press, and New Delhi: Penguin Random House, 2018).
3. Letter from A.C. Datta, president of the East Bengal Minority Welfare Central Committee, Calcutta, to Rajendra Prasad, 12 May 1948, CA/9/FR/48, Election Commission of India Record Room (hereafter ECIR).
4. Ibid.
5. Letter from the Reforms Commissioner of Assam to all district officers, 28 May, CA/1/FR/48-II, ECIR.
6. Internal note, 8 June 1948, CA/9/FR/48, ECIR.
7. This was the East Bengal Minority Welfare Central Committee.

8. Resolution No. 2, Assam Bengalee Association, in internal discussions, CAS, 28 August 1948, CA/9/FR/48, ECIR.

9. Letter from Tinsukia Bengali Association to the deputy commissioner of Lakhimpur district, Assam, 4 September 1948, CA/9/FR/48, ECIR.

10. Letter of the Assam Citizens Association, Nowgong, to the district magistrate, Nowgong, Assam, 30 September 1948, CA/9/FR/48, ECIR.

11. Later legal adjustments were made in the Representation of the People Act to align with the procedures that were employed for the registration of the refugees and relax the residential date for them.

12. S. Radhakrishnan, 'Democracy: A Habit of the Mind' (presidential address at the annual session of Andhra Mahasabha, Madras, September 1938) in *Education, Politics and War* (Poona: The International Book Service, 1944), p. 16.

The First and Last General Election in Hyderabad State

1. Government of India, *White Paper on Hyderabad* (New Delhi, 1948).

2. A brief note on the work of enumeration of voters for elections to the Hyderabad Constituent Assembly, (undated), National Archives of India, Ministry of States (hereafter NAI, MoS), f.11(3)-H/49.

3. Report of the progress of the work for the elections to the Constituent Assembly for the Hyderabad State, from 1 March to 15 September 1949, by S.W. Shiveshwarkar, election commissioner and joint secretary to the Government of Hyderabad, elections department, (undated), NAI, MoS, f.10 (80)-H/49.

4. Ibid.

5. Ibid.

6. A brief note on the work of enumeration of voters for elections to the Hyderabad Constituent Assembly, (undated, 1949), NAI, MoS, f.11 (3)-H/49.

7. Extract from fortnightly report for the second half of November 1950, 9 December 1950, NAI, MoS, f.1 (7)-H/50.

8. *Siasat*, 29 September 1951.

9. L.G. Rajwade, chief secretary to the chief civil administrator, Government of Hyderabad, to N.M. Buch, joint secretary to the Government of India, Ministry of States, 22 August 1951, NAI, MoS, f.17(7)-H/51.

10. L.G. Rajwade, chief secretary to the chief civil administrator, Government of Hyderabad, to N.M. Buch, joint secretary to the Government of India, 8 October 1951, NAI, MoS, f.17(7)-H/51.

11. See Ravi Narayana Reddy, *Heroic Telengana [sic]: Reminiscences & Experiences* (New Delhi: Communist Party of India, 1973), pp. 70–71.

12. L.G. Rajwade, chief secretary to the chief civil administrator, Government of Hyderabad, to N.M. Buch, joint secretary to the Government of India, 8 October 1951, NAI, MoS, f.17(7)-H/51.

13. *Siasat*, Editorial, 11 December 1951.

14. *Siasat*, Deccan Desh page, 30 September 1951.

15. M.K. Vellodi, chief minister, Chief Minister M.K. Vellodi, Hyderabad, to C.S. Venkatachar, secretary, Ministry of States, 2 November 1951, NAI, MoS, f.6(20)-H/51.

16. P. Sundarayya, *Telangana People's Struggle and Its Lessons* (Calcutta: Cambridge University Press, 1972), p. 114.

17. The President, Agriculturalists' Association, to the Prime Minister of India, 27 December 1948, NAI, MoS, f.3 (4)-H/49.

18. L.C. Jain, chief secretary to the Government of Hyderabad, to S. Narayanaswamy, deputy secretary to the Government of India, Ministry of States, 10 September 1949, NAI, MoS, f.1(56)-H/49.

19. Radio talk by M. Seshadri, 10 June 1950, NAI, MoS, f.10 (4)-H/50.

20. M.K. Vellodi, chief minister, Hyderabad, to P.V. Subba Row (sic), member, Board of Revenue, NAI, MoS, f.10 (4)-H/50.

21. Extract from secret communist document, enclosed in S.B. Shetty, deputy director (B), Intelligence Bureau, Ministry of Home Affairs, to S. Narayanaswamy, deputy secretary to the Government of India, Ministry of States, 7 January 1952, NAI, MoS, f.1 (21)-H/50.

22. Note indicating the changes proposed in the amending legislation to the Hyderabad Tenancy and Agricultural Lands Act, (undated), NAI, MoS, f.10(4)-H/52.

23. Note by L.C. Jain, chief secretary, to the Government of India, 7 November 1948, NAI MoS, f. 10(38)-H/49 NAI.

24. *Siasat*, 15 Jan 1952.

25. L.C. Jain, chief secretary to chief civil administrator, Government of Hyderabad, to M.K. Vellodi, secretary to the Government of India, Ministry of States, 29 May 1949, NAI, MoS, f.11(3)-H/49.

26. Extract from fortnightly report from the Bombay outpost, no. 6 (II)/52 for the period 10th to 23rd March 1952, National Archives UK, DO 35/3264.

27. L.C. Jain, chief secretary to chief civil administrator, Government of Hyderabad, to M.K. Vellodi, secretary to the Government of India, Ministry of States, 29 May 1949, NAI, MoS, f.11(3)-H/49.

28. Swami Ramanand Tirtha, *Memoirs of Hyderabad Freedom Struggle* (Mumbai: Popular Prakashan, 1967), p. 65.
29. L.G. Rajwade, chief secretary to chief civil administrator, Government of Hyderabad, to N.M. Buch, joint secretary to the Government of India, Ministry of States, 21 December 1951, NAI, MoS, f.17(7)-H/51.
30. L.G. Rajwade, chief secretary to chief civil administrator, Government of Hyderabad, to N.M. Buch, joint secretary to the Government of India, Ministry of States, 6 December 1951, NAI, MoS, f.17(7)-H/51.
31. *Deccan Chronicle*, 21 December 1951, NAI, MoS, f.1 (30)-H/51.
32. *Statistical Report on the General Election, 1951, to the Legislative Assembly of Hyderabad*, http://eci.gov.in/eci_main/StatisticalReports/SE_1951/StatRep_51_HBD.pdf, accessed on 11 December 2010, p.12.
33. *Statistical Report on General Elections, 1951, to the First Lok Sabha I*, http://eci.gov.in/eci_main/StatisticalReports/LS_1951/VOL_1_51_LS.PDF, p. 6.
34. *New Standard (Bombay)*, 25 December 1951, NAI, MoS, f.1 (30)-H/51.
35. Ibid.
36. *Siasat*, Editorial, 6 January 1952.
37. *Siasat*, Editorial, 24 January 1952.
38. *Deccan Chronicle*, 21 December 1951, NAI, MoS, f.1 (30)-H/51.
39. Press Information Bureau, Government of India, Hyderabad State Assembly Elections, Election Analysis, 1 March 1952, NAI, MoS, f.1(5)-H/52.

A Tumultuous and Glorious Seventy Years

1. V.S Ramadevi (in office from 26 November 1990 to 11 December 1990). She was the law secretary who was made to officiate as CEC. There's no constitutional provision for this.
2. Article 324 gives complete charge of 'superintendence, direction and control of all elections' to the ECI. But government paid no heed to many of its proposals, e.g., introduction of voter identity card. https://indiankanoon.org/doc/950881/.
3. David Gilmartin, 'One Day's Sultan: T.N. Seshan and Indian democracy', *Contributions to Indian Sociology* 43 (2009): 247–84.
4. *Election Commission of India v. Union of India and Others* (Writ Petition No. 606 of 1993), the Supreme Court observed in its order dated 30 August 1993: ' . . . we reiterate the judicial perception as to the constitutional

position and the plenitude of the powers of the Election Commission as a high and exclusive body charged with the duty, at once sensitive and difficult, of overseeing the free and fair elections in the country and that its perceptions of the imperatives for a free and fair elections are not to be interfered with by the courts . . . '

5. *T.N. Seshan Chief Election Commissioner of India etc. v. Union of India & Ors [1995]* INSC 313 (14 July 1995), http://www.advocatekhoj.com/library/judgments/index.php?go=1995/july/22.php.

T.N. Seshan and the Election Commission

1. *Constituent Assembly Debates* 1 (New Delhi: Lok Sabha Secretariat, 1989), p. 918 (debate of 29 July 1947).
2. Election Commission, *Report on the General Elections to the House of the People* (Jaipur: Government Central Press, 1980), pp. 113–14.
3. Harsh Sethi, 'Notes on Electoral Violence', *Seminar*, no. 368 (April 1990), p. 42.
4. *National Mail*, 8 May 1991.
5. Barbara Crossette, 'Wounded India Candidate Is Reported Near Death', *New York Times*, 24 November 1989, https://www.nytimes.com/1989/11/24/world/wounded-india-candidate-is-reported-near-death.html.
6. *Report of Justice Saikia Commission of Inquiry on Meham Incidents Submitted to the Central Government on May 31, 1994* (New Delhi: Government of India Press, 1994), https://www.abebooks.com/Report-Justice-Saikia-Commission-Inquiry-Meham/681102822/bd
7. *Frontline*, 4 June 1993, p. 25.
8. This judgment is not devoid of flaws: in fact, it can encourage future governments to appoint as many commissioners as they consider necessary for ensuring the Election Commission's tilt or for paralysing it (see the *India Today* debate on this point, 15 August 1995, p. 99).
9. Supreme Court of India, *T.N. Seshan Chief Election Commissioner vs. Union Of India & Ors*, 14 July 1995, https://indiankanoon.org/docfragment/525269/?formInput=article%20319%20.
10. Video cameras were used to film the election campaign so as to exert psychological pressure on the candidates and their party workers (*Economic Times*, 14 March 1996).
11. *National Mail*, 2 May 1996, p. 1.
12. *Madhya Pradesh Chronicle*, 7 May 1996.

13. Ibid., 4 and 5 May 1996; *Times of India*, 5 May 1996; and *National Mail*, 30 April 1996.
14. Ibid., 8 May 1996; *Times of India*, 8 May 1996, p. 1.
15. During the 1985 state elections, sixty-nine people were killed in election-related violence and 242 people were wounded (*Madhya Pradesh Chronicle*, 30 April 1996).
16. 'T.N. Seshan's Electoral Reform Initiatives Made Him the Darling of Urban Middle Class', *India Today*, 15 July 1994, https://www.indiatoday.in/magazine/nation/story/19940715-t.n.-seshans-electoral-reform-initiatives-made-him-the-darling-of-urban-middle-class-764810-2012-11-15.
17. The post-Iftikhar Chaudhry Supreme Court of Pakistan illustrate very well this point.

Participation Revolution With Voter Education

1. Francesca R. Jensenius and Gilles Verniers, 'Election and Turnout Data', (Sonepat: Trivedi Centre for Political Data, Ashoka University, 2017).
2. Official website of the Systematic Voters Education for Electoral Participation, http://ecisveep.nic.in/.
3. Election Commission of India Turns 60—President to Launch Diamond Jubilee Celebrations ahead of Electoral Bodies from across the World to Participate', press release by the Election Commission of India, 19 January 2010.
4. https://www.poverty-action.org/sites/default/files/day_2_s0_quraishi_0.pdf.
5. Katie Beck, 'Australia Election: Why Is Voting Compulsory?' BBC, 27 August 2013, https://www.bbc.com/news/world-asia-23810381.
6. S.Y. Quraishi, *An Undocumented Wonder: The Making of the Great Indian Election* (New Delhi: Rainlight Rupa, 2014).
7. Bharti Jain, 'Highest-ever Voter Turnout Recorded in 2014 Polls, Govt Spending Doubled Since 2009', Times of India, 13 May 2014, https://timesofindia.indiatimes.com/news/Highest-ever-voter-turnout-recorded-in-2014-polls-govt-spending-doubled-since-2009/articleshow/35033135.cms.
8. Chintan Chadrachud. 'A Draconian Ban on Prisoner Voting', The Hindu, 7 October 2015, https://www.thehindu.com/opinion/columns/The-draconian-ban-on-prisoner-voting/article10142992.ece.
9. Ritika Chopra, 'Should Prisoners Be Allowed to Vote? EC Panel Seeks Answers', *Indian Express*, 14 September 2016,

https://indianexpress.com/article/india/india-news-india/should-prisoners-be-allowed-to-vote-ec-panel-to-seek-answer-3029960/.

10. Maninder Dabas, '70% of the Undertrials Are from the Minority Communities, or the Marginalized Sections', Indiatimes, 2 November 2016, https://www.indiatimes.com/news/nearly-70-inmates-in-country-s-jails-are-undertrial-and-most-of-them-are-muslim-tribals-and-dalits-264711.html.

11. The data for voter turnout has been taken from the National Election and Turnout Database by Jensenius and Verniers (Sonepat: Trivedi Centre for Political Data, Ashoka University, 2017).

12. This Wikipedia entry summarizes the unique aspects of GE 2014, https://en.wikipedia.org/wiki/Indian_general_election,_2014.

13. S.Y. Quraishi, *An Undocumented Wonder: The Making of the Great Indian Election* (New Delhi: Rainlight Rupa, 2014).

14. Ibid.

15. Ibid.

16. 'Voter Education for Inclusive, Informed and Ethical Participation' (conference reader published by the ECI, New Delhi, 2016), http://voicenet.in/data/Conference_Reader.pdf.

17. The Election Commission of India's national and regional icons list, http://ecisveep.nic.in/approach/national-regional-icons/.

18. A collection of 101 stories related to India's elections: *Belief in the Ballot*, published by the Ministry of Information and Broadcasting, Government of India, in 2016.

19. Publications Division, *Belief in the Ballot: 101 Human Stories from India's Elections* (New Delhi: Ministry of Information and Broadcasting, Government of India, 2016).

The Election Commission as Producer of Political Data

1. See S.Y. Quraishi, *An Undocumented Wonder: The Making of the Great Indian Election* (New Delhi: Rainlight Rupa, 2014), p. 103.

2. The link between safer elections and women's participation has been empirically established by Divya Singh, 'Safer Elections and Women Turnout: Evidence from India' (New York: Columbia University, 2017).

3. This landmark judgment came from a public-interest litigation filed by the Association for Democratic Reforms in December 1999. The 2002 judgment led to the publication of the August 2002 ordinance on electoral

reforms, which was eventually passed as a bill in December 2012. For more information on election reforms related PILs and court cases, see https://adrindia.org/legal-advocacy/judgements-and-orders.

4. For a detailed description of the ECI vulnerability mapping and on the general question of securing elections, see Quraishi (2014), chapter 6.

5. For a detailed discussion on the ECI's code of conduct, see David Gilmartin, 'One Day's Sultan: T.N. Seshan and Indian democracy', *Contributions to Indian Sociology* 43 (2009): 247–84; A. McMillan, 'The Election Commission of India and the Regulation and Administration of Electoral Politics', *Election Law Journal: Rules, Politics, and Policy* 11 (2012): 187–201.

6. See: https://eci.nic.in/eci_main1/ElectionStatistics.aspx.

7. The NES was interrupted for fifteen years, between 1980 and 1995.

8. See: http://lokdhaba.ashoka.edu.in/LokDhaba-Shiny/.

9. In 2007, a Delhi University statistician was deputed to the Commission at the request of the CEC but estimated that he could not fulfil its mission and therefore resigned.

10. Incidentally, the ECI had decided in 1971 to count votes in district headquarters, to avoid electoral fraud and misuse of local electoral data by parties and candidates. Ballots were mixed up by constituency to avoid identification of voting behavior at the local level. Under pressures from political parties, the ECI reversed its decision by the end of the 1970s. It resumed this practice under the tenure of T.N. Seshan, in 1996 (Jaffrelot 2007).

11. Christophe Jaffrelot, '"Voting in India": Electoral Symbols, the Party System and the Collective Citizen', in *Cultures of Voting*, eds. Romain Bertrand, Jean-Louis Briquet and Peter Pels (London: Hurst & Publisher, 2007), pp. 78–99.

12. This decision proceeds from a 2009 judgment of the Madras High Court, Madurai bench.

Indian Elections: Lessons for and from Nepal

1. The official website of the FEMBoSA, http://www.fembosa.af/fembosa.

2. The official website of the IIDEM: http://iiidem.nic.in/.

3. The setup of the ECI, https://eci.nic.in/eci_main1/the_setup.aspx.

4. Election Commission, Nepal, https://en.wikipedia.org/wiki/Election_Commission,_Nepal.

5. Surya P. Subedi, 'Post-Conflict Constitutional Settlement in Nepal and the Role of the United Nations', *Kathmandu Law Review* 1 (2008), http://www.asianlii.org/np/journals/KathSLRS/2008/2.pdf.

6. The Constitution of Nepal, *Nepal Gazette* (2015), http://www.wipo.int/edocs/lexdocs/laws/en/np/np029en.pdf.

7. Local Level Election Act, 2073 BS; Local Level Election (1st Amendment) Act, 2074 BS.

8. President and Vice-president Election Act, 2074 BS.

9. https://timesofindia.indiatimes.com/world/south-asia/bidya-devi-bhandari-relected-as-nepal-president/articleshow/63286452.cms.

10. 'Nepal's Locally Elected Women Representatives', The Asia Foundation (2018), https://asiafoundation.org/wp-content/uploads/2018/07/Nepals-Locally-Elected-Women-RepresentativesExploratory-Study-of-Needs-and-Capacity-Assessment.pdf.

11. GESI Policy, Strategy of Election Commission Nepal

12. National Assembly Member Election Ordinance, 2074 BS; State Assembly Election Act, 2074 BS. Nepal Sambat is a solar calendar based on ancient Hindu tradition (see Hindu calendar and Vedic timekeeping). The Bikram Sambat calendar is 56.7 years ahead (in count) of the solar Gregorian calendar.

13. House of Representative Election Act, 2074 BS.

14. Election Commission Act, 2073 BS ; Voter Roll Related Act, 2073 BS.

15. The set-up of the Election Commission of Nepal, http://election.gov.np/election/np/.

16. A report on SAARC training. Election Management: Principles and Practices, New Delhi, 5–15 December 2016, https://eci.nic.in/eci_main1/current/SAARCTraining_02012017.pdf.

Part Three: People and Perspectives

Civil Society in Elections in India

1. The Center for Civil Society, UCLA School of Public Policy and Social Research, http://www.sppsr.ucla.edu/ccs/default_body.cfm?body=11

2. The World Bank, http://web.worldbank.org/WBSITE/EXTERNAL/TOPICS/CSO/0,,contentMDK:20101499~menuPK:244752~pagePK:220503~piPK:220476~theSitePK:228717,00.html.

3. It can be argued that the raison d'être for the existence of political parties is to mobilize and consolidate public opinion, get in power, and then provide *good* governance to the state or country.
4. https://www.britannica.com/topic/Shiromani-Akali-Dal.
5. http://www.bjp.org/images/bjp_infographics.jpg.
6. http://www.bjp.org/images/bjp_infographics.jpg
7. Citizens for Democracy, *Report of the Committee on Election Expenses*, (1978).
8. Citizens for Democracy, *Report of the Committee on Election Expenses*, (1978).
9. http://adrindia.org/sites/default/files/Dinesh%20Goswami%20Report%20on%20Electoral%20Reforms.pdf.
10. http://adrindia.org/sites/default/files/VOHRA%20COMMITTEE%20REPORT_0.pdf.
11. http://adrindia.org/sites/default/files/Indrajit_Gupta_Committe_on_State_funding_of_Elections.pdf.
12. http://lawcommissionofindia.nic.in/lc170.htm.
13. Ibid.
14. https://adrindia.org/
15. Writ petition (civil) number 7257 of 1999 filed in the Delhi High Court.
16. AIR 2001 Delhi 126, 2000 (57) DRJ 82.
17. https://www.sci.gov.in/jonew/judis/18463.pdf.
18. Ibid.
19. Article 123 of the Constitution gives the president the power to issue an ordinance '(1) If at any time, except when both houses of Parliament are in session, the president is satisfied that circumstances exist which render it necessary for him to take immediate action, he may promulgate such ordinances as the circumstances appear to him to require'.
20. The Ordinance was subsequently presented to Parliament, as required by the Constitution, and unanimously passed as the Representation of the People (Third Amendment Act), 2002.
21. https://adrindia.org/sites/default/files/Supreme_Court's_judgement_13th_March_2003.pdf.
22. https://www.sci.gov.in/jonew/judis/40545.pdf.
23. https://www.sci.gov.in/jonew/judis/40835.pdf.
24. https://www.sci.gov.in/jonew/judis/40768.pdf.
25. https://www.sci.gov.in/supremecourt/2015/32225/32225_2015_Judgement_16-Feb-2018.pdf.
26. http://www.commoncause.in/.

27. http://mkssindia.org/about/.
28. http://www.humanrightsinitiative.org/.
29. S.Y. Quraishi, *An Undocumented Wonder: The Making of the Great Indian Election* (New Delhi: Rupa Publications, 2014), pp. 285–86.

Women Vote 'Yes' to Empowerment

1. http://pib.nic.in/newsite/erelcontent.aspx?relid=34850; https://capitalkhabar.in/index.php/lead/2328-women-s-participation-in-quit-india-movement-a-story-of-valour-and-patriotism.
2. That year, the colonies were embroiled in the French and Indian War, and—legend has it—the town of Uxbridge held a vote on 30 October 1756 to appropriate funds for the war effort. Josiah Taft had been one of the largest landowners in the town, and since his widow was the legal representative of his estate, the town selectman allowed her to vote on whether to tax the local citizens to pay for the war. Lydia Taft voted in favor of the tax—casting the tie-breaking vote, per historical legend, http://mentalfloss.com/article/94209/5-very-early-stories-about-american-women-and-voting.
3. 'Commemorating Women's Day, Annan Calls for Prioritizing Women's Needs', UN News, https://news.un.org/en/story/2003/03/61252-commemorating-womens-day-annan-calls-prioritizing-womens-needs.
4. Latest figures (November 2018). Women members: 65 (12.20%) Lok Sabha; http://164.100.47.194/Loksabha/Members/GenderWiseStatisticalList.aspx; Rajya Sabha women members: 28; http://164.100.47.194/Loksabha/Members/GenderWiseStatisticalList.aspx

A Modern Miracle

1. https://www.goodreads.com/quotes/7135958-democracy-is-eternal-and-human-it-dignifies-the-human-being.
2. https://bobsnewheart.wordpress.com/tag/rodney-dangerfield/.
3. Joseph Brant, http://www.greatthoughtstreasury.com/government/quotes-1.
4. https://www.rbth.com/education/327163-in-soviet-russia-jokes.
5. 'Elections in India, the World's Largest Democracy', Brookings Institution, 13 December 2013, https://www.brookings.edu/events/elections-in-the-worlds-largest-democracy/.
6. Freda Bedi. *Dawn of Freedom in Rhymes for Ranga* (Noida: Random House India, 2010).

Bollywood Goes to the Polls

1. I have discussed this in greater detail in my book *Nehru's Hero: Dilip Kumar in the Life of India* (New Delhi: Roli Books, 2004).

Part Four: The Path Ahead

Elections, Exit Polls and the Electronic Media

1. This essay is an abridged version of the problem statement published in the August 2016 issue of *Seminar*.
2. Kaushik Basu made a similar remark about economic forecasting.
3. The evidence to support this claim, at least in India, is thin.
4. Jill Lepore, 'Are Polls Ruining Democracy? Politics and the New Machine', *New Yorker*, 16 November 2015.
5. The empirical evidence for this claim is thin. However, it is possible that some voters may be shifting towards parties performing well in initial phases.
6. There would a huge academic cost of not conducting polls at the time of elections.
7. Of course, there are other polls (surveys) that are conducted for the purpose of market research or purely for academic or for evaluation of public policies.
8. Many of these market-research firms are not sensitive to the nuances of conducting election-related polling in diverse and competitive political environment such as India.
9. Many have made a plea to various polling agencies to be transparent with their methodology. See, for example, Yogendra Yadav, 'Opinion Polls – The Way Forward', *The Hindu*, 12 November 2013; Karthik Shashidhar, 'How to Make Opinion Polls More Honest', *Livemint*, 27 February 2014.
10. Also, voters from weaker sections of society may not wish to reveal their vote choice in public.
11. Fly-by-night operators generally function as workforce aggregators supplying field researchers to large market-research firms.
12. Pollsters often complain that media houses invest in low-cost polls, which means that investigators and data analysts are poorly trained, survey instruments poorly designed, and the achieved sample not representative. It is no surprise then pollsters in India often fail.

13. The one-time infrastructure cost is high, but the same call centre can be used for a variety of other business purposes. CATI data often tends to oversample urban, male, educated and socio-economically well-off individuals.

14. Even if a researcher successfully manages to target a representative sample, they often fail to meet every sampled respondent on the ground due to various reasons. And if there is a systematic bias in who is responding to the poll, the analysis based on such data is erroneous.

15. The use of sampling weights to correct skewness in data has an established tradition in statistics. This is not data massaging or manipulation, as it is sometimes called.

16. In an interview with Yogendra Yadav on the 1989 and 1991 Lok Sabha election predictions, Prannoy Roy put this point very succinctly: 'When you get something spot on it's bound to be a bit of fluke: the methodology doesn't allow you to get anywhere but within twenty seats of the final result.' See, Yogendra Yadav. 'Interview with Prannoy Roy', *Seminar* 385 (1991): 61–63.

17. Margin of Error is a statistical expression and means that the estimate from a random sample would differ from 'truth' or actual reality, simply due to chance. The higher the sample size, the lower the margin of error.

18. Methodological issues related to survey research have long been debated among scholars. See, Yogendra Yadav, 'Whither Survey Research: Reflections on the State of Survey Research on Politics in Most of the World'. Malcom Adiseshiah Memorial Lecture, 2008.

19. See Chhibber Pradeep and Rahul Verma, *Ideology and Identity: The Changing Party Systems of India* (New York: Oxford University Press, 2018).

20. See the discussion between Yogendra Yadav and Ranjit Chib, 'Psephology Is Not a Science Like Microbiology . . . It's Poll Studies. But Everyone Thinks Only of Seat Forecasts', *Indian Express*, 27 January 2008.

Confronting the Challenge of Money in Elections

1. Adam Przeworsk, Michael E. Alvarez, Jose Antonio Cheibub, and Fernando Limongi, *Democracy and Development: Political Institutions and Well-Being in the World, 1950–1990* (New York: Cambridge University Press, 2000).

2. Milan Vaishnav and Danielle Smogard, 'A New Era in Indian Politics?' Carnegie Endowment for International Peace, 10 June 2014, https://carnegieendowment.org/2014/06/10/new-era-in-indian-politics-pub-55883.

3. The 2009 and 2014 estimates were calculated by the Centre for Media Studies (CMS), a New Delhi–based think tank. See Niraj Sheth, 'Corruption Mars Image of Change in India Elections', *Wall Street Journal*, 9 April 2009; Sruthi Gottipati and Rajesh Kumar Singh, 'India Set to Challenge U.S. for Election-Spending Record', *Reuters*, 9 March 2014.

4. This section draws heavily on Devesh Kapur and Milan Vaishnav, 'Introduction', in Devesh Kapur and Milan Vaishnav, eds. *Costs of Democracy: Political Finance in India* (New Delhi: Oxford University Press, 2018), pp. 1–14

5. This section draws on the findings contained in Milan Vaishnav, *When Crime Pays: Money and Muscle in Indian Politics* (New Haven: Yale University Press, 2017).

6. Eswaran Sridharan and Milan Vaishnav, 'Political Finance in a Developing Democracy: The Case of India', in Devesh Kapur and Milan Vaishnav, eds. *Costs of Democracy: Political Finance in India* (New Delhi: Oxford University Press, 2018), pp. 15–35.

7. For instance, the Association of Democratic Reforms found that incumbent Lok Sabha members of Parliament elected in 2009 and running for re-election in 2014 saw their assets grow by as much as 145 per cent during their five years in office. See Association for Democratic Reforms, 'Analysis of Assets Comparison of Re-Contesting MPs in the 2014 Lok Sabha Elections', 9 May 2014, https://adrindia.org/research-and-report/election-watch/lok-sabha/2014/analysis-asset-comparison-re-contesting-mps-lok-sa.

8. Eswaran Sridharan and Milan Vaishnav, 'India', in Pippa Norris and Andrea Abel van Es, eds. *Checkbook Elections? Political Finance in Comparative Perspective* (New York: Oxford University Press, 2016), pp. 64–83.

9. For more on these stylized facts, see Devesh Kapur, Eswaran Sridharan, and Milan Vaishnav, 'Conclusion: Implications for Research and Policy', in Devesh Kapur and Milan Vaishnav, eds. *Costs of Democracy: Political Finance in India* (New Delhi: Oxford University Press, 2018), pp. 273–98.

10. For more on electoral bonds, see Milan Vaishnav, 'Electoral Bonds Prize Anonymity, You Won't Know Who's Bought Them', *Indian Express*, 8 January 2018.

11. In the 2017 Finance Act, Parliament eliminated the cap on corporate giving (which earlier stood at 7.5 per cent of a corporation's net profits over the previous three years). It has also retrospectively changed provisions in the Foreign Contributions Regulation Act (FCRA) to expand the definition of a 'foreign' company (previously, there was a strict prohibition on foreign funding). For more, see Milan Vaishnav, 'Don't Believe the BJP and Congress Claims That They're Cleaning Up Poll Funding', The Print, 6 February 2018, https://theprint.in/opinion/dont-believe-the-bjp-and-congress-claims-that-theyre-cleaning-up-poll-funding/33671/.

12. Eswaran Sridharan and Milan Vaishnav, 'Political Finance in a Developing Democracy: The Case of India'.

13. Devesh Kapur, Eswaran Sridharan, and Milan Vaishnav, 'Conclusion: Implications for Research and Policy'.

14. Association for Democratic Reforms, 'Analysis of Election Expenditure Statements of MPs: 2014 Lok Sabha Elections', 1 August 2014, http://www.governancenow.com/files/Analysis%20of%20Election%20Expenditure%20Statements%20of%20MPs%20from%202014%20Lok%20Sabha%20Elections%20(English).pdf.

15. Eswaran Sridharan and Milan Vaishnav, 'Political Finance in a Developing Democracy: The Case of India'.

16. Press Council of India, 'Report on Paid News', 7 July 2010, http://presscouncil.nic.in/oldwebsite/councilreport.pdf.

17. Baijayant 'Jay' Panda, 'Now Reform Political Funding', *Times of India*, 23 November 2016; and M.V. Rajeev Gowda and Varun Santhosh, 'A Proposal for Public Funding of Elections and Political Parties in India', Ideas for India (blog), 21 April 2017, http://www.ideasforindia.in/topics/governance/a-proposal-for-public-funding-of-elections-and-political-parties-in-india.html.

18. Milan Vaishnav, 'Votes for Crooks and Cricket Stars', *New York Times*, 9 May 2014.

19. Archana Masih, 'Demonetization Gives Modi A Powerful Narrative for 2019', Rediff.com, 6 September 2018, http://www.rediff.com/news/interview/demonetisation-is-modis-powerful-narrative-for-2019/20180906.htm.

How India Should Fund Its Democracy

1. According to election watchdog, Association for Democratic Reforms, between 2004–05 and 2014–15, national and regional parties in India received Rs 11,367 crore of donations and of which only Rs 1835 crore was from known sources. See the report in *The New Indian Express*, 24 January, 2017, http://www.newindianexpress.com/nation/2017/jan/24/69-of-funds-for-india-political-parties-from-unknown-sources-report-1563076.html.
2. See a detailed story in *Livemint*, 2 February 2017, http://www.livemint.com/Politics/D3amBITlx7UglrLWXm9UIO/Budget-2017-Arun-Jaitley-announces-political-funding-curbs.html.
3. Niranjan Sahoo, 'Reforming Campaign Finance', *DNA*, 14 February, 2017, http://www.dnaindia.com/analysis/column-reforming-campaign-finance-2321937.
4. See John Hudson, 'The Most Expensive Elections in History by Numbers', *Atlantic*, 6 November, 2012, https://www.theatlantic.com/politics/archive/2012/11/most-expensive-election-history-numbers/321728/.
5. See the report carried out by *Time* (11 April 2014), http://time.com/33062/india-elections-expenditure/.
6. See a detailed story in *The Hindu*, http://www.thehindu.com/news/national/tamil-nadu/Rs.-150-crore-2-lakh-dhotis-why-EC-pulled-the-plug-on-polls-in-2-TN-constituencies/article14344249.ece.
7. The said figure is of last four years (2012–16). For details, see ADR report, https://adrindia.org/research-and-report/political-party-watch/combined-reports/2014/corporates-made-87-total-donations-k.
8. M. Rajsekhar, 'How Coal Scam in Linked to Political Funding', *Economic Times*, http://economictimes.indiatimes.com/industry/energy/power/how-corruption-in-coal-is-closely-linked-to-political-funding/articleshow/15381252.cms.

Contributors

BHIKHU PAREKH, political theorist and a Labour member of the House of Lords, UK

Parekh is an emeritus professor at University of Hull, England. He is also a visiting professor at several universities, including Harvard, McGill and Pennsylvania. He is the vice chancellor of University of Baroda; a professorial fellow at the Centre for Study of Developing Societies; and a fellow of the British Academy as well as the European Academy. He has authored several widely acclaimed books on political philosophy and modern India. Parekh is also the recipient of BBC's lifetime achievement award and the Padma Bhushan.

CHRISTOPHE JAFFRELOT, senior professor of Indian politics and sociology at King's India Institute, UK

Jaffrelot is a senior research fellow at CERI-Sciences Po/CNRS, and a professor of Indian politics and sociology at King's India Institute, London. Among his publications are *The Hindu Nationalist Movement and Indian Politics: 1925 to the 1990s, India's Silent Revolution: The Rise of Lower Castes, Dr. Ambedkar and Untouchability, The Pakistan Paradox: Instability and Resilience, Armed Militias of South Asia: Fundamentalist, Maoists and Separatists* (co-edited with L. Gayer), *Muslims of India's Cities: Trajectories of Marginalization* (co-edited with L. Gayer) and *Pan-Islamic Connections: Transnational Networks between South Asia and the Gulf* (co-edited with L. Louër).

DASHO KUNZANG WANGDI, former chief election commissioner of Bhutan

Wangdi is a member of the Royal Research and Advisory Council, His Majesty's Secretariat, Bhutan. As the first chief election commissioner of Bhutan, he conducted the first-ever parliamentary elections of 2008. He served another term to conducted the first local government elections in 2011 and the second national parliamentary elections in 2013. Wangdi has studied at St Stephen's College, India, and Pennsylvania State University, USA. He served as the auditor general for the Royal Audit Authority of Bhutan (2000–05). He was conferred the title of 'Dasho' by the King and is the recipient of the Druk Thuksey medal and the Lifetime Royal Civil Service Award. He is married to Pem Tandi and has five daughters and five grandchildren.

DAVID GILMARTIN, distinguished professor of history, Northern Carolina State University, USA

Gilmartin received his PhD from the University of California, Berkeley, and is a professor of history at North Carolina State University. His publications include *Empire and Islam: Punjab and the Making of Pakistan*, *Civilization and Modernity: Narrating the Creation of Pakistan*, and *Blood and Water: The Indus River Basin in Modern History*. His current research focuses on the intersection of elections and law in twentieth-century South Asian history, and his recent publications include, 'The Paradox of Patronage and the People's Sovereignty', in Anastasia Piliavsky, ed., *Patronage in South Asia*; and 'Towards a Global History of Voting: Sovereignty, the Diffusion of Ideas; and the Enchanted Individual', *Religions*.

ELA R. BHATT, founder of SEWA (Self-Employed Women's Association)

Bhatt is a Gandhian, who is always clad in khadi and is widely recognized as one of the world's most remarkable pioneers and entrepreneurial forces in grassroots development. In 1972, she founded the Self-Employed Women's Association (SEWA), a trade union with more than 2 million members. In 1974, she founded SEWA Cooperative Bank, which has an outreach of 3 million women. She was nominated as a member of Parliament, Rajya Sabha; she was also a member of the Planning Commission; and has served as trustee of the Rockefeller Foundation for a decade. Bhatt has received several awards, including the Padma Shri, the Padma Bhushan, the Ramon Magsaysay Award and the Right Livelihood Award.

GILLES VERNIERS, assistant professor of political science at Ashoka University and co-director, Trivedi Centre for Political Data, Sonepat

Verniers is an assistant professor of political science at Ashoka University; he is the founder and director of the Trivedi Centre for Political Data; and a research associate at the Centre de Sciences Humaines, New Delhi. His research focuses on the study of India's political class, matters of political representation, and the intersection between electoral politics and local and state governance in India. He is a regular contributor to the *Indian Express*, and is based in New Delhi since 2005.

ILA SHARMA, election commissioner, Nepal

Sharma is an election commissioner of Nepal and has over twenty-eight years of experience in law, media, public relations and development. She has an undergraduate degree in bioscience and an LLB in common law. She also has a diploma in journalism from the Nepal Press Institute and a bachelor's degree in Sanskrit literature. After an LLM in public international law and human rights from Tribhuvan University, Nepal, she practised as a consulting lawyer. She continued writing editorials for newspapers on political, developmental and gender issues. She is also a British Chevening scholar and holds an LLM in international business law from University of Hull. She's been involved with policy advocacy, networking and lobbying at national and international levels. Before her appointment as a commissioner, she was pursuing a doctoral research from the Centre for International and European Law, Vrije Universiteit Brussel on an Erasmus Mundus fellowship.

JAGDEEP S. CHHOKAR, former professor of management and organizational behaviour at Indian Institute of Management, Ahmedabad

Chhokar has been a professor, manager and engineer. He was professor, dean, and director in-charge at Indian Institute of Management, Ahmedabad, and is a founder member of the Association for Democratic Reforms (www.adrindia. org), and the founding chairperson of Aajeevika Bureau (www.aajeevika.org). He is now a concerned citizen, lawyer, and birdwatcher, working on political

and electoral reforms, and transparency, among other social issues. He lives in
New Delhi.

KABIR BEDI, Indian television and film actor

Bedi is an international actor, producer and columnist. His career in film,
television and theatre spans across India, Europe and America. He has been
a voting member of the Academy of Motion Picture Arts and Sciences for
almost three decades. In 2010, the Italian government bestowed on him a
knighthood, 'Cavaliere'—its highest civilian honour. His last film was *Mohenjo
Daro*, with Bollywood actor Hrithik Roshan. He is based in India and lives in
Mumbai, while continuing with his worldwide career.

KARAMJIT SINGH, former member, Electoral Commission of the UK

Singh was born and educated in the UK. He keeps in touch with his ancestral
roots in a Punjab village, from where his parents migrated. His career has
encompassed a number of national positions in the public sector; he was
awarded the Commander of the Most Excellent Order of the British Empire
or CBE for services to the administration of justice by Her Majesty The Queen
in 2000. He was one of the five founding commissioners of the UK Electoral
Commission (2001–10) and in this role, developed personal links with the
Election Commission of India from 2001 onwards.

PRAMOD KUMAR, director, Institute of Development and Communication,
Chandigarh

Kumar is the director of the Institute for Development and Communication,
Chandigarh. His work focuses on three interrelated themes: the politics
of development and governance, the politics of conflict management and
resolution, and the practice of democracy through empirical methodologies
and analysis of public policy and peoples' movements. He has published books
and articles on communal violence, terrorism in Punjab and the criminal justice
system. He has contributed research articles on electoral politics in India in
books such as *Indian Politics and the 1998 Elections: Regionalism, Hindutva
and State Politics* (edited by Paul Wallace and Ramashray Roy), *India's 1999
Elections and 20th Century Politics* (edited by Paul Wallace and Ramashray
Roy), *India's 2004 Elections: Grassroots and National Perspectives* (edited by Paul

Wallace and Ramashray Roy), and *Coalition Politics in India: Selected Issues at the Centre and the States* (edited by E. Sridharan).

(LATE) SOMNATH CHATTERJEE, former speaker of Lok Sabha

Chatterjee (25 July 1929–13 August 2018) was an Indian politician, who served as the Lok Sabha speaker from 2004 to 2009. He studied at Presidency College and University of Calcutta. He also studied law at Jesus College, University of Cambridge. He was awarded an honorary fellowship by Jesus College in 2007. He was called to the bar from the Middle Temple in London and took up legal practice as an advocate at the Calcutta High Court. In 1996, he won the Outstanding Parliamentarian Award and received the Living Legend Award at the prestigious Bharat Nirman Awards in 2013.

MARK TULLY, former bureau chief of BBC New Delhi, writer, and broadcaster

Tully was the former bureau chief of BBC New Delhi from 1972 to 1994. He is still based in the capital and is a presenter on BBC Radio 4's weekly programme 'Something Understood' since 1995. He holds an MA in history and theology from Trinity Hall, University of Cambridge. He has authored more than eight books, including *Amritsar: Mrs Gandhi's Last Battle*, *No Full Stops in India* and most recently *Upcountry Tales: Once Upon a Time in the Heart of India*.

MEGHNAD DESAI, British economist and a Labour member of the House of Lords, UK

Desai is a British economist and Labour politician. He has a bachelor's degree in economics from Ramnarain Ruia College and a master's degree in economics from University of Mumbai. He won a scholarship to University of Pennsylvania in 1960. Desai has written over 200 articles in academic journals, and was a regular columnist for the British radical weekly *Tribune* during (1985–94), and continues writing for *Business Standard*, *Indian Express* and *Financial Express*. He was co-editor of the *Journal of Applied Econometrics*. Desai retired from London School of Economics in 2003. Since then he has published notable works such as *Rethinking Islamism: Ideology of the New Terror*, *The Route to All Evil: The Political Economy of Ezra Pound*, *The*

Rediscovery of India, and a novel *Dead on Time*. He was awarded the Padma Bhushan in 2008.

MILAN VAISHNAV, director and senior fellow, South Asia Programme, Carnegie Endowment for International Peace

Vaishnav is a senior fellow and the director of the South Asia Programme at the Carnegie Endowment for International Peace. His primary research focus is on the political economy of India, and he examines issues such as corruption and governance, state capacity, distributive politics, and electoral behavior. He is the author of *When Crime Pays: Money and Muscle in Indian Politics*. He is also co-editor (with Devesh Kapur) of *Costs of Democracy: Political Finance in India* and *Rethinking Public Institutions in India* (with Pratap Bhanu Mehta and Devesh Kapur). He is currently an adjunct professor at Edmund A. Walsh School of Foreign Service at Georgetown University, Washington.

MUKULIKA BANERJEE, director of South Asia Centre and associate professor of social anthropology at London School of Economics, UK

Banerjee is the inaugural director of the South Asia Centre and an associate professor of social anthropology at London School of Economics and Political Science. She studied in New Delhi and Oxford University, and taught at Oxford and University College London before joining LSE. She has conducted ethnographic research in Khyber Pakhtunkhwa (NWFP), Pakistan, between 1990 and 1993 and India since 1998. Her publications include *Why India Votes?*, *The Pathan Unarmed*, *The Sari* and *Muslim Portraits*. She has also made a documentary called *Sacred Election* for BBC Radio 4 (with CultureWise) on Indian elections.

NAINA LAL KIDWAI, chairman of Altico Capital India Ltd and Advent Private Equity India advisory board

Kidwai is chairman of Altico Capital India Ltd and Advent Private Equity India advisory board. He is a non-executive director on the boards of Max Financial Services, CIPLA, Nayara Energy, and Larsen and Toubro; she was the former president of Federation of Indian Chambers of Commerce and Industry (FICCI). She retired on December 2015 as the executive director on the board of HSBC Asia Pacific and chairman HSBC India, and from the global board of Nestle in April 2018. An MBA from Harvard Business School, she is the recipient of awards and honours in India and abroad, including the Padma Shri. She has authored three books, including *30 Women in Power: Their Voices, Their Stories* and *Survive or Sink: An Action Agenda for Sanitation, Water, Pollution, and Green Finance.*

NIRANJAN SAHOO, senior fellow, Observer Research Foundation, India

Sahoo is a senior fellow with Observer Research Foundation's governance and politics initiative. He anchors studies and programmes on democracy, human rights, federalism, electoral reforms (particularly issues related to political funding), exclusion, insurgencies and affirmative action. A recipient of the Asia Fellowship (2009) and a former Sir Ratan Tata Fellow, he currently serves as the South Asia member for the Carnegie Rising Democracies Network. He has authored two books: *Politics of Power Sector Reforms in India* and *Reservation Policy and Its Implementation across Domains in India: An Analytical Review.* His latest (co-authored) monograph 'Funding India's Democracy' will be published soon. He regularly contributes for academic and current affairs journals, newspapers, think thanks, and media programmes.

ORNIT SHANI, senior lecturer at the department of Asian studies, University of Haifa, Israel

Shani is a senior lecturer in the politics and modern history of India at the department of Asian studies, University of Haifa. She is the author of *How India Became Democratic: Citizenship and the Making of the Universal Franchise,* and *Communalism, Caste, and Hindu Nationalism: The Violence in Gujarat.* She is currently working on a history of India's first elections. Her other areas of research are the history of India's constitutionalism, and identity and caste politics. Shani received her PhD from University of Cambridge, and was a research fellow at St John's College, University of Cambridge.

PAUL WALLACE, emeritus professor, University of Missouri, USA

Wallace is emeritus professor of political science at University of Missouri. He served as the expert witness on Sikhs at the Air India trial in Canada in 2003 and at the Supreme Court of British Columbia in 2017. He has been a consultant to the US and Canadian government agencies. He has received five Smithsonian-funded awards for national election studies; and he frequently delivers lectures throughout India and in other parts of the world. His publications include nine books and contributions to over forty other books and articles. His latest book is *India's 2014 Elections: A Modi-led BJP Sweep*.

RAHUL VERMA, University of California, Berkeley, USA

Verma is a PhD candidate in political science at University of California, Berkeley. His doctoral dissertation examines the historical roots of elite persistence in contemporary Indian politics. He is a regular columnist for various news platforms. His book *Ideology and Identity: The Changing Party Systems of India*, co-authored with Pradeep Chhibber, develops a new approach to defining the contours of what constitutes an ideology in multiethnic countries, such as India.

RATAN TATA, industrialist, investor, philanthropist

Ratan Tata is an industrialist, investor and philanthropist. He was the former chairman of Tata Group, a Maharashtra-based global business conglomerate, from 1991 till 2012 and from 24 October 2016 for an interim term. He has continued as the head of its charitable trusts. He has studied at Cornell University and Harvard Business School. He received the Padma Bhushan in 2000 and the Padma Vibhushan in 2008.

SHASHI THAROOR, member of Parliament since 2009, former career international diplomat

Tharoor is an award-winning author of eighteen books of fiction and non-fiction, including *The Great Indian Novel*, *Pax Indica: India and the World of the 21st Century*, *An Era of Darkness: The British Empire in India*, *Why I Am a Hindu* and the recently published *The Paradoxical Prime Minister*. He has won numerous literary awards, including Commonwealth Writers' Prize. A second-term MP representing Thiruvananthapuram, and chairman of the Parliamentary Standing Committee on External Affairs, he has served as the Minister of State for Human Resource Development and for External Affairs in the Government of India. During his nearly three-decade-long career at the United Nations, he served as a peacekeeper, refugee worker, and an administrator at the highest levels, serving as Under-Secretary General during Kofi Annan's leadership.

TAYLOR C. SHERMAN, associate professor, department of international history, LSE, UK

Sherman is the author of two books on the history of the transition from the colonial to the postcolonial in India: *State Violence and Punishment in India*, and *Muslim Belonging in Secular India: Negotiating Citizenship in Postcolonial Hyderabad*. Her current research is a critical examination of the central tenets of what is known as the Nehruvian consensus in the first two decades after independence in India.

TIRUNELLAI NARAYANA IYER SESHAN, tenth chief election commissioner of India (1990–96)

Seshan is a 1955 batch Indian Administrative Service officer of the Tamil Nadu cadre. He is best remembered for his contributions to the cleaning up of the elections in India. He was the tenth chief election commissioner of India from 1990–96. He reformed elections by largely ending rampant malpractices in the country. He redefined the status and visibility of the Election Commission of India, the constitutional body responsible for conducting free, fair and transparent elections in India. He earlier served as the cabinet secretary of India in 1989. He won the Ramon Magsaysay Award for government service in 1996.

YOGENDRA YADAV, social activist and senior fellow, Centre for the Study of Developing Societies

Yadav is an Indian politician, psephologist and renowned academic, whose primary interests lie in advocacy and social sciences. He is a senior fellow at the Centre for the Study of Developing Societies, New Delhi, since 2004. He is a former member of the University Grants Commission and the National Advisory Council on the Right to Education Act. He was a member of the national executive of the Aam Aadmi Party until 2015. Yadav is also a founding member of Swaraj Abhiyan and Jai Kisan Andolan.

Index

Aam Aadmi Party (AAP), 155
Aandhi (1975), 189, 190, 192, 195
accountability and responsiveness in
    politics, 10, 40, 47, 86
Administrative Reforms Commission,
    Second (2007), 238
affirmative action, 64
agriculture reform in Hyderabad,
    92–93
Ahmadi, Justice Aziz Mushabber, 110
Akali movement, 154
alcoholism, 25–26
Ali, Aruna Asaf, 164
All India Radio, 176, 180, 239
Amina Begum, 120
Amir Singh, 106
Anantnag, Jammu and Kashmir:
    general elections, 1989, low voter
    turnout, 112
Andhra Mahasabha, 88, 90, 92
Annadurai, C.N., 188
Annan, Kofi, 165
anti-incumbency, 213
antisocial elements, 25
Arjun Rampal, 191
Arya Samaj, 26
Assam

assembly elections 1983, 41
refugees' registration issue, 82–83
voters' turnout, 116
Assam Bengalee Association, 83
Assam Citizens Association Nowgong,
    83
Associate Chambers of Commerce of
    India (Assocham), 239
Association for Democratic Reforms
    (ADR), 125, 158
authoritarianism, 5, 22–23, 208,
    236
Awasthy, Malini, 119
Azad, Abul Kalam, 183

Bahadur Osman Ali Khan, Nizam of
    Hyderabad, 88
Bajajs, 197
Bajpai, Manoj, 191
Bansi Lal, 24–25
Baramullah, Jammu and Kashmir:
    general elections, 1989, low voter
    turnout, 112
BBC World Service, 176, 178–81
Benegal, Shyam, 189
Besant, Annie, 164
Bhajan Lal, 24–25